D0328828

*f*P

Also by Dina Temple-Raston

A Death in Texas:
A Story of Race, Murder, and a Small Town's Struggle for Redemption

JUSTICE ON

Free Press • *New York London Toronto Sydney*

THE GRASS

Three Rwandan Journalists, Their Trial for War Crimes, and a Nation's Quest for Redemption

DINA TEMPLE-RASTON

FREE PRESS
A Division of Simon & Schuster, Inc.
1230 Avenue of the Americas
New York, NY 10020

For information about special discounts for bulk purchases,
please contact Simon & Schuster Special Sales at
1-800-456-6798 or business@simonandschuster.com

Designed by Leslie Phillips
Map copyright © Lisa Jordan Illustrations

Manufactured in the United States of America

1 3 5 7 9 10 8 6 4 2

Library of Congress Cataloging-in-Publication Data

Temple-Raston, Dina.
Justice on the grass: a story of genocide and redemption / Dina Temple-Raston.
p. cm.
Includes bibliographical references and index.
1. Rwanda—History—Civil War, 1994—Atrocities.
2. Genocide—Rwanda—History—20th century. 3. Tutsi (African people)—Crimes against—Rwanda—History—20th century. 4.Hutu (African people)—Rwanda.
5. Rwanda—Ethnic relations—History—20th century. I. Title.
DT450.435.T47 2005
967.57104'31—dc22 2004063587

ISBN 0-7432-5110-5

For Flora, Obed, and the people of Rwanda
who told their stories to a stranger

Contents

Glossary

Akazu: The entourage of President Habyarimana's intimates and people linked with the president's high-powered wife. Mrs. Habyarimana now lives in France.

Arusha Accords: An internationally brokered plan aimed at defusing tensions between Hutu and Tutsi in Rwanda by forging a power-sharing agreement. The accords never came to fruition and instead became a rallying point for Hutu extremists.

Jean-Bosco Barayagwiza: Rwandan lawyer, one of the founders of RTLM and of the extremist CDR party. Defendant in the media trial.

CDR: Coalition for the Defense of the Republic, a stridently anti-Tutsi political party that sometimes worked together with the MRND.

***Inkotanyi*:** Term used to identify members of the Rwandan Patriotic Front army or RPF sympathizers.

Interahamwe: Young toughs who came together in a "civil defense" force on behalf of the MRND, President Habyarimana's party. They went door-to-door killing Tutsi and moderate Hutu during the genocide.

Inyenzi: Its literal translation from Kinyarwanda is "cockroach." During the 1959 revolution refugees, mainly Tutsi, fled the country. In subsequent incursions, refugees entered and left Rwanda under cover of darkness. The activity was likened to that of cockroaches, which are rarely seen during the day but often are discovered at night. Unlike the term *Inkotanyi*, the term Inyenzi had a negative connotation.

Paul Kagame: The president of Rwanda and key leader and strategist of the Rwandan Patriotic Front.

***Kanguka*:** Its literal translation from Kinyarwanda is "Wake Up." *Kanguka* was the mainstream newspaper Hassan Ngeze sought to parody with his *Kangura* tabloid. He purposely chose to call his newspaper by a similar name to confuse readers.

Kangura: Its literal translation from Kinyarwanda is "Wake It Up." It was Hassan Ngeze's extremist newspaper.

Kubohoza: Its literal meaning is to liberate someone against his or her will. A political term applied originally to people who were forced to change political parties, Kubohoza was later used to describe the rapes of Tutsi women during the genocide.

Simone Monasebian: Key member of the media trial prosecution team.

MRND: National Republican Movement for Democracy and Development. President Habyarimana's party. Its power base was in the northwest. The president made all Rwandans automatic members when he created it.

MDR: Democratic Republican Movement. It began as a Hutu Power party that led the revolution in 1959 and overthrew the Tutsi aristocracy. It had a moderate wing in the run-up to the genocide and afterward. Faustin Twagiramungu was a leader of this party, as was Bonaventure Ubalijoro.

Ferdinand Nahimana: Professor of history at the University of Rwanda, one of the founders and directors of RTLM. Defendant in the media trial.

Hassan Ngeze: Founder of *Kangura* newspaper and defendant in the media trial.

Damien Nzabakira: Teacher and deputy director of a Kigali orphanage. He helped evacuate forty children from the capital to Butare.

Stephen Rapp: Senior prosecutor of the media trial.

RPF: Rwandan Patriotic Front, initially composed of Rwandans who had lived in exile for a generation. The RPF is credited with ending the genocide with its march on Kigali.

RTLM: Radio-Télévision Libre des Mille Collines, an ostensibly private radio station known in Rwanda as "Radio Hate" for its fiery broadcasts in the run-up to and during the genocide.

Faustin Twagiramungu: Leader of MDR and moderate Rwandan politician. He would have been the interim prime minister of Rwanda if the Arusha Accords had been put in force.

Bonaventure Ubalijoro: Former Rwandan ambassador to Washington and Paris. Key moderate politician before and after the genocide.

Umunganda: Government-ordered labor said to be for the common good. Sometimes it involved clearing fields or digging ditches. During the genocide the term was used to refer to killing Tutsi.

UNAMIR: The United Nations Assistance Mission for Rwanda, a U.N. peacekeeping force meant to help the implementation and transition of government in keeping with the Arusha Accords. Ten Belgian peacekeepers, who were part of the UNAMIR, were killed in the early days of the genocide.

Blood, no matter how little of it,
when it spills, spills on the brain,
on the memory of a nation.

Mongane Wally Serote,
South African poet

Justice on the Grass

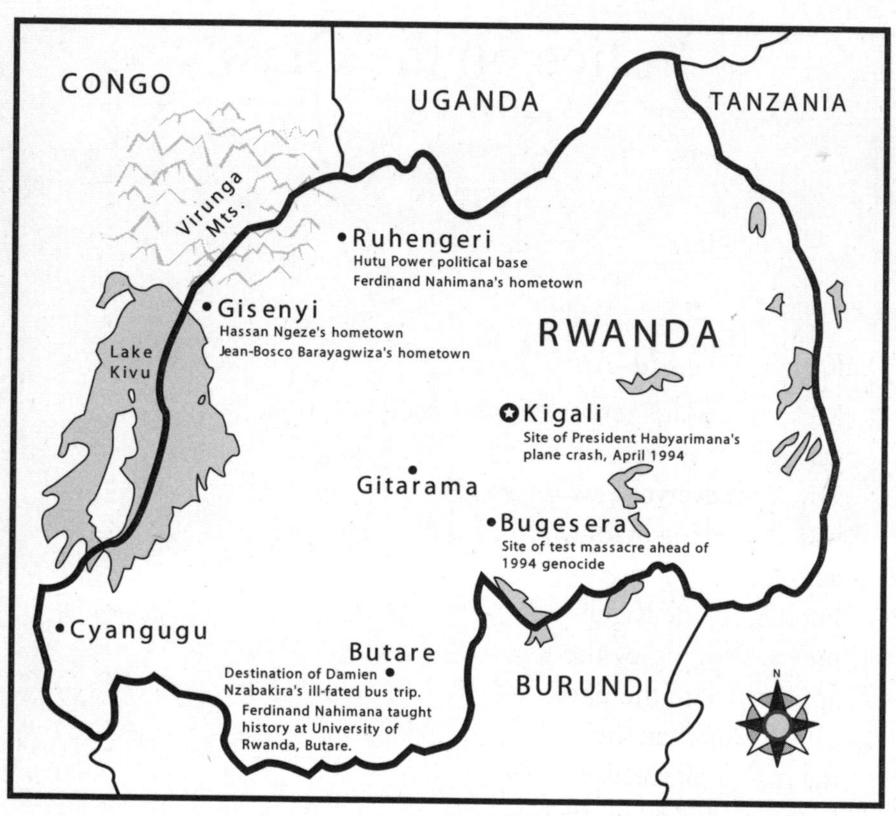
CONGO
UGANDA
TANZANIA
Virunga Mts.
Ruhengeri
Hutu Power political base
Ferdinand Nahimana's hometown
Gisenyi
Hassan Ngeze's hometown
Jean-Bosco Barayagwiza's hometown
Lake Kivu
RWANDA
Kigali
Site of President Habyarimana's plane crash, April 1994
Gitarama
Bugesera
Site of test massacre ahead of 1994 genocide
Cyangugu
Butare
Destination of Damien Nzabakira's ill-fated bus trip.
Ferdinand Nahimana taught history at University of Rwanda, Butare.
BURUNDI
N

Prologue

Kigali, Rwanda–April 6, 1994

Most Rwandans remember April 6, 1994, as if they were under water. Sounds were oddly distorted, movements were unnaturally slow, as if everyone were pushing against a great unseen force. It was an evening of long shadows and an eerie pinkish light melted across the cool night sky. Residents in the Macombe neighborhood, near the Kigali International Airport, later recalled a slight breeze washing by the curtains as the hills winked and then disappeared into the darkness. The pale outlines became ghosts of hills, rather than the actual thing. Then, as happened every night, the hissing of voices rose up from the shadows. Women in the district had clicked on their transistor radios to listen to the national broadcast.

A year earlier they might have tuned the dials to FM 101, the government station, Radio Rwanda. But more recently, FM 106, Radio Mille Collines—or Radio of a Thousand Hills—had become the sound track of the nation. The first private radio station allowed to broadcast in Rwanda, its call letters, RTLM (Radio-Télévision Libre des Mille Collines), had become a ubiquitous part of the

Rwandan vocabulary. The letters were said so quickly, in such comfortable and familiar succession, they sounded more like an invented word than a slow recitation of an acronym.

RTLM's popularity had as much to do with its lack of competition as with the programming choices its directors made. Instead of staid government fare, or replays of long-winded speeches by President Juvénal Habyarimana, RTLM listeners were treated to Congolese music, call-in shows, and shock jocks who used bawdy language and told off-color jokes. For the first three weeks it was on the air, the station played nothing but music. Rwandans tuned in in droves. Then they began to pick up the phone. At first they shyly called to request a song. Then they started making elaborate dedications.

For the first time, Rwandans suddenly were offered an opportunity to express themselves, to hear their own voices over the airwaves. Unhappy about a neighbor? Call your complaint in to RTLM. Was a prefect of your commune taking advantage of his position? A phone call to the radio station could elicit some empathy; maybe it would even kick-start change. RTLM offered a taste of freedom, the sweet satisfaction of momentary fame as one's voice traveled the country from end to end. At first the radio station made Rwandans a little giddy. Who could not love such a radio station? How could one resist embracing such a novelty? Rwandan radio, the people giggled among themselves, had finally come of age.

That was not to say that RTLM focused exclusively on the frivolous. It was helpful. Announcers provided direction, broadcasting details of the latest village meeting or government reshuffle. RTLM aired phone numbers and addresses of government ministries. In a poor nation with few televisions and even fewer literate citizens, the station provided wisdom for a people otherwise starved of information. That was why the early crackles of a broadcast beckoned Rwandans to come closer and caused them to haunt neighbors' houses at news time. Radio Mille Collines pulled citizens in like moths to a flame, until they congregated in small knots on street corners, with transistor sets clamped to their ears, arms fluttering like wings as they called for silence.

In a country where secrets were legion and half-truths told, it seemed that Radio Mille Collines was out of step. It was willing to tell its listeners what was really happening. It didn't sugarcoat the latest decrees. It didn't embrace President Habyarimana as a great leader. Instead, it gave a mute population voice. And as the months went on, RTLM began to take on an oddly paternalistic role. It seemed to be watching out for regular citizens. In fact, to the initiated listener, RTLM revealed secrets. It predicted the future. It questioned mysterious disappearances. It reported on clandestine meetings convened in the darkness. Something menacing was brewing, broadcasters warned. Our investigations tell us there is trouble afoot, RTLM said in early 1994; we must be vigilant, we must prepare. Listeners needed to steel themselves in case they were called to service and asked to protect the nation from the evil growing within.

Anyone who was outside the April evening when it all began, would have been able to follow the moth-pale contrails of the two shoulder-launched missiles across the night sky above Kigali. The rockets roared out from under the waxy leaves of the banana trees in Masaka commune—exploding from a cozy huddle of houses less than a mile from the presidential palace—and sped toward a small private jet preparing to land at Kigali International Airport.

There was an explosion as the missiles met their mark. A fiery ball that lit the darkness like daylight was followed by the sound of falling metal, the high-pitched screech of crumbling steel that makes molars ache. The noise echoed through the Macombe district as bits of plane rained down on the grounds of the president's residence. Then followed a moment of silence. The quiet of rural Africa. It took a minute to process what had just occurred. Pots bubbled on the fire. Radios hissed. Quiet conversations continued floating just below the volume of understanding, and then the night suddenly exploded with activity.

The families in the Macombe district, in their ramshackle mud houses, were the first to realize something momentous had just taken place. They were the first to see the commotion. Burning debris had set fields ablaze. The presidential guard burst from their barracks. Heavy boots thudded across grass, sounded across the dirt, then hit the pavement, echoing in the direction of the wreckage.

RTLM was the first to report the news. "President Habyarimana's plane has been shot down," the first bulletin said. "The president is dead." The sleek and expensive Mystère-Falcon 50 jet had been a present to the Rwandan government from French president François Mitterrand. It was carrying, the radio voice said, Rwandan president Habyarimana and his Burundian counterpart, Cyprien Ntaryamira, back from Tanzania, where they had signed the latest iteration of the Arusha Accords. There are no survivors, the voice continued. The Tutsi, the station accused from the darkness, have killed our president.

How RTLM came to the conclusion, so quickly, that the nation's minority Tutsi had killed the Hutu president is still a mystery.

Even ten years later no one could say with absolute certainty who assassinated President Habyarimana that night. The government-backed Rwandan army blamed the Tutsi-led Rwandan Patriotic Front, or RPF. The RPF said extremists in the Rwandan army ranks had staged a military coup. The men charged with protecting the president, they claimed, were the ones who killed him. What was sure was that the Arusha Accords, the pact that would have allowed the majority Hutu and the minority Tutsi to rule side by side, had inspired some faction to take matters into its own hands. And now the president was dead. What no one realized at the time was that the downing of the presidential aircraft was the least of anyone's concerns. The plane crash was a coda to months of escalating tension in Rwanda. A sense that something awful was about to happen had been spreading across the land.

Rwandans needed little convincing at the beginning of 1994 that something was terribly wrong. In early January there had been unexplained grenade explosions several times a week. By mid-month a concussion shook Kigali every night. Then the frequency built to explosions sounding several times a night. In early February RTLM reported that a group of Belgian soldiers, sent by the United Nations to ensure Rwandans forged a coalition government between Hutu and Tutsi, had roughed up a man named Jean-Bosco Barayagwiza, one of the directors of radio station RTLM. The foreign soldiers had objected to anti-Belgian broadcasts, and they wanted Barayagwiza to know it. The soldiers broke into Barayagwiza's house, beat him in front of his family, and before they departed, aimed a gun at his head and told him that if he or RTLM ever insulted or threatened the Belgians again, they would return to finish him off. The soldiers were in civilian dress. They were never apprehended. Days later, a convoy carrying Faustin Twagiramungu, a leading moderate politician, had been ambushed by what RTLM called "unknown assailants." Twagiramungu escaped, but one of his bodyguards was killed.

By far the most frightening episode, however, happened at the end of February: the lynching of the national president of the Hutu extremist party, the Coalition pour la Défense de la République, or CDR. When the news arrived in Kigali, the city exploded. Young toughs melted out of the hills like ghosts and blocked all the major intersections and routes out of the capital city. For two days the young men rampaged on the streets of Kigali: thirty-five people died and 150 were injured before calm was restored. Even when the barriers disappeared and the young men folded themselves back into the crowds, Rwandans knew something was amiss.

For months government forces had been recruiting young men into a ragtag army while regular Rwandans pretended not to notice. Bands of unemployed young men, known as Interahamwe, or "those who attack together," had been fashioned into a menacing force. They swaggered around the streets of Kigali, all appetite and bravado, game for anything. They sang at the top of their lungs, blew whistles, and wore colorful uniforms. They hung machetes from their belts and grenades around their necks. In early 1994, there was a roaring business in grenades. Rwandans could buy one for the equivalent of $3.00 No one dared ask why, suddenly, they were so prevalent or so cheap.

There were rumors that the young militiamen were given free guns by their political patrons. New machetes were imported from China. Hutu officials were given weapons for "self-defense."

While Kigali residents didn't say as much aloud, the presence of the grenades and the appearance of these bands of men suffused them with a kind of abstract dread. There was an end-of-the-world tenor in the air that made the reports of progress in the implementation of the Arusha Accords ring hollow. Something was not right. There was the musky odor of defeat in the air mixed, the Tutsi said later, with the tang of revenge. The ranks of Interahamwe continued to swell. Among the young men, any remaining sense of individual responsibility fell away as their numbers grew. They were a mob in search of pleasure, and it was clear their desire would not be denied.

When people thought of the Tutsi and the Hutu at all, it was on the divide between them that everyone concentrated. But for all that was made about their differences, Tutsi and Hutu had a great deal in common. They spoke the same language (Kinyarwanda). They practiced the same religion (Catholicism). And as far as anyone could tell, for no history of it was written down, they had both arrived in the hills of Rwanda around the same time. As long as Hutu had been on this land, Tutsi had been there too. It is human nature, though, to focus on what sets us apart, not what brings us closer. And in Rwanda it was the often taller, fairer-skinned Tutsi who seemed to be at the receiving end of the majority Hutu's bitterness and resentment.

What outsiders didn't understand was that the root of this conflict was not prejudice so much as a competition for resources. Rwanda, a nation the size of Maryland, has little land. And when there is no room, something has to yield. Hutu and Tutsi had taken turns massacring each other over the years because the nation was unable to accommodate both the Hutu farmers and the Tutsi herders. The killings were not fueled by hate. They were fueled by politics and power. RTLM told Rwandans quite plainly what was at stake: Hutu brothers, they said, it is them or us.

That is why those dark hours of April 7 when the killing began were not met with cries of outrage or surprise. They were greeted instead with a kind of naked silence. Villagers counted the dead not so much to mourn, but to measure this massacre against the others that had preceded it. As the casualties mounted, villagers searched their leaders' faces for cues on how to react. Who had seen Pierre the night the killing started? Where had Emmanuel gone? In the weeks that followed, each moment of the massacre was pieced together by those who were left to tell the story.

Within hours of the plane crash, Rwandan authorities (they called themselves the Crisis Committee) set a curfew. Radio Rwanda and Radio Mille Collines told listeners to return to their homes. The order was part of the plan. It made finding Habyarimana's opposition that much easier.

In no time the militia were in their vehicles, springing from the truck beds like cats, surrounding the residences of those who had advocated moderation and peace and power sharing. The young toughs went from house to house, banging on doors with the butts of their rifles, demanding to see identity cards that labeled one Hutu or Tutsi. They skulked at hastily erected roadblocks with machetes in one hand and a radio in the other—taking big, hard breaths of air and long, slow swigs of banana beer. There was the faraway sound of grenades exploding and shots fired. To the trained ear, this was not the sound of war. Military battles had return fire. The screams and sounds of running feet made clear that this was a conflict of the armed against the unarmed. Those who were ready for battle clashed with those who were not.

Phones at the U.N. Assistance Mission for Rwanda (UNAMIR) in Kigali began ringing within minutes of the crash. Moderate politicians across the city were looking for help. Faustin Twagiramungu, who led the moderate wing of a political party known as the MDR, went into hiding. Prime Minister Agathe Uwilingiyimana, a leading moderate who had become the lawful head of state with the death of Habyarimana, had had a contingent of U.N. peacekeepers guarding her twenty-four hours a day for months. She worried a military coup was under way. She knew for certain, whatever was unfolding, that she was a marked woman.

"Mrs. Uwilingiyimana is alerting people that she saw a person with a dagger near her house," RTLM had told listeners just four days earlier. "Imagine that this is the first time she sees a person carrying a weapon. Now if you go to visit Mrs. Uwilingiyimana you have to be thoroughly searched. She is terrified by a knife. What would have happened if they had seen a gun? There must be something in the wind for those people who think they could be killed. They should not think they are wanted because of their power sharing, but it is rather because of their treachery. They should be afraid since they have betrayed the people."

Hours after the crash, a U.N. peacekeeper was trying to hike the prime minister over a wall separating her house from the compound occupied by the U.N. Development Program when the presidential guard arrived. The Rwandan militiamen entered the yard. The prime minister and her husband surrendered. Moments later there was a crack of gunfire, the sound of bullets meeting meat. Then there was cheering. The prime minister was dead.

Across town, the militia had surrounded the barracks of U.N. peacekeepers. They rounded up the blue helmets and took them to military headquarters. By evening the peacekeepers, too, were in twisted, bloody heaps outside the barracks. In less than a day, the death list had grown to include the chairman of the Liberal party, the minister of labor, the minister of agriculture, and dozens of others. Cause of death: murder by presidential guard.

Monique Mujawamariya, Rwanda's most famous homegrown human rights activist, could see the distant cloud of conflict when it was only beginning to form. She had long believed that ethnic divisions in her country flared only when those in power used them for political advantage. When Hutu began pitting themselves against the Tutsi in the early 1990s, she blamed President Habyarimana. "People don't get up every morning thinking, I am a Hutu, he is a Tutsi. Someone has to put those thoughts there," she said. Monique tried to take the correct avoiding action by founding a series of monitoring groups to keep track of the Habyarimana regime's anti-Tutsi offenses.

Monique realized right away the plane crash would be used as a pretext to set something sinister in motion. Monique called Rwandan scholar Alison Des Forges at home in Buffalo, New York, on April 7. Habyarimana's presidential guard were ransacking Kigali, Monique whispered into the phone. They were targeting all the leader's opponents, Tutsi and moderate Hutu. Monique dispassionately described their movements as they went from house to house in her neighborhood. On the line from Buffalo, Des Forges could hear gunfire. By the next day, when Des Forges spoke to Monique again, the presidential guard was next door. Then she heard a crash.

"They're here, they are coming in," Monique told Des Forges. Then, before she hung up, she said, "I don't want you to hear this. Take care of my children."

Then the line went dead.

The killing had become more widespread. Tutsi identity-card holders were stopped by militia, pulled out of cars, picked from crowds, summarily killed. As the number of murderers swelled, it was collectively decided that the Tutsi as a whole were responsible for any suffering or slight a Hutu might have felt in a lifetime. And their victims' resignation, their downcast eyes as they were tugged from buses, seemed like collusion in their fate, an admission of guilt. There were single gunshots, then the smack of machetes on flesh, then the sound of wailing children.

For the outsiders, those watching events unfold from the sidelines, it was difficult to keep all the players straight. Rwanda had its Tutsi and Hutu and Twa—names with so many vowels they ran together in a blur. Westerners used mnemonics to tell them apart. Tutsi, with a *T*, were tall and fair-skinned, and made up about 15 percent of the Rwandan population. Hutu, with an *H*, were hydrant-shaped, stocky people, darker than their Tutsi neighbors. They were the majority. They were built like big boat sailors, all broad shoulders and thick forearms. The Twa, a forest people, known for their pottery and representing about 3 percent of the population, were not party to the argument. They were left to their own devices.

By April 10, four days into the killing, the Red Cross estimated tens of thousands were dead, eight thousand killed in Kigali alone. The counting was made easier by the fact that none of this was done in secret. There were corpses stacked in front of houses, laid in the street; and according to one report, a pile of bodies six feet high was outside the main hospital. A genocide, though it would take the world months to call it that, had begun.

* * *

To make sense of killing, historians often make comparisons: 43,000 dead in the London blitz; 100,000 dead in Tokyo in 1945; 200,000 perished in Nagasaki and Hiroshima. Still, the mind had trouble counting to 800,000, twice the number of civilians who died in the Vietnam War. The rounded-off figures were only educated guesses, of course. And with their attendant zeros, lined up like soldiers neatly one after another, they seem inconceivable. Others tried to make the unfathomable accessible by tying the figures to particular towns. There had been 250,000 Tutsi in Kibuye in March of 1994. When the authorities counted again, after the families who had fled had returned, they could find only 8,000. The best the government figures could do was convey horror in an abstract way.

For people who were closer to it all, who spent time in Rwanda during the genocide or picked up the pieces in its aftermath, the deaths had no zeros. Instead, casualties were counted on their hands. They remembered the brothers and sisters and mothers and fathers who had disappeared. Once the figures were tabulated, one in every ten people in the country had been killed in the space of a hundred days.

Every Tutsi, every Hutu, every neighbor, every friend knew (or thought they knew) precisely who had done what. In a country so small, there could be no real secrets. That's why when the killing stopped, and residents emerged from beneath houses and climbed down from their hiding places in the rafters, they carried their accusations with them. Jean-Baptiste had killed Odette and her family. Pierre had escaped. No one knew where Marie-Rose had gone. There was confusion. And hope. And dread.

The most fortunate had unexpected reunions. Those who were taken for dead appeared, suddenly, on doorsteps, thin and tired, looking much as they had before the massacre but for the flat emotionless expressions they now wore. And there were fruitless searches for family members who had fallen, or run away to the Congo and Zaire, or just vanished.

Rwandans numbly accepted the tally of the dead or the nearly daily news of an identified body recognized from the piles stacked in the streets. Often a relative simply bobbed to shore, surfacing in the waters of Lake Kivu. After a time there were so many dead that the numbers lost all real meaning. "Where there is war, there are also killings," Radio Mille Collines told its listeners. "That's how it goes."

By July, people were tired of killing. The inventory in Kigali had become the same as in any country under siege: burned-out buildings, smoldering fires, shell-shocked citizenry. A journey across the city became uncomfortably reflective. The RPF, which marched on Kigali July 4 and sent the Hutu extremists fleeing for their lives, began the clean-up. They had dug mass graves on the side of the road and pushed the corpses into the long ditches, sweeping death beneath a dirt rug. The addresses of the dead piled up. The roadblocks disappeared. In their place, catacomb-like gatherings sprang up: all hushed voices, subdued lighting, bowed heads. From such an event, they said, how could anyone hope to recover?

[illegible]

[illegible]

[illegible]

[illegible]

[illegible]

1

Beginnings

The wreckage of President Habyarimana's plane was still smoldering when Damien Nzabakira put the last of the children at the orphanage in Kigali to bed. Damien was a strong, solid man who could shush one child while rocking another to sleep. He could inspire trust with a gesture or the tone of his voice. As a result, the children tended to take their cues from him. They loved him enough to decide that if he was not worried, they should not be either. So even though they had all heard the explosion, even though they jumped at the sound of gunfire, they collectively decided to put their faith in Damien and let him, as a grown-up, do their worrying for them. Damien, for his part, tried to minimize what they could hear or see. He read them books. He spoke quietly. He tried to make his calm infectious.

Damien was a compact man with shiny eyes and a cleanly shaven dome of a head. He laughed easily, had a smile that lit up a room, and obviously loved to be around his charges. Damien began his career in teaching because he was determined to pass on the advantages he had had—an education at elite Catholic elementary and high schools, and a year at the seminary—to those who might otherwise have no future in a country like Rwanda.

Damien was sensitive to how alien the world must look to these orphaned children. They lived in a constant state of flux, with none of the familiar objects or routines of home to calm them. Their lives were an unending series of new circumstances and new people. Damien knew that his presence provided a modicum of stability. And on that April evening he sensed, without being fully aware of the details, that he was all that stood between the children and chaos. He was equally sure that God had put him there at that moment to protect them all.

As the children slept, Damien stood vigil. He cocked his head to listen to the gunfire and tried to map from the sounds how close the violence was to the orphanage. The crack of each gun's report was magnified by the darkness. Damien found himself starting involuntarily with each shot. He walked into one of the orphanage's small classrooms, his shoes chirping over the linoleum, and fished a small radio out of a lower drawer in his desk. He clicked it on. There was a warbling and then a hum and then the sound of RTLM.

He moved toward the window without switching on a light. Outside he could see young men sitting in circles, lit up by bonfires. They passed around large bottles of beer. Some fired their pistols toward the heavens. He watched as the muzzle flashes lit them in brief silhouette.

* * *

What Damien didn't know was that a genocide had been launched and all Tutsi, typically the tall, slender minority and anyone who appeared to support them, were targets. Over the course of a week, the murders had become a kind of sport for the Interahamwe militiamen, like hunting. Rooting out the hiding Tutsi had become a battle of wits—Hutu extremists versus their prey. At first, the Tutsi ran to the predictable places: the churches and government compounds. That made them easy to kill. It was more difficult, however, to ferret out the craftier Tutsi. They hid in the vestibule closets of churches. They found refuge behind false ceilings. They clung to rafters. They lay on the ground, unmoving, hoping their pursuers would think them already dead. Those who twitched, or fell from the ceilings, or moved from their hiding places at the wrong time, paid for their mistakes with their lives.

The Tutsi did not beg to be spared. Instead they asked for a merciful end. They offered money to be shot instead of hacked to death. Killing Tutsi had become the law, a duty. It was not disorder, it was order—they were all *Inkotanyi*, accomplices of the invading Rwandan Patriotic Front army, the radio said.

"There will be no more *Inkotanyi*; there will be none in this country anymore," RTLM told its listeners. "When you see how many of them die, you would think that they come back to life. They themselves believe that they come back to life, but they deceive themselves, they are disappearing. They disappear gradually as bombs continue to fall on them and as they are killed like rats."

Damien watched from the orphanage window as people began moving to the outskirts of the capital, carrying their belongings on their heads. There were bodies in the street, swimming in sticky pools of blood. There were so many people pouring out of the city, Kigali was becoming deserted—like a remote hill village instead of a capital. For days now, Damien's full-time occupation was to calm the children. But after so many concussive explosions and so many cracks of gunfire, even Damien was losing his grip. The children began to shriek with every grenade blast. They exchanged worried glances when shots were fired. Damien cursed himself for not having taken the group out of Kigali before the fighting started. They would have been in the countryside, safe, if only he had acted sooner. Radio Mille Collines journalists had been beating the war drums for months, ramping up concern that something evil was coming. It had named names. It singled out traitors, enemies, and plotters—their names rolling out of the radio speakers in an endless stream.

"Jeanne is a sixth-form teacher at Mamba in Muyaga commune," one broadcast had said. "Jeanne is not doing good things in this school. Indeed, it has been noted that she's the cause of the bad atmosphere in the classes she teaches. She urges her students to hate the Hutus. These children spend the entire day at that, and it corrupts their minds. We hereby warn this woman named Jeanne; and indeed, the people of Muyaga, who are well known for their courage, should warn her. She is a security threat for the commune."

The station made clear who could be trusted and who could not. It lauded the vigilant who had found Tutsi hiding in the fields. It wooed the Hutu who were torn about the tastiness of the hunt. Damien listened as young militiamen breathlessly told the listening audience about the impending extermination of the Tutsi. One day slipped into the next as Damien held his radio to his ear and listened as RTLM reported every twist and turn of the unfolding war. And it would have continued that way had it not occurred to him one morning that RTLM offered something more than a blow-by-blow of a massacre. It provided the careful listener with clues. The Interahamwe calls gave Damien a good sense of who was where. He mapped out in his mind which roadblock patrols seemed especially vigilant or deadly. Those who called often to report their progress were to be avoided. Those who phoned in occasionally to say their posts were quiet offered hope of a less explosive confrontation.

Six days after the crash, Damien left one of the nuns in charge of the children and began to walk up the hill toward the Red Cross headquarters where he had once worked. The Red Cross volunteers were sure to help, he thought, as he picked his way through banana groves. He avoided the main roads, moving through the dirt alleyways between the houses. He tried not to look inside the houses, with their doorways open like dark mouths. The walk took about half an hour, and the Belgian volunteers, frightened themselves, were happy to see a familiar face. Damien gave them a wave as he came up the dirt drive and hugged them when he arrived at the door. He needed their help, he said. And he began to lay out his plan.

Less than an hour later, Damien was behind the wheel of a school bus, Red Cross flags snapping from the bumpers, driving back to the orphanage. We will leave all this, he decided, in the morning.

* * *

History in Rwanda has always been malleable, growing out of story lines of one's own choosing. If one was Hutu, then heroes were Hutu. If one was Tutsi, the opposite was true. In that storytelling, that exaggeration and embellishment, came the seeds of conflict.

When the colonialists came, to "civilize the savages," the differences between the Hutu and the Tutsi were formalized. It was the colonizers who took two people who had more in common than not and taught them to loathe each other. In the late 1800s and early 1900s, the nearby Congo offered rubber and slaves to Belgium's King Leopold. Rwanda, on the far side of the Ruwenzoris, or Mountains of the Moon, offered only proximity. From 1895 to 1916, Rwanda was a German colony. In 1916, in the midst of the First World War, Germany pulled out of the East African territories and Belgium took on the responsibility for Rwanda and neighboring Burundi. Belgian paternal rule lasted forty-five years.

In the late 1800s, race science was in fashion, and no one was given more credit for making sense of the dark continent than British explorer John Hanning Speke. Speke was best known for finding the source of the Nile in a wild and adventurous competition against the more intellectual and taciturn Captain Richard Burton. Speke, ever the glad-hander willing to slap fellow members of the Royal Geographical Society on the back and stand them a pint at the nearby pubs, was decidedly more popular than Burton. British society embraced his theories as gospel. Rwanda would suffer the consequences of Speke's popularity more than a century later. His doctrine, known as the Hamitic theory, laid the foundation for the 1994 genocide.

On his travels in Central and East Africa, Speke came to classify Africans into orders. He decided that all culture and civilization in Central Africa by 1863 had been the work of a taller, sharper-featured people who he decided must have come from a Caucasoid tribe in Ethiopia. This "higher order" of African descended from Noah's son, Ham, who married a Cainite woman, he said. These special Africans had a royal family and a semblance of a government and were, as a result, superior to the native Negroids. The other black Africans, the majority, he casually classified as subhuman. They were the savages who could be taken as slaves without troubling issues of conscience. "In these countries," he wrote of East Africa,

> the government is in the hands of foreigners, who had invaded and taken possession of them, leaving the agricultural aborigines to till the ground, while the junior members of the usurping clans herded cattle—just as in Abyssinia, or wherever the Abyssinians or Gallas have shown themselves. There a pastoral clan from the Asiatic side took the government of Abyssinia from its people and have ruled over them ever since, changing, by intermarriage with the Africans, the texture of their hair and color to a certain extent, but still maintaining a high stamp of Asiatic feature, of which a marked characteristic is a bridge instead of bridgeless nose.

For posterity, Speke drew his vision of these two Africans in one of his notebooks. On the last page of a sketchbook filled with watercolors of antelope and African birds, there is a quick drawing. On the left-hand side there is a rendering of a small, stocky African. There are dark lines and smudges around the nose as Speke used his chalks to flatten the bridge and flare out the nostrils. Behind that small African man, Speke drew another. Nearly twice the first one's size, this figure was what any European at the time would have drawn to capture the image of an African king: he looked like a slender, regal European in African garb, with a long nose and thin lips.

Taking their cues from the famous British explorer, white rulers in Rwanda decided that the Tutsi were destined for great things. The Tutsi were given administrative duties and the Hutu were shunted aside. They were given menial tasks. In most instances, the Hutu were obliged to work for Tutsi. They tilled their land or grazed their cattle. Enlisting the Tutsi as de facto rulers allowed the Belgians to develop and exploit an enormous network of tea and coffee plantations without having to install a contingent of Belgians on the ground. The Belgians appreciated the natural orderliness of this so much that they institutionalized the differences between Hutu and Tutsi in a series of administrative measures between 1926 and 1932. They issued identity cards, dividing everyone as either Hutu or Tutsi. No one is altogether sure how the distinction was made. Some stories said that anyone who owned ten cows was automatically designated a Tutsi, so that the system was based more on caste than on ethnicity.

However the ethnicity was assigned, it came to be the basis for determining everything from enrollment in the school system (only Tutsi were worth educating, Hutu were too stupid) to civil service jobs (also reserved for the Tutsi). The very act of recording the ethnic groups not only made them more important but fundamentally changed their character. The Hutu and Tutsi designations were no longer amorphous categories; instead, they became inflexible. Europeans began to refer to them as ethnic differences. The elite, the Tutsi, were the immediate beneficiaries, and they played that superiority to its best advantage. By the same token Hutu, officially excluded from power, began to take on the hallmarks of the oppressed. They banded together against the Tutsi. They groused about the unfairness of it all, and they plotted revenge.

The culmination of all this resentment came in November 1959 when an attack on a Hutu political activist sparked the first modern recorded violence of Hutu against Tutsi. Rumors of the attack sent bands of Hutu into the streets. They organized themselves into groups that were eerily like the Interahamwe militia who would succeed them. Splitting up into groups of ten, the Hutu men hunted Tutsi neighbors. Tutsi were summarily murdered. The episode was called the "wind of destruction."

It was after this killing spree that Rwanda's Belgian administrators decided to replace about half the local Tutsi authorities with Hutu. Popular elections were held the following year. It came as a surprise to no one that the Hutu, as the majority, won most of the seats. In September 1961, 80 percent of Rwandans voted to end recognition of the Tutsi monarchy entirely. The Belgians allowed Rwandans to claim a republic and retired from the colony completely. Their system of identity cards, however, remained in force. Maintained over sixty years, it eventually became one way Hutu killers identified Tutsi during the genocide. But that would come later. In the meantime, the Hutu consolidated their power in Rwanda by installing a charismatic Hutu leader named Grégoire Kayibanda as president. Thousands of Tutsi fled for their lives. They became stateless refugees in Burundi, Uganda, and Zaire. The revolution of 1959 forever cleaved Rwandan history into a before and an after. The uprising was popularly known as the Hutu Revolution.

From 1959 to 1994, victims and killers were slowly prepared for the coming genocide. Day after day at every level of Rwandan society the seeds of distrust and hatred were sown. Newly empowered, Hutu teachers would make Tutsi children stand up in the classrooms before their schoolmates. "Look at these Tutsi," the teachers would sneer, as the Tutsi children stood uncomfortably at their desks. "They think they are better than we are." The Tutsi students would try to protest and then would go silent. They were only children. Certainly, they could not be blamed for the crimes that came before them?

And yet they were blamed. Ethnicity came to trail the Tutsi minority like a tin can tied to the tail of a dog. While outsiders assumed that the Hutu and Tutsi were differing tribes, their differences were more superficial than that. While many Tutsi were tall and fine-featured with delicate hands and fingernails the color of blanched almonds, they did not all look that way. It was a stereotype. Similarly, while many Hutu were ebony black, short, and powerfully muscled, some belied the classification on their identity cards. Many looked Tutsi. Tutsiness or Hutuness was as much a state of mind as it was some closely tracked lineage. There were intermarriages that begot Hutu-looking men whose fathers had been Tutsi but who favored their Hutu mothers. Technically, their identity cards would read "Tutsi" since one was assigned the designation of one's father. And there were tall, thin Hutu, the offspring of Hutu fathers and Tutsi mothers, who were also caught between the two groups. Residual Belgian perceptions of Tutsi and Hutu found a place in the Rwandan psyche. Tutsi were seen as a handsomer people, a smarter people. Never mind that there was nothing to substantiate either claim. It was enough that people believed it to be true.

* * *

Rwandan mornings smell sweet and sour. The tang of fresh fires mixes with the salt of old sweat and the sweetness of fresh-cut grass. The air is thick and cool. The ground is soft and mossy. Fog gathers thick and white in the valleys and envelops hills sculpted by thousands of gardens. The mist softens the hard edges of the coffee plants and plantain trees. It muffles sound. Children in limp, colorful T-shirts balance on makeshift bicycles made of wood, swimming in and out of focus, taking shape out of the whiteness. Teenagers pulling bullock carts suddenly appear at close range. In every direction the view is the same: coffee plants, mud huts, green hills.

Before the genocide, Rwanda was known as the Tibet of Africa, the land of a thousand hills. The name came from the peaks and valleys of the Virunga Mountains, a volcanic chain that forms the continental divide between the Nile and the Congo river basins. The hills give the Rwandan landscape an enchanting quality, more Central America than Africa. For anyone on foot, however, the hills quickly become oppressive. They make one feel closed in, suffocated. Car engines strain going up the inclines and brakes smoke going down. It is difficult to get anywhere in Rwanda without running out of breath. One hill is left behind only to be followed by ten more ahead. The rolling lushness makes an already tiny place seem that much smaller. Hills are a curse in a place where size really matters. Rwanda is one of the most densely populated countries in Africa. Its ten thousand square miles hold almost 8 million people, all of whom seem to be clinging to the sides of the hills. Houses lean at angles, small patches of crops struggle to take root.

In one way or another all of Rwanda's battles seemed to spring from the ground on which its people stood. Geographers joke that Rwanda is so small there is no room for its name on a map. Atlases draw arrows—or allow RWANDA to slip into the Democratic Republic of the Congo (the former Zaire) on one side or into Tanzania on the other: a cartographic metaphor for the Rwandan condition. In the waning days of the genocide, ten thousand Rwandans spilled over the Zairean border every hour, as if Rwanda had filled to capacity and was letting the excess run off. The feet of millions of exiles padded into neighboring countries packing the cinder plains near the Virungas to an asphalt hardness.

There had been other exoduses. Hutu would flee on one occasion, Tutsi would flood the borders on another. It was an endless seesaw of political fortunes—when one group was down, the other was up. And while those in power jockeyed for advantage, the Rwandan people, resigned to this endless push and pull of politics, would load or unload their worldly possessions onto or off cattle and cart and make the pilgrimage to wherever safety beckoned.

Paul Kagame, a young Tutsi who had grown up in a refugee camp in Uganda, was one of those refugees. His parents had fled Rwanda in 1961, when Kagame was only three years old, amid a rash of anti-Tutsi violence in Rwanda. With little else to do but long for a country that refused to welcome him back, Kagame followed hundreds of other young Rwandan men into the forest to join a Ugandan anti–Idi Amin rebel force led by Yoweri Museveni. When that force succeeded in installing Museveni as the new Uganda president, Kagame was made the head of Uganda's army intelligence.

As highly regarded as Kagame was, however, he still had the sense that he would only be permitted to go so far in his adopted country: he was not, after all, Ugandan; he was Rwandan. He was part of a lost generation who had grown outside Rwanda looking in. And it was out of this general longing to return home that the Rwandan Patriotic Front was born.

More than twenty years before the genocide, in July 1973, General Juvénal Habyarimana, the army's most senior officer, toppled Grégoire Kayibanda in a coup d'état. He assumed the presidency and vowed to end the cycle of violence. He said he would allow those who had fled to neighboring nations out of fear to return. He called on Rwandans to welcome the exiles. He promised that Rwanda's future would be brighter. A trickle of humanity took him up on his offer and returned.

It took only two years for Habyarimana to decide that the returnees were not really so welcome. Rwanda didn't have the resources to absorb them. There were battles over land. Squatters fought for their houses. Exiles demanded the government make good on its promises of right of return. Habyarimana, concerned the violence would shake his hold on power, took drastic action. He closed the borders and made Rwanda a one-party state under the National Republican Movement for Development, or MRND. All local leaders, by default, were decreed MRND members. Overnight, everyone was dubbed an ally of the president. Ensuring that everyone adhered to Habyarimana's political reorganization was relatively easy: Rwanda's communities had been divided and subdivided and cut into so many overlapping pieces, it was easy to keep track of everyone. The nation was divided into ten prefectures, each of which included subprefectures and communes, which usually encompassed about forty thousand residents. The communes themselves were led by burgomasters. They held court once or twice a week to receive citizens and explain the latest news from the capital. More than a mayor, the burgomaster was all-powerful. He determined land use, mediated property conflicts, settled family disputes, placed children in secondary schools, and decided whether cases ought to go to a higher court. Below the level of communes, the communities were further divided into sectors of about five thousand people. Community cells sliced that population even thinner.

The structure made the administration of authoritarian rule child's play. Keeping tabs on citizens and, more important, mobilizing them against threats required a single phone call. And to make sure that the people were ready to follow orders at all times, the government instituted a system called *umunganda*, literally "work for the public good." Rwandans were compelled, with a simple request from the burgomaster, to repair roads or clear brush. Rwandans were conditioned to do as they were told and not ask questions.

Contrary to popular lore, when the RPF made its first small invasions into Rwanda, in 1990, Rwandan refugee Paul Kagame was not in charge. He was in the United States for a course at the Army's Command and General Staff College in Fort Leavenworth, Kansas, and rushed back to Uganda, cutting his studies short, so he could help organize the RPF. Hutu leaders in Rwanda immediately worried that Kagame would be a force to be reckoned with. He was considered the military brains behind Museveni's successful overthrow of the Ugandan government. The mere mention of his name frightened regular Rwandan citizens and his battlefield prowess started to take on mythic proportions.

It wasn't until January 1991, when the Rwandan Patriotic Front raided the town of Ruhengeri, the birthplace of the Hutu Power movement, that members of Habyarimana's cabinet made their plan for a counteroffensive public. "Go do a special *umunganda*," the prefect in Ruhengeri told local residents.

"Destroy all the bushes and all the *Inkotanyi*. And don't forget that those who are destroying weeds must also get rid of the roots." The roots, presumably, were the Tutsi civilians who might secretly support the RPF. Rwandans who took part in the genocide said later they could hardly be blamed for their actions. They were only following orders.

* * *

It is easy to underestimate the damage historical confusion can wreak. For that reason Rwanda needed responsible academics to help set the record straight. University of Rwanda history professor Ferdinand Nahimana believed he was the man to do just that. Born in 1950 to a farming family, Nahimana was the youngest of nine children. He managed to get an education in spite of the fact that he was poor and Hutu. He even received a doctorate in France, where his study of Hutu history was lauded as a step toward helping peace return to his country.

A slender man with a wide forehead and sympathetic eyes, Nahimana spoke in the soft, even tones of an intellectual. He saw no need to raise his voice. Some said his gentle demeanor belied the turmoil that raged inside him. People said that he secretly harbored hatred of the Tutsi and he had come to the conclusion that a history needed to be written that extolled the virtue of the majority people, the Hutu. Nahimana had focused his research on what he perceived were the overlooked contributions the Hutu had made to Rwandan culture.

Nahimana's "new history" was a rejection of an inherited body of understandings that could be traced back to Speke's writings from the Mountains of the Moon. Nahimana felt the Tutsi were not just wrongheaded about their perceived right to pull the levers of power in Rwanda; they were a natural enemy of the Hutu majority. Anything that provided a boost to the Tutsi came at the expense of the Hutu, he said. The Tutsi had no right to rule. Their goal was to return Rwanda to its days as a monarchy. Nahimana had taken his theory to the University of Paris in 1986 and written a dissertation on the Hutu kingdoms of northwest Rwanda. His professor, Jean-Paul Chrétien, awarded him the highest honors for "demystifying Rwandan history."

Nahimana returned from abroad just as the Tutsi-led Rwandan Patriotic Front began forcing Habyarimana's hand on the right of Tutsi exiles to return. The Tutsi offensives had sparked a rapid militarization of Rwandan society by 1990. Sides were chosen along familiar lines: it would be Hutu against Tutsi. Recruits to the Rwandan army grew at breakneck speed. The ranks grew from a few thousand soldiers to forty thousand in just three years. By 1992, the military consumed almost 70 percent of the Rwandan government's budget. Between 1985 and 1990, the military gobbled up 1.6 percent of the nation's GNP; by 1993, three times that amount.

Nahimana might have labored on in relative anonymity had it not been for President Habyarimana. A stalwart supporter of the president's party, the MRND, later renamed the MRNDD in 1991, Nahimana offered to help Habyarimana unite the nation's Hutu majority. He saw it as an opportunity to teach unlettered people about their past, to replace historical rumor and innuendo with fact. He began to educate the masses from a seat at Radio Rwanda, the nation's only government-sponsored station, in 1992. Before Nahimana's arrival Radio Rwanda's broadcasts were mind-numbing. The airwaves were filled with only the dullest fare. There were excerpts of President Habyarimana's political speeches or a recitation of the latest news from an MRND political meeting. When the news was particularly slow, Radio Rwanda would rebroadcast presidential speeches in their entirety—hours and hours of monotone from a man who seemed to love the sound of his own voice. In comparison, anything Nahimana decided to broadcast would be an improvement.

For a man who was used to speaking to a rarefied audience of intellectuals, Nahimana found himself able to find the right words to reach the eager ears of ordinary Rwandans, men and women who were more characterized by action than reflection.

The potential of such an audience was not lost on Nahimana. It was clear that, properly presented, his vision of the Hutu would pour from the speakers of Radio Rwanda into the ears of a receptive audience who could easily turn theory into actual practice. It was not until Nahimana blamed Tutsi rebels for a series of killings in a small swampy town called Bugesera in 1992 that people began to notice that this Hutu professor had been given such a broad portfolio and powerful position.

Initially, all that was known for sure about the events in Bugesera was that some killings had taken place there. Armed men had arrived, and villagers, a lot of them, had been murdered. How the details were filled in beyond that depended on your point of view. Among the Tutsi community, word spread that members of the Rwandan army had arrived and killed hundreds of Tutsi. Hutu heard that the Rwandan Patriotic Front army had arrived and hundreds of Hutu had been killed.

At the broadcast studios of Radio Rwanda, Ferdinand Nahimana handed journalists a communiqué from the Commission Inter-Africaine pour la Non-Violence, a human rights organization said to be based in Nairobi. The communiqué warned that the low-boil fighting in Bugesera was about to change into something bloodier. It would escalate, the communiqué said, from guerrilla warfare to a rash of assassinations. Property would be destroyed. After the battle took place, the RPF would blame the violence on the Hutu, the journalists reading from the communiqué told listeners.

Radio Rwanda decided to air the contents of the communiqué without making a single attempt to corroborate it. Journalists didn't even make the cursory phone call to the Commission Inter-Africaine pour la Non-Violence to ask them about their sources. Had they done that most basic of journalistic checks, they would have discovered that the human rights organization didn't exist at all. Officials in Bugesera had made it, and the communiqué, up.

Hours after the communiqué was broadcast, Ferdinand Nahimana's voice came over the radio. "Annihilate these Machiavellian plans of the enemy Inyenzi-Inkotanyi," the director of the nation's Bureau of Information said, using the Kinyarwandan-language nickname for the Tutsi: "cockroach." The Tutsi were preparing to overthrow the country, he said.

A short time later a truck filled with young toughs from the Interahamwe militia and the presidential guard arrived in Bugesera. Residents recalled the first sounds that evening were the wheezing of truck engines and the clattering of metal. There was the dead sound of boots on the dirt. Orders barked. Then the tangled, unmistakable sound of commotion: short gasps, bare feet thumping across soft earth, small shrieks, and then the dull thud of body meeting ground.

When the work was done, and it didn't take long, corpses lay along the streets frozen in twisted poses, limbs missing, eyes open in startled surprise. At first glance it might have appeared indiscriminate, proof of a world gone mad. Many of the dead looked of a piece: they were tall, thin, fine-featured, the color of café au lait. They lay in delicate repose, floating in muddy circles of blood. Truck engines roared back to life. Metal blades fell with a clatter into the truck beds. The killers melted back into the eucalyptus groves and the bottle green hills without a trace.

This was a dress rehearsal for a genocide.

Nearly two hundred Tutsi and moderate Hutu were dead and fifteen thousand people had simply disappeared. "It was the first time that the radio was used to incite people to violence," the Rwandan expert for Human Rights Watch, Alison Des Forges, would testify later.

What she didn't know was that a young Rwandan journalist named Hassan Ngeze was also using the media, a newspaper called *Kangura,* to stir up the people of Bugesera. Witnesses would say later that they saw him in Bugesera two weeks before the violence offering passersby copies of the *Kangura* tabloid. The banner headline read: THE BATUTSI, GOD'S RACE! Beneath the sixteen-point type was an image of the former Hutu president of Rwanda, Grégoire Kayibanda. The caption under the photograph was fiery: "How about relaunching the 1959 BaHutu Revolution so we can conquer the Inyenzi-BaTutsi?" Another large headline beneath the caption went a step farther. WHAT WEAPONS SHALL WE USE TO CONQUER THE INYENZI ONCE AND FOR ALL?

The newspaper helpfully supplied an answer: beside the headline was a drawing of a machete. While it suggested one ought to take matters into one's own hands, it never directly advocated that anyone kill. It was a fine distinction that would arise when *Kangura* was the subject of discussion in a court of law years later.

* * *

As Bugesera began to bury its dead, a group of men in Kigali were watching the events with satisfaction. Bugesera was their experiment. It was the first phase in a grander plan meant to end this Tutsi problem in Rwanda once and for all. But that was revealed only later. What alarmed moderate forces at the time was Nahimana's decision to broadcast his version of the events. Radio Rwanda had fomented tensions in Bugesera, they said, and Nahimana had intended to whip up residents when he broadcast news of the communiqué out of Nairobi. Why had he not directed journalists to check the veracity of the report? Why had he decided to make a personal appearance on the radio to turn up the heat on the situation? Putting the best face on it, the moderates said, Nahimana exercised bad judgment. At worst, he knew precisely what he was doing and his actions had cost hundreds of Tutsi lives. President Habyarimana bowed under pressure and fired Ferdinand Nahimana from the top job at the Rwandan Bureau of Information (ORINFOR) and Radio Rwanda.

"I was a scapegoat," Nahimana would say later. "I learned that I had been sacked from my position from Radio Rwanda. Then the radio said the council of ministers was appointing me as first adviser, or first consular, for the Rwandan embassy in Bonn, Germany, instead." Witnesses would say later that Germany told the government in Kigali that it would not accept Nahimana into the country because he was a known racist. Nahimana said the job change never occurred because he didn't want it.

Six months later Nahimana would find a handful of people to help him with a new venture. He decided to start his own radio station, a creation he would call Radio-Télévision Libre des Mille Collines, or RTLM. The idea came, he said later, when he was having coffee with several friends in the fall of 1992. The conversation had turned to the rise of an RPF radio station called Radio Muhabura. It had started broadcasting in the western part of the country and into the Congo. And while the new station's signal was not strong and its following was not large, it rankled the men sitting around the table drinking coffee. Radio Muhabura gave the Rwandan Patriotic Front a voice. It had been calling on Rwandans, or more precisely Tutsi, to return from their countries of exile. This right of return angered the men. There was barely enough in Rwanda for the people who were already there.

What concerned those aligned with the president most was Radio Muhabura's support of the U.N.–supervised Arusha Accords. The plan outlined a twenty-two-month timetable for Rwanda's political parties, including the RPF and the president's Mouvement Républicain National pour la Démocratie et le Développement (MRNDD), to form a transitional government that would lead, eventually, to democratic, multiethnic elections. The plan was to reintegrate the refugees and the RPF into Rwanda—to demobilize the government and RPF troops, draft a new constitution, and rebuild the economy. The goals would have been ambitious even if everyone concerned had been eager to make them work. Those who supported them saw the accords as Rwanda's best chance for a new social contract. Those who loathed them, Habyarimana and his supporters among them, couldn't think of anything worse than the plan's implementation.

Their objections came on many levels. Habyarimana didn't trust the RPF and felt that the MRNDD, the only party in Rwanda for decades, was getting short shrift. He felt that the

MRNDD deserved more weight in any transitional government and should not share power equally with the political upstarts that had only recently emerged in Rwanda. Members of the ruling MRNDD had another very real concern: they worried that once the transitional government was in place, the RPF would see to it that the president and his entourage would be charged for crimes they committed in the nearly twenty years they had been in power.

"If Radio Muhabura was not doing this major propaganda on behalf of the RPF, and showing that the government and Rwanda was the one who was in the wrong, I think the company, RTLM, would not have been established," Nahimana said later. "This is what motivated people to establish this company; at least in my view it's these factors which dictated my involvement in the establishment of this company."

* * *

Jean-Bosco Barayagwiza was the chief ideologue for the stridently anti-Tutsi Coalition for the Defense of the Republic, or CDR, and he made no secret about how he personally felt about the Tutsi and the RPF. He didn't like them.

To follow Barayagwiza's progression through life was to follow the typical path followed by any of Rwanda's Hutu elite since independence. He was educated at a seminary, as many bright Hutu had been, and later was permitted to study law in the Soviet Union in the 1970s at a time when the state in the Soviet Union ranked supreme and when laws were not in place to protect individuals. They were there to protect the state. In postcolonial Rwanda the opportunity to study abroad, much less travel abroad, was limited, and those who returned to Rwanda from such adventures were rewarded. Barayagwiza's experience rather naturally opened the door to politics. On his return several years later to Rwanda, he became a senior official in the Ministry of Foreign Affairs and eventually worked as director of political affairs for the Habyarimana government.

Barayagwiza and Nahimana were an odd pair. The lawyer was as fiery as Nahimana was quiet. Barayagwiza was a man who seemed to create a blast area around his beliefs, and Nahimana seemed to be perennially musing. "I can go up the genealogy of my family back to about the ninth generation," Barayagwiza said. "They are Hutus. They brought me up as a Hutu. I grew up in a Hutu culture. I was born before the 1959 revolution. My father did forced labor. My mother used to weed in the field of the Tutsis who were in power. My grandfather paid tribute money. They would tell me: 'That is how things are: we must work for the Tutsis.'"

Barayagwiza, like all true believers, allowed his hatred of the Tutsi to become all-consuming, and because he was the kind of man who inspired people to join his crusade, his passions consumed everyone in the vicinity. His simmering hatred for the Tutsi came to a rolling boil soon after the announcement of the Arusha Accords. He saw Nahimana's RTLM project as an antidote—a way to avoid the worst of all possible fates: sharing power with the Tutsi. He helped Nahimana find investors for the new venture. The radio station incorporated in April 1993 and was broadcasting by that summer.

"RTLM is a radio station with objectives," one 1993 broadcast said. "Its aim is to tell the truth, all the truth. There are people who call us on the radio and talk to us. Others write to us. Some come to see us, while we meet others and discuss the station with them. Anybody can be an RTLM correspondent, whether they come from Rwanda or are foreigners, whether they are in Burundi, in Uganda, or anywhere else in the world."

2

Murderers or Patriots

In March 1994, RTLM unveiled a new contest. Listeners who read the *Kangura* newspaper and answered a few questions had an opportunity to win money, an all-expenses-paid weekend on the shores of Lake Kivu, electronics, clothing, or food. All that was required was a little close reading of old issues of the newspaper. Contestants needed to answer eleven questions, the correct responses could be found in the pages of back issues of *Kangura*. Contestants had to send an original entry form (no photocopies accepted) with their answers to RTLM's broadcast headquarters in downtown Kigali. First prize was 25,000 Rwandan francs, the announcers said. That was the equivalent of several months' salary.

The contest was far from easy. In which issue of *Kangura* will you find the sentence "We have no more Tutsi because of Kanyarengwe"? one question read. "When did *Kangura* become the voice to wake up the majority people and defend their interests?" queried another. The questions related to some thirteen different issues of the newspaper. To come up with the answers entrants would likely have to pore over at least three times that many copies of the paper. The founders of *Kangura* helpfully suggested that anyone who had thrown out past issues could buy back copies at their local newsstand. It was a boon for circulation.

RTLM also asked contestants to complete an opinion poll attached to the entry form. "Since RTLM began broadcasting in Rwanda, tell us what you think of its activities," the survey began. "Tell us what you would want to change. Tell us what you consider to be its strong points and its weak points." The survey asked readers to rank the various RTLM personalities. The questions seemed innocent enough, but this was more than simple market research. It was an attempt to see if the fiery rhetoric of RTLM was effective.

* * *

Human rights activist Monique Mujawamariya sensed trouble was coming long before the violence began.

She had noticed the Habyarimana government's tendency to target Tutsi and she tried to draw world attention to it. Those who knew her described her as fearless. She spoke her mind and showed little deference to the rank or standing of those who she believed were doing wrong.

The daughter of a Hutu father and a Tutsi mother, she was married to a senior Rwandan army officer, with whom she had three children. From the start, she chafed under the traditional roles she was expected to assume. Women in Rwanda were treated and regarded as dependents of their male relatives. They were expected to be protected, and managed, by their fathers, their husbands, and even their male children. Women were valued for the number of children they produced, and in Rwanda, that was many. Before 1994, the average number of children per woman was 6.2.—the highest in the world.

Monique wasn't built that way, and when her husband responded by trying to tame her, to beat her into submission, she left him and took her children with her. In Rwandan society that was just not done. Many women, while they admired Monique's tenacity, were also frightened of her. Men were a little rattled by her defiance too. To keep herself occupied as her marriage unraveled, Monique began working with AIDS victims. She opened her home to other battered women and their families. One thing led to another and before she knew it, she had become a champion of human rights in Rwanda—not just an advocate for women but a piercing voice that questioned the Habyarimana regime and its followers. In 1990, the seventeenth year of President Juvénal Habyarimana's regime, there was an alarming outbreak of politically motivated kidnappings and murders. Political opponents went missing. Moderate Hutu turned up dead. Monique worked hard to make sure the international community took notice.

Monique was certain there was a pattern to the murders that had been occurring across the country. She began to see, in the early 1990s, what she came to believe were tentative, trial massacres. There were unexplained killings in small towns where extremists thought no one would notice. These were training missions of sorts, allowing those in the upper echelons of the extremist Hutu movement to see what worked and what didn't when trying to launch a grassroots campaign against the Tutsi. In each case the pattern was much the same. Authorities used false rumors and misinformation ("The Tutsi rebels are invading our nation" or "We have heard the RPF are planning an offensive") to promote ethnic hatred and incite local residents. Government leaders called political meetings and warned of Tutsi soldiers ready to attack.

Because the Rwandan Patriotic Front had been launching small offenses into Rwanda, planting such seeds of fear was easy. The Hutu were genuinely afraid of the RPF. They believed the Tutsi would stop at nothing to regain the power they lost after independence. And who was to say whether one's Tutsi neighbor, the man or woman who seemed so nice, so helpful, during harvest time, wasn't secretly in alliance with the RPF, awaiting an opening?

Alison Des Forges, who headed Rwandan studies at Human

Rights Watch in New York, was one of Monique's secret weapons against such excesses of the Habyarimana regime. The two women had met in 1991 when Des Forges was on a fact-finding tour of Rwanda. They ran into each other by accident at the Kigali International Airport. Monique had heard of Des Forges, a Yale University scholar and fluent Kinyarwanda speaker who had had a thirty-five-year relationship with Rwanda, and Des Forges had heard of Monique. The two women instantly felt a connection. So much so, they spent the next two weeks together, traveling along the green hills of the interior speaking to citizens who worried aloud that there would soon be violence in Rwanda.

The massacre in Bugesera, a year later, showed those early fears were well founded. Much to the chagrin of the Kigali government, Monique immediately set to work organizing diplomats and foreign observers to join her on a field trip to Bugesera so they could see the devastation for themselves. Just days before one group arrived, Monique flagged a taxi outside her offices in Kigali. As she buried herself in the details of the visitors' itinerary, she noticed that the taxi was picking up speed. The driver was steering erratically. A moment later, the passenger side of the speeding cab careened into a tree. The driver fled the scene.

Monique was thrown through the windshield. Her face was badly cut. Less than a week later, she met the human rights representatives at the Kigali International Airport as scheduled, covered in bandages. It was never clear who was behind the accident, but the incident solidified her reputation as Rwanda's most unflappable human rights activist.

The decision to escort foreigners to Bugesera turned out to be a boon for Monique's effort to show the world that Habyarimana's government condoned a roster of human rights abuses. Human rights groups and diplomats strongly condemned what they concluded was government-sponsored violence in Bugesera. What is more, they singled out Radio Rwanda for having encouraged the massacres. The killing was a "logical and direct response to the mysterious communiqué that had been broadcast several times," they said in a written statement later. Their displeasure and the political pressure that followed led to the dismissal of Ferdinand Nahimana from the Bureau of Information. Ever after, there was no love lost between Monique and Nahimana. She would discover later quite a few high-ranking members of the Habyarimana regime felt the same way.

Concerned that Monique's taxi accident would be followed by other attempts on her life, Des Forges decided to raise Monique's international profile, to redirect world attention to the human rights abuses in Rwanda. So she invited Monique to represent Rwanda at a White House ceremony in December 1993 to commemorate the forty-fourth anniversary of the United Nations Universal Declaration of Human Rights, a common standard of human rights achievement to which all nations should aspire. Des Forges hoped that Monique's highly visible meeting with President Clinton would shield her from future reprisals when she returned home.

When Rwandans shake hands, they often continue to hold the other person's hand, reluctant to break the human contact once it has been established. While it is unclear whether Monique clutched President Clinton's hand, or he hung onto hers, the two shook hands for more than ten minutes. Standing in a receiving line, she told him that Rwanda needed his help. She told him about the human rights abuses in her country and her fear that mass violence was close at hand.

President Clinton listened in rapt attention. It was not only Monique's story that intrigued him. It was her tenacity. President Clinton was so taken with her that he singled Monique out from all the other human rights activists in attendance during his remarks later that morning. "Your courage is an inspiration to all of us," he told her. Four months later Habyarimana's plane crashed.

* * *

Asked to describe his life, Hassan Ngeze's response was a long recitation of accomplishments that were difficult to verify. Hassan

Ngeze liked to embellish. One moment he would talk about growing up in Uganda, the next moment one would hear about his rise from bus token collector to investigative journalist. Ngeze would tell anyone who would listen that he spoke twelve languages fluently, could troubleshoot a computer, and was (almost) a soccer player on the national team. He was (almost) a graduate from middle school. He was (almost) a key player in Rwanda's first private radio station, Radio Mille Collines.

Hassan Ngeze's stories rarely came out the same way twice. People from his village of Gisenyi said he had a minimal education and what he learned he learned on the streets. Hassan Ngeze's motivation was simple: he wanted money and was willing to get it through whatever means were necessary. Ngeze wasn't exactly a charlatan, but he was close. He was always working on some great scheme, jockeying for position so some combination of people and events could be used to his best advantage. He had a kiosk in downtown Gisenyi where people gathered just to talk or gossip, and it may have been the information he picked up there—the grumbling of office workers, the grousing of government officials—that led him to the conclusion that he would make a first-rate investigative reporter. Ngeze knows a story, he would say, referring to himself in the third person. He quickly came to hold his own reportorial talents in such high regard that he decided to start his own newspaper just to showcase them.

Kangura, or "Wake It Up," was born out of vengeance. Ngeze had been a reporter at a popular newspaper in Rwanda called *Kanguka* ("Wake Up") until he got in a fight with the editor over a story. Ngeze's newspaper mission was twofold: it was meant to take a bite out of *Kanguka*'s sales and it was aimed at a natural readership—the majority people. Ngeze's propensity toward exaggeration may not have made for the best journalism, but it sold newspapers. What is more, Ngeze saw nothing wrong in radically inflating the circulation numbers for his creation. Who would it hurt? he reasoned. So though he claimed he was printing thirty thousand copies of the paper by January 1994, the true number, when the newspaper came out at all, was closer to two thousand. "It was a gossip rag," one neighbor of Ngeze's said. "What people don't understand about Hassan Ngeze is that he wasn't political at all. All he was interested in was money, and he thought this newspaper would make him money. If he didn't think that it was going to bring him cash, he wouldn't have done it."

Ngeze claimed to have started his journalism career by launching a press agency in Gisenyi. He built a network of contacts by paying people to bring him news from wherever they were. He said he approached ministers' secretaries and offered to double their salaries on the condition that they provide him with a copy of whatever they typed for their bosses. He would offer huge bonuses for those who made photocopies. That's how, he said, he could report on events before they actually occurred. The star of *Kangura*, though, was not the news so much as Ngeze himself. There were full-page pictures of him and recitations of his many (embellished) accomplishments. He implied he had friends, many friends, in high places and, for the sake of his craft, he had taken information they had imparted and provided a summary for his readers. When there were rumors, he reported them. And there was hardly a story heard on the streets of Rwanda that Ngeze didn't claim to know, or claim to report, first.

Hassan Ngeze liked to be in the middle of things, even if those things weren't good for him. Nothing puts a man in the thick of events more than newspaper work. *Kangura* became Ngeze's bully pulpit, a platform for extolling his own virtues. Ngeze is a good guy, he would say. Ngeze is a good-looking guy. "Hassan Ngeze wants to be the corpse at every funeral," those who knew him would add, laughing.

Still, there was something oddly winning about Ngeze. He had a wide, friendly face and an easy smile. Semiliterate but well sourced, he was good at conversation and was particularly deft at working contacts in the government intelligence services. Over time he was able to extract, either through charm or cash, meaty tidbits for his newspaper.

The first issue of *Kangura* hit the streets of Rwanda in May 1990. It was clear from the start that Ngeze intended to take easy shots at the Tutsi. There were cartoons spoofing them, screeds slamming them for controlling 70 percent of the country's wealth. The Tutsi would never be satisfied, he wrote in unsigned editorials, until they ruled Rwanda again. They would try, he said, to overthrow the government and regain the reins of power. That kind of thing, in 1990, was enough to get Ngeze thrown in jail for violating the nation's media rules. The authorities said he was guilty of "divisionism." The rift between Hutu and Tutsi, though ever present, was not supposed to be alluded to.

Ngeze had trouble walking that fine line. He received a two-year suspended sentence for his transgressions in 1990 only to be detained again in August of 1991 for accusing the leadership in neighboring Burundi of providing arms for the RPF. Ngeze was in prison for several months before he won his release. For all the trouble Hassan Ngeze was getting himself into, there was, in his view, one very good thing to come of it: he was getting noticed.

In January 1994, the banner headline in *Kangura* attracted the attention Ngeze so openly craved. WHO WILL SURVIVE THE WAR OF MARCH? the headline read. Given there was no war going on at the time, aside from skirmishes with the RPF along the border, the question naturally attracted readers. The article claimed that the Rwandan Patriotic Front was preparing an offensive. RPF commanders were planning to send three thousand troops to the presidential barracks in Kigali instead of the six hundred agreed upon in the Arusha Accords, the article warned. The boost in manpower was aimed at massing the forces necessary for a coup. The article concluded: "If the RPF have decided to kill us . . . then let us kill each other. Let whatever is smoldering erupt."

The Arusha Accords permitted the RPF to station a light battalion of six hundred soldiers in Kigali to protect their high-ranking officials, who would end up in the future transitional government. They were stationed on one side of a hill in Kigali, and the presidential guard, the government troops, were stationed on the other. If the RPF had tried to station more than the permitted number of soldiers in the Kigali compound, the government forces would have seen it. Even more to the point, the United Nations, which was monitoring the interim stages of the peace pact, would not have permitted it. But that hardly mattered. Rwandans had been so conditioned to expect the worst from the Tutsi that no one needed to have proof that they were up to something.

In February 1994, *Kangura* published another frightening article entitled "Final Attack." "We have indications that the RPF will soon launch other attacks in Kigali from all sides. We know where the cockroaches are. If they look for us, they had better watch out."

To anyone reading *Kangura,* it seemed clear that Ngeze was leveling a threat. Ngeze would say later that the articles were misunderstood. He was trying to let the RPF know that if they tried to start a war, they would be wiped out. Ngeze even predicted how the war was going to start. "Last month we saw undeniable signs showing how Habyarimana is going to be killed . . ." Ngeze's February 1994 article read. "He'll be shot dead by a person taken from the Rwandan Armed Forces. That person will be a Hutu bought by the Inyenzi." The genocide started two months later. The violence made it impossible for *Kangura* to publish. The February 1994 issue was Ngeze's last in Rwanda.

This apparent clairvoyance, the prediction of how and when the most sinister events would unfold, was too precise to be coincidental. Radio Mille Collines possessed a similar gift. Three days before Habyarimana's plane was shot out of the sky, alarming reports began to float from the RTLM airwaves. The RPF was planning to overthrow the Rwandan government, the station said. "The RPF rebels want to take power. Take it by the use of arms. They want to do a 'little something,'" the radio told Rwandans. "They have dates. They tell us this: on the third, fourth, and the fifth there will be a little something here in Kigali City. And also on the seventh and the eighth. . . . You will hear the sound of bullets or grenades explode. But I hope that the Rwandan armed forces are on alert."

RTLM's power to predict the future would have been written off were it not for one thing: on April 7, President Habyarimana was dead.

* * *

If someone had peered into the law offices of Michael Kennedy, P.C., on Manhattan's Upper East Side, just as Habyarimana's plane went down, they would have seen Simone Monasebian's face aglow with the light from her computer screen. A junior attorney at the top-shelf New York firm, Monasebian was at the office late, working on a tax fraud case. The firm told its lawyers that if they took on a share of corporate and white-collar cases—the bread and butter of the firm—they could work pro bono cases to their heart's content. "Those white-collar types subsidized our tilting at windmills," Monasebian said later.

The firm's Park Avenue offices were not typical law firm fare. Every morning the attorneys would file by the trompe l'oeil rendering of Picasso's *Don Quixote* in the office lobby. They would pass trompe l'oeil books on trompe l'oeil shelves. People would comment later that Monasebian, like the paintings in the lobby, was not as she first appeared.

Monasebian stumbled into lawyering through an unlikely route: hip-hop radio. She had been a sixteen-year-old reporter at *RadioScope*, a nationally syndicated urban entertainment program. Though she was a young woman of Iranian descent, the first child in her family to be born in America, she became one of the nation's first journalists to cover rap music and hip-hop culture. As *RadioScope*'s East Coast correspondent, she began reporting on a case in the Southern District Court of New York involving a 1983 copyright suit between Sugar Hill Records, the first rap label, and Grandmaster Flash and the Furious Five. At issue: who owned the moniker Grandmaster Flash—the artist or the label?

Monasebian's reportage on the case was more enthusiastic than impartial. She clearly thought Grandmaster Flash deserved to own the name and reported the story that way. Grandmaster Flash and the Furious Five credited her in the liner notes of their *They Said It Couldn't Be Done* album. The title could have been a shorthand summation of Monasebian's future career.

The experience at *RadioScope* led to a number of unlikely jobs. Spike Lee offered her a job as a script supervisor. She sang backup vocals on Chuck Brown and the Soul Searchers' 1985 recording "Back It on Up (Sho' Yuh Right)." Eventually though the young New Yorker made the leap from hip-hop culture to the courtroom. The Grandmaster Flash case had peaked her interest in the law. She graduated from New York University and decided to enroll in Syracuse University College of Law. She wanted to defend artists instead of just write about them.

In particular, Monasebian found herself drawn to cases where there was an intersection of journalism and the law. For her senior thesis at Syracuse she questioned, for example, the impartiality of press coverage in some of the nation's best-known racially explosive gang rapes—chief among them the 1989 Central Park jogger case in which five men were charged with raping a jogger in New York City's biggest park. Ten years after Monasebian wrote her thesis, the Central Park jogger verdicts were reversed. There had been, among other things, too much media hype around the incident. The men who confessed to attacking a lone woman jogger in the park weren't guilty; another man subsequently confessed to the crime. There was such intense public pressure to find the perpetrators, the young men who were convicted were convenient culprits. The Manhattan district attorney asked a judge to vacate the convictions of the five men in 2002.

With an interest in the rights of defendants, Monasebian focused with single-minded zeal on getting a job with one of Manhattan's best criminal defense attorneys, Michael Kennedy. Monasebian wanted to make her application stand out. So in addition to her résumé, she sent Kennedy a selection of her salty hip-hop-style poems. Her moxie, and a poem called "GhettOver Girls," which focused on feminism and urban politics, landed her the job. Once at the Kennedy firm, Monasebian became an expert on federal sentencing. She represented the political head of the Islamic resistance movement, Hamas, in an extradition case involving alleged crimes against humanity and defended a photographer at *High Times* magazine who had taken centerfold pictures of the marijuana weed. To that point in her legal career, Monasebian had sat on the defense side of the table. It took a plane crash in East Africa to make her a prosecutor.

* * *

Stephen Rapp, the U.S. attorney for the Northern District of Iowa, had just turned out the light in the bedroom and switched on a late-night BBC broadcast when he heard the news of massacres in Rwanda. It was April 7, 1994, and the announcer called the killings part of a civil war. Years later, Rapp would wonder why the bulletin registered. While his wife was an expert in African affairs at the University of Iowa, Rapp had generally limited his focus on the continent to the polite interest spouses have in the specialties of their other halves. His wife, Dolly, held a mild interest in the law enforcement changes he championed, and he made due with a good general knowledge of the African issues that interested her. At the time, he was completely unaware of the difficulties Rwanda faced.

A tall, lanky man with thinning blond hair and fair skin, Rapp had an infectious laugh and the easy gait of a high school athlete. A Harvard Law School graduate, he had risen through the ranks to become an attorney who thrived at the intersection of law and politics. Iowa's future senator Tom Harkin was a friend. In the 1970s, Rapp had run against future senator Chuck Grassley for a congressional seat. There was something immensely likable about Steve Rapp, and that quality made him effective as an attorney.

On the evening of the Habyarimana plane crash, Rapp was

focused on an upcoming visit to the White House—his first. It was National Crime Victims' Rights Week, and President Clinton was trying to garner support for a crime bill. Rapp was part of his strategy. He was singled out for his work in Iowa prosecuting criminals under the Brady Law. A controversial statute named after Ronald Reagan's press secretary James Brady, who was shot during a presidential assassination attempt, the law stiffened the sentences of any criminal who used a gun while committing a crime. The Clinton White House wanted Rapp in the Rose Garden for a ceremony to drum up support for what it saw as the next step: a three-strikes provision in the crime bill before Congress that would put repeat felons away for life. Eventually, Rapp would become the first U.S. attorney to prosecute someone under the three-strikes law. But all that lay ahead.

* * *

Three days later and half a world away, Ferdinand Nahimana emerged from behind the walls of the French embassy. Nahimana had been bedridden with malaria since the end of March and had left his home, he said later, only to seek refuge in the French mission after the genocide began.

Nahimana said he went to the market to buy food for his family and stopped by the offices of RTLM. No one was entirely sure why he was there. Later, prosecuting attorneys would say that Nahimana had arrived to ensure that journalists were doing their jobs according to plan, a plan aimed at eradicating the nation of Tutsi. Defense attorneys said it had been unclear that Nahimana was there at all. Witnesses could have been confused, and certainly he hadn't been there for long. By then, they said, the army had taken over the radio station and Nahimana wouldn't have been able to say much about what was unfolding anyway.

There would be an argument later, too, about whether Ferdinand Nahimana arrived at the Hôtel des Diplomates to attend the official swearing-in of the new, interim government. With Habyarimana dead and his prime minister also murdered, the power vacuum needed filling. The slight, quiet Nahimana picked his way down the main boulevard in Kigali toward the Hôtel des Diplomates. He must have seen the bodies piled by the roadsides. Trucks with young militia rumbled up the hills. The streets, but for fighters and corpses, were deserted. If the scene upset him, Nahimana never said. He was focused on the swearing-in of a new president. That night, after hands were placed on the Bible and the oaths were taken, the leadership served champagne.

3

"Contours of the Monster"

The first time Georges Ruggiu met Ferdinand Nahimana, the men were as far from Rwanda as one could imagine. It was March 1993 and the pair were attending a human rights conference in Liège, Belgium. Ruggiu was a young bureaucrat, an employee of the Belgian social security administration. Nahimana was an internationally recognized professor of Rwandan history who had arrived to disabuse conferees of the notion that there were human rights abuses in Rwanda. Georges Ruggiu, a small, slight white man who had visited Rwanda the previous summer, immediately felt a kinship with Nahimana. Ruggiu had spent his time in Africa with Rwandan friends who had been influential members of the MRNDD party, led by President Habyarimana. Ruggiu believed that the Hutu had long been discriminated against by the Tutsi and only now, as leaders of Rwanda, had the Hutu been able to level the field. Ruggiu was so taken with his Rwandan experience he had already planned a second trip, to Kigali, the following July. He decided a move to Africa would help him break out of a life of obscurity.

A friend of his had suggested he look into job opportunities at an upstart radio station called Radio Mille Collines. Ruggiu was told to look up a professor named Ferdinand Nahimana, and now Nahimana was here, in Liège, where Ruggiu would have an opportunity to lobby for a job in person. Ruggiu had only limited success. While he and Nahimana discussed a job, he didn't get a firm commitment. He decided to return to Rwanda anyway.

Nearly six months later, Georges Ruggiu was walking through the streets of Kigali, weighing whether he should give up on RTLM, when he stumbled upon President Habyarimana's motorcade. Not sure what else to do, the little white man waved, and much to his surprise, the convoy stopped, a door opened, and he was invited to climb into the presidential car. That was the moment when Georges Ruggiu's life changed forever. He told the president that he had come to Rwanda counting on a job at RTLM and that up to now he had been foiled at every turn. "He told me that he would sort things out. As far as I know, he telephoned Ferdinand Nahimana on the very same day to order him to hire me," Ruggiu said.

Days later, Ruggiu was summoned to Nahimana's office. "He told me that he had received a very important telephone call and that he was to solve my problem," Ruggiu said later. Ferdinand Nahimana hired the young Belgian before the month was out.

"I started work as a journalist on January 6, 1994. I didn't have a contract, only a letter of employment signed by the director," he said. Ruggiu, with no journalistic training and no radio experience, was made a cub reporter. He took his orders from the station's editor in chief, a man named Gaspard Gahigi. It was Gahigi who decided the editorial line of the day, and the journalists on staff responded to his marching orders.

The other key player at the station was Phocas Habimana, a proud, authoritarian man who had been a civil servant at the Ministry of Finance. Habimana was married to one of President Habyarimana's cousins and was a member of the MRNDD central committee. He had become the director general at the radio station just days before Ruggiu started his job.

* * *

Mornings at RTLM started in much the same way they do at media outlets the world over. Journalists wandered into the morning editorial meetings, with sleep in their eyes, sipping cups of coffee or strong milky Rwandan tea. The papers had been read and wire stories digested. Government press releases were skimmed and dispatched. Gaspard Gahigi was responsible for doling out the assignments—a ministerial press conference on one side of town, a meeting of human rights officials on the other. And then, just as quickly as they arrived, the journalists disappeared to cover their various stories, returning hours later with notebooks full of scribbled quotes and sound captured on their cassette tapes.

Until early 1994, the work was largely routine. RTLM opened its broadcasts at seven-thirty in the morning with a Kinyarwanda-language show that lasted until midday. Journalists took their lunch for an hour and then returned to the station at one o'clock to gather news for the evening newscast. The station was back on the air at five o'clock with another Kinyarwanda broadcast. The night shows were in French and ran from 8 to about 10 p.m. Between these times the air was dead. That was the schedule at RTLM until April 6. Then everything at RTLM seemed to change.

Although RTLM was ostensibly a private enterprise, started to oppose the Tutsi-led Radio Muhabura, in reality it got a lot of support from the Habyarimana government. The president was the largest shareholder in the venture; he held a million shares. The station was also linked in a number of ways to the national station, Radio Rwanda. It was allowed to broadcast on the same frequencies as the national radio station between 8 a.m. and 11 a.m., the hours when Radio Rwanda itself wasn't on the air. The two stations often shared staff. Their technicians swapped parts for repairs. Sometimes journalists worked at one station and then at the other. That made it difficult for Rwandans to know the difference between the national station and the upstart.

If the stations had ever fought for ratings, RTLM would have won hands down. It had become a tabloid of the airwaves, covering everything from rumors circulating in the villages to news from the national radio and local newspapers to the back-and-forth between government officials jockeying for power. Callers passed along local gossip and their words went right on the air. The veracity of what they said was never checked or commented upon. It was simply broadcast, live. Tutsi rebels were drawing up lists of Hutu they intended to attack, Philippe from Ruhengeri said. Someone else, from Cyangugu, called a short time later. He had heard rumors about hit lists too.

"To be honest with you, even though it sounds frightening, these lists exist," RTLM told its listeners in March 1994. "They have been drawn up and shall be used even if they are not used at the time of the killing. People will be arrested and thrown into prison for many years without trial. The Inkotanyi still have a single objective: to take back the power that the Hutu seized from them, the Tutsi, in 1959. They tell you that the transitional period will last for two years, but it could last a hundred years."

The switch in format came without explanation in early March. Listeners knew something was up when the signal on the RTLM broadcasts, once spotty and difficult to tune in, became clear and unwarbling. RTLM radio personalities talked about invasions. The RPF, they warned, were coming. No one would be safe.

* * *

When Bonaventure Ubalijoro was growing up in Rwanda in the 1950s, most Hutu could not aspire to an education beyond primary school. Hutu who showed an aptitude joined the seminaries. Ubalijoro had such ambitions. His intelligence won him a place at the prestigious Séminaire Saint-Léon, from which he graduated at the top of his class. He then embarked on the career path of all successful Hutu at the time: he joined the class of officers in the Rwandan military academy. His classmates included Juvénal Habyarimana, the man who would become Rwanda's second president in 1973.

Rubbing elbows with the elite in a country like Rwanda

inevitably leads to key connections. Ubalijoro got the first of a series of lucky breaks in his late twenties. It came in the form of a phone call from President Grégoire Kayibanda in the early 1960s. He asked Ubalijoro, who spoke beautiful French, to head the Rwandan intelligence service, working with the Belgian authorities as their colonial aspirations winked out in Africa. The president needed a man with diplomatic finesse to assure the Belgians that Rwandans were perfectly capable of governing themselves. Ubalijoro led the service for five years and then left to become director of the first national savings bank, the Caisse d'Épargne du Rwanda, another presidential appointment. Ubalijoro excelled at his new assignment as well.

Many of Ubalijoro's classmates at the seminary and military academy were rising through the government ranks. As time went on, they became increasingly focused on what they perceived as the injustices visited upon the Hutu by the Tutsi. The nation began to split along regional lines. The northern part of the country became a stronghold for Hutu extremists. The Tutsi were run out of some northern towns. They began to settle in the south or along the border with Burundi. Ubalijoro noticed a growing institutionalization of the anti-Tutsi policies, something that he worried could lead to Rwanda's undoing. Disillusioned by the policies his friends in the Rwandan government were pursuing, Ubalijoro quit his job at the bank in protest and began pursuing his own private business career. He didn't want to be part of this government, he told his friends.

Two years later, Ubalijoro's former classmate General Major Juvénal Habyarimana overthrew President Kayibanda. Ubalijoro, hopeful that the new president would end the anti-Tutsi policies, agreed to join his administration. He was appointed ambassador to neighboring Uganda, where he served from 1973 to 1976, navigating the difficult years of Idi Amin's rule. He was rewarded with a succession of high-visibility diplomatic posts. He served as ambassador to the United States from 1976 to 1983, and then was transferred to Paris.

Five years later, however, Ubalijoro began to notice that the balanced tone of the Habyarimana government was shifting. Hard-liners in Kigali were winning the president's ear. Ubalijoro, marked as a moderate in the Hutu administration, was called back to Rwanda in 1987 and installed in a junior position in the Rwandan Tourism Office. "It was when I knew that Rwanda was changing for the worse," he said later.

During all this time, Ubalijoro kept a house just outside of Kigali, in Rutongo commune. It was decorated with all the souvenirs one collects in an interesting life. The Ubalijoro kitchen rarely smelled of African food. Instead there was always the smell of French cooking: white-wine sauces and cheese. By 1994, though he was out of favor with the Habyarimana regime, Ubalijoro had all the creature comforts of the nation's elite. His house was large and overlooked Kigali. He had servants. And cows. And when cooler heads prevailed, he was seen as one of the elders to whom Rwanda's leadership turned as it tried to negotiate peace between the Hutu and the Tutsi. In time, Ubalijoro was named to lead the moderate wing of the MDR party, and though he didn't find the Arusha Accords to be a panacea for what ailed Rwanda, he did see the pact as a start toward a cure, so he supported it.

By 1994, there were three main political parties in Rwanda. The MRNDD, the National Republican Movement for Democracy and Development, was Habyarimana's party, the single party (originally the MRND) that he had created and told all Rwandans they automatically belonged to. Its power came from the northwestern part of the country, the president's home prefecture. Similar to the MRNDD, the most stridently anti-Tutsi party was the Coalition for the Defense of the Republic, or CDR. It often worked together with Habyarimana and, historians testified later, was created so the MRNDD could propagate its extreme ideas without leaving fingerprints.

The MDR, or Democratic Republican Movement, got its start in the Parmehutu, the party that led the 1959 revolution and overthrew the Tutsi aristocracy. Its power base was in the center of the country. As the Arusha Accords negotiations drew to a conclusion, the MDR splintered between a radically anti-Tutsi faction and a more moderate wing. Ubalijoro was the leader of the kinder, gentler MDR. He was one of several MDR members who were outspoken and publicly expressed views opposing the Habyarimana government. He called for elections and criticized Habyarimana's policies on democracy and reconciliation.

The evening of April 6 had started for him like any other. He had sat down for dinner with his wife, Madeleine, a big woman with an easy laugh, and was about to open a beer (he allowed himself one with dinner) when Madeleine began to have difficulty breathing. Though she had never showed any signs of asthma in the past, Ubalijoro was worried. He didn't want to take any chances. He packed his wife a bag, cajoled her into the car, and drove down to the hospital, where doctors could find out what was the matter. They left dinner, uneaten, on the table. It was about 9 p.m.

Half an hour later, there was a thumping of boots on the stairs outside, followed by cracking of wood as the front door was kicked in. A dozen members of the Interahamwe had arrived, exploding into the house with a concussion. They ransacked the place looking for Ubalijoro. All they found was his mother. When the Interahamwe departed, Ubalijoro's mother was dead, lying facedown in the yard. The militiamen began a citywide search for Ubalijoro's car.

* * *

There was room enough on the bus for the forty children and a handful of the adults who had taken refuge at the orphanage. Damien Nzabakira had calculated the fit precisely. He loaded the group early on April 12, 1994, just as the sun was adding color to an otherwise slate sky. The children were sleepy, and damp with the kind of heat children generate after a night's rest. They climbed aboard the school bus without much fuss. They were too drowsy. No one seemed concerned about where they were going. Instead, the focus was simply on leaving.

Damien had been through Rwanda's periodic eruptions of violence before. Usually the killing was isolated, limited to a single town or a commune or two. He felt sure that there would be no violence outside of Kigali. Safety awaited them in the countryside. Damien had friends in Butare. It was a university town and less likely to be subject to extremist violence, so he decided that he would take the children there. He knew the roads. They would drive all day if they needed to. He was certain that once they arrived, the children would be safe.

With everyone aboard, Damien started the bus, said a prayer, and crossed himself.

He ground through the gears, rolling down the smooth blacktop highway heading south. For all of Rwanda's problems, its roads were top flight, making it one of the easiest African countries to traverse. Or so it could have been, were it not for the Interahamwe roadblocks that dotted the landscape. Damien had driven less than a quarter of mile when he was asked to pull over by a knot of young toughs. They seemed like college kids on a bender, except they were carrying machetes. Their eyes rolling back into their sockets and their legs unsteady, as if they were about to pass out, they leered at Damien and demanded his identity card. There was little need for it; with his dark skin and stocky, solid frame, Damien was a Hutu out of central casting. Still, the young men, emboldened by beer, had power and they intended to wield it. They had been kings for a week. Just days earlier, before the violence began, they had had nothing: they were unemployed, poor, hungry. Now, with machetes on their hips and a radio pressed to their ears, they were in charge. This strip of land around the barricade had become their domain.

The young men gathered, standing in rows, chins high, eyes suspicious, mouths soft and sullen. They had added banana leaves to their uniforms, an accouterment that could have looked good only to a drunken eye. They wore them as headdresses and around their waists, like skirts. They called out to a man who seemed to be in charge, and waved Damien's identity card in his direction. The older Interahamwe leader could not have been more than twenty years old. He walked over to the bus, his quick strides swallowing ground.

Damien was suddenly surrounded by a dozen militiamen armed with machetes and *masus*, clubs fashioned with spikes at the end. They were protecting their leader, in case Damien made a false move. Damien explained the situation, looking down as if addressing his shoe tops. He hoped this would make the young man feel that he was showing deference. The leader told Damien to go back downtown. The rebels were infiltrating from the hills, he said. The Tutsi were invading from Uganda. In the distance, Damien could hear the sharp sound of single gunshots. They were finding the accomplices hidden among them and ensuring that they would no longer be a problem. This was, as the radio said, their work.

Damien was a patient man, so he waited for the group to talk among themselves. The Interahamwe asked whether he could be a collaborator. What could he be doing with this busload of children? Damien could smell the beer on their breath. He could smell the skunky scent of marijuana on their clothes. At this point in the morning only doctors and soldiers had the right to be out and about, they said to him. Why does a schoolteacher need to be out so early?

"Who are these children?" a young man demanded, waving his rifle in the direction of the bus.

"Orphans," Damien said. "We are on our way to Butare. It is a field trip. They are waiting for us at the university there."

"Take the Tutsi off the bus," the leader said to Damien. "There are Tutsi children and Tutsi women on the bus."

Damien's heart started to race. "I have been instructed to bring them all to Butare," he said. "I am not allowed to break up the group. They are expecting them all in Butare."

The soldiers' eyelids were at half-mast. Damien smiled and

handed a fistful of Rwandan francs to the leader. "As I said, I must get them all to Butare."

Damien lived a thousand lifetimes in the next few moments as the leader tried to work out what to do. Damien, for his part, was trying to strike a pose of firmness without looking threatening. He wasn't sure how he was doing. There would be, he decided to himself, no one taken off the bus. Other cars had pulled up in the meantime and a line had begun to form at the roadblock. As the line grew longer, stopping Damien and the children began to seem like more trouble than it was worth. Besides, the officers seemed to be thinking that Damien and his children were a problem other Interahamwe, farther up the road, could wrestle with. They tossed Damien's papers back at him and waved him through.

The bus engine coughed to life. Damien could hear the whine of a radio at the roadblock below. He heard the broadcast voices rise and fall, like wind coming from a distance. He couldn't make out the words, but he recognized the sound. It was RTLM.

The second roadblock was as haphazard as the first. Damien hoped to be lucky again. Then two trucks loaded with presidential guard troops surged ahead, cutting off his bus. The troop convoy stopped momentarily, chatting up the Interahamwe at the barriers. Damien pulled up close behind the troop trucks. Four Interahamwe youth began lifting the logs out of the road to let the troops pass. Damien opened his window and motioned to the trucks ahead of him. "We're with this convoy." He waved his papers without permitting the guard to see them and pulled into the small space between the bus and the army vehicle. The guard waved him through. Damien and his children made it through the next three roadblocks the same way. By the time they arrived in Butare, normally a three-hour journey, it was nightfall. Damien pulled the bus into the compound of Sainte-Famille, a Belgian Catholic school he had attended as a child. They welcomed him and his charges with open arms. Here, Damien felt certain, it wouldn't matter if one were Hutu or Tutsi. Here, everyone would be protected by God.

The children were gently removed from the bus so as not to disturb their sleep. The adults brought them into the school and put them on the floor side by side.

Damien lay awake wondering how it had come to this. His instinct to bring the children to Butare was almost right. He would learn years later that there was only one documented case of a government official refusing the orders to kill. It came from Jean-Baptiste Habyarimana (no relation to the fallen president). He was the only Tutsi prefect in the country, and when he was ordered to kill, to send his people in a frenzy of violence into the streets, he refused. And for two weeks he was able to hold out. And for two weeks there was no killing in Butare.

The president of the interim government that followed Habyarimana's assassination—Théodore Sindikubwabo, a Butare native—was furious. He went to Butare himself and accused the people in the area of "sleeping." They needed to rise up, he told them. They did as they were told. Prefect Habyarimana was dismissed and replaced with an extremist. Days later presidential guard troops arrived, flown in from Kigali by helicopter. They wasted no time. The Butare massacres began the moment they touched down on April 25, 1994.

* * *

Faustin Twagiramungu, the man who had been chosen in Arusha to lead the transitional government when it was formed, was lying low with a radio to his ear. In the days after the plane crash, RTLM had been providing bulletins of the murders of his moderate friends. Twagiramungu remembered thinking the apocalypse had begun.

Twagiramungu was one of Rwanda's elite. He had been given the opportunity to study abroad and had studied and worked in Quebec, Canada, for eight years, from 1968 to 1976. His stay had given him an opportunity to see Québécois separatism up close. He had attended a rally for the "Français" at McGill University and listened as the French Québécois tried to drum up support for a seccession from English-speaking Canada. He saw this as a seminal event in his political life, and when he returned to Rwanda he began to take on the responsibilities—such as running a state-run company—that, in his country, naturally allowed him to rise through the ranks of political power where he believed he could eventually make a difference.

Twagiramungu's time in Canada was especially fortuitous because it gave him common cause with the leader of the U.N. peacekeeping contingent, a Canadian general named Roméo Dallaire, who had arrived in Rwanda intending to help the nation put the Arusha Accords in place, in October 1993. Like Twagiramungu, Dallaire, a Québécois, had been deeply affected by Canada's separatist movement. That commonality allowed the two men to talk easily and they spent many evenings watching the sun slip below the hills, discussing old times in Canada and the way forward in Rwanda.

But that seemed long ago as Twagiramungu huddled in a friend's house hoping for rescue. He could hear gunshots and grenades and his prospects seemed bleak. Evil was triumphing. Just as despair had started to take over, a knock came on the door. He swallowed hard and resigned himself to his fate. He opened the door expecting Interahamwe and found instead blue helmets, U.N. forces. They had come to take him to force headquarters, they said. It was one of the few successful rescues of Rwanda's moderate politicians during the genocide. Twagiramungu snapped off the radio. RTLM had started playing killing songs, such as Simon Bikindi's reggae-rap song "I Hate These Hutu." Twagiramungu thought the lyrics were aimed at moderate Hutu like himself. It called on the majority people to kill them. The Bikindi tunes were playing at roadblocks when a U.N. troop transport, secreting Twagiramungu, drove by. He arrived in Nairobi without incident.

* * *

Monique Mujawamariya, listening from behind a false ceiling in her house, could hear a melee below her. The sound of boots on the floor, the splintering of furniture. She pushed herself up against the rafters, barely able to breathe. The Interahamwe talking below her radiated menace. They began to rough up her gardener, demanding to know where Monique had gone. The gardener, doing his best not to look heavenward to where she was hiding, told them that she had run away days before.

Concerned that the young hoods' next move would be to torture her employee, Monique decided to escape. Lowering herself down from the ceiling she went around the house pulling small bundles of money out from their hiding places. She took a family photo off a shelf. It was her wedding picture: Monique was standing beside her husband, an officer in the Rwandan army. It was her passport out of chaos.

Stepping out into the street, she walked directly up to several young army men who were guarding a nearby roadblock. They didn't recognize her. She held out the photograph and showed them to the officer. She said she needed to get downtown and asked them to let her pass. They were loath to do so but quickly changed their minds when she offered them $700 for passage. As she picked her way past the roadblock their main concern had become how to divide the money. It sounded like it was going to come to blows.

Monique had already mapped out her next move. She needed to get to the Hotel des Mille Collines, a SABENA-owned establishment on the other side of town. Foreigners were gathering there for a convoy to the airport where they would board evacuation planes. Monique was determined to be on one of those flights. Monique had hoped to get a U.N. escort to the hotel but a call to General Dallaire made clear that was impossible. He said that his troops were stretched too thin as it was. So Monique was left to her own devices to find a way to cover the ten kilometers to the hotel. More cash, she found, judiciously doled out to military men at the roadblocks, made the trip easier. Eventually, they drove her to the luxury hotel.

The foreigners awaiting evacuation had already left the Mille

Collines by the time Monique had arrived. They had now gathered at the L'École Française, closer to the airport. Just as Monique felt the window had closed on her escape, another opened. A Canadian priest who had been a longtime friend of Monique's said he would help her find a car to get to the school. He had been ferrying foreigners out to the school all morning, he said, so his car was out of gas. If Monique could find a car, he said he would drive her to safety. It took Monique less than an hour to find a man with a car who was willing to help. Monique, and a man she had known just long enough to ask for a favor, slouched in the backseat as the priest took the wheel. The Interahamwe were hesitant about stopping a man of the cloth. They waved him through the roadblocks.

The Belgian military were organizing the foreigners for the flight when Monique arrived at the school. They were willing to take Monique on the plane, they said, but her friend, this man with whom she had arrived in the car, was not welcome. Monique refused to take "no" for an answer. Instead, she marched up to the soldier in charge and said that she had arrived with her husband. If he was not permitted to board the plane, she would not do so either. The ploy worked. Monique and her husband of convenience were flown to Nairobi. By April 13, Monique was in Belgium. Four days later she arrived in Canada and by the end of the month she was testifying before Congress in Washington, D.C. Clinton aides said later than when President Clinton heard about the killing in Rwanda his chief concern was for Monique's safety. At the beginning of every briefing he asked one question, "Where is Monique? Have they found Monique?" When he heard she had safely escaped, he seemed to lose interest in what was unfolding in East Africa.

* * *

"The Tutsis are very few in number," an RTLM broadcast said in May. "They were initially estimated at ten percent, but the war must have reduced that figure to eight percent. Will they really continue with their suicide? Don't they run the risk of disappearing if they continue trying to commit suicide by locking horns with people who are by far numerically superior to them?"

By that time, Rwanda looked like a country at war. Buildings—low and mud brown—were burned or razed. The structures wore the blank faces of conflict, their windows blown blind by rocks or fire. Mud huts crouched open and vulnerable by the road, their doors just fabric or plywood. Laundry hung in bright flags. In normal times, children would be standing by the roadside, watching as strangers drove through their open lives. Instead, the streets were eerily deserted. Stores wore faded advertisements for cell phone cards. Billboards called to Rwandans, *Écoute ta soif* ("Listen to your thirst").

The violence had cast a ghastly magic over Rwanda. Everything seemed to be holding its breath against another wave of killing. Everyone was waiting, watchful, and suspicious. Farmers in southern Rwanda would occasionally stumble on ghost camps in the woods. The cold fires, empty tins, and crushed grass provided evidence of the enemy among them. In the urban areas, there was an uneasy sense that a thousand backstreet armies could be mobilized with just a whisper.

* * *

Concern in Rwanda about a possible Tutsi invasion was made all the more stark by problems in neighboring Burundi. Six months before the plane crash, in the autumn of 1993, a band of Tutsi soldiers assassinated their Hutu president, Melchior Ndadaye. It was a bloody end to Burundi's first successful democratic elections since independence. The successful assassination of the Burundian leader sent shock waves through Central Africa. In many parts of Burundi, Hutu authorities led attacks on Tutsi, while the Tutsi-dominated army launched massive reprisal killings. The massacres left Burundi's rivers full of bloated bodies. An estimated fifty thousand people, both Hutu and Tutsi, were murdered. Some three hundred thousand refugees had crossed into Rwanda.

The assassination in Burundi provided all the proof the Hutu extremists in Rwanda needed to show power-sharing agreements like the Arusha Accords would never work. The Tutsi couldn't be trusted. The Hutu had to act. It was a question of self-defense. Overnight, the death of the Burundian president turned a fringe preoccupation into an organizing ideology, and that ideology came to be known as the Hutu Power movement. It provided a unifying theory for those who opposed any move toward ethnic reconciliation.

The vocabulary shifted first. It returned to the bitterness of the colonial period. Habyarimana, when he was first elected, had spoken of the Tutsi as an ethnic group, not a race. They were Rwandan, he had said, not an alien minority. After the assassination in Burundi, the mantra changed. It revolved around the belief that even in their most legitimate and daily actions, the Tutsi were trespassing.

The coup d'état in Burundi provided a cautionary tale, RTLM said. Rwanda was next. There were massive revenge killings in Burundi in the days that followed. There were some fifty thousand dead. It wasn't the Burundian army that was behind the killing, RTLM said. It was the Tutsi generally. According to RTLM, the massacres of Hutu in Burundi were the first step in a larger Tutsi plot to eliminate Hutu from the region altogether. While they didn't say genocide, it was what they meant.

Alarmed by the content of such broadcasts, the Ministry of Information summoned Ferdinand Nahimana and Jean-Bosco Barayagwiza to their offices. "The kind of press I strongly wish to see in Rwanda is the one that supports democracy and peace," the minister of information told the RTLM founders. "As for the type of press that sets one ethnic group against the other, which sets the heads on fire, sets one region against the other, or causes strife between Rwandans and their friends, this has no place and should never have any in this country."

He continued to chastise Nahimana and Barayagwiza about RTLM's propensity to focus on the Hutu side of the story. When they started the radio station, he continued, they had said they were an independent station and would report the news faithfully, and they hadn't done so.

Nahimana spoke up. "Our radio cannot be held responsible for the present state of affairs in this country," he said. "We only report on current facts and events, but people are not happy when their wrongdoings are brought out into the open."

The situation, the RTLM contingent continued, was a difficult one. Democracy and the press were suddenly at odds. The type of democracy that the government of Rwanda was striving for was the kind that would muzzle the press, they said. "This leads to the question of asking what type of democracy our current leaders preach, and the type of press that befits it," they said.

The RTLM directors left the Ministry of Information with a warning. There would be action taken, the government officials said, if the tone at RTLM didn't change. Their threats meant nothing. In fact, the broadcasts got worse.

"The thing you gave me to smoke," one RTLM journalist began after visiting the Interahamwe at the roadblocks, "it had a bad effect on me. I took three puffs. It is strong, very strong, but it appears to make you quite courageous. So guard the trenches well to prevent any cockroach passing there tomorrow. Smoke that little thing, and give them hell. Suppliers should give you a sizable quantity to make you tough, to make you enraged so we can fight for our town and for our country, my dear brothers. You're listening to RTLM, a private radio station broadcasting from Kigali. The time is now 12:02 p.m."

John Shattuck, U.S. assistant secretary of state for human rights, would say later that the State Department was also focused on Radio Mille Collines by that time, the spring of 1994. "RTLM was seen to be at the heart of the genocide from the start, certainly by me," Shattuck said. "I was involved in a very early effort to have the U.S. government look into jamming RTLM. And it was a hard sell. Truth was, at that time the post–Cold War world was throwing up entirely new challenges and we didn't know how to deal with them. Rwanda was the perfect human rights storm."

* * *

Raphael Lemkin was an unremarkable man who managed to do a remarkable thing: he anchored an unspeakable crime with a name. A small gentleman with thinning hair and thick-rimmed glasses, Lemkin's inspiration can be traced back to the 1920s, when as a young linguistics student in Poland he began to read about the Armenian genocide. An Armenian rebel was being held in prison at the time for the assassination of a former Turkish interior minister named Talaat Pasha. Talaat had presided over the 1915 massacre of over a million Armenians, the newspapers reported, because Talaat had decided that murder was the best way to rid Turkey of its Armenian "problem." The young Armenian rebel vowed to avenge the loss of his parents in the violence, and the assassination was an attempt, he explained, to even the score.

What struck Lemkin was not the young Armenian's desperate act, but rather the fact that no law existed to hold Minister Talaat accountable for the killing of thousands of Armenians. "I felt that if the killing of one man was a crime, and is not a matter of negotiations between the guilty and the policeman, the destruction of millions of people should also be a crime," Lemkin wrote in his unpublished autobiography. "Killing of nations is not a political matter which permits interpretations and negotiations."

Winston Churchill, in August of 1941, defined what would become Lemkin's mission. "The whole of Europe has been wrecked and trampled down by the mechanical weapons and barbaric fury of the Nazis," Mr. Churchill told the Allies over the BBC. "As his armies advance, whole districts are exterminated. We are in the presence of a crime without a name."

Lemkin—a lawyer, a linguist, and a human rights crusader—

decided he possessed just the tools to remedy that. Naming the crime, giving it a definition, he decided, might make it that much harder for it to be committed again. Lemkin began his search for a word that would resonate. He wanted a word that stung simply by its utterance. His creation, as it turns out, needed two civilizations, and two languages, to do the job. He combined the Greek derivative *geno*, meaning "race," with the Latin derivative *cide*, meaning "killing." His race killing became "genocide."

In his book *Axis Rule in Occupied Europe*, Lemkin said that "genocide" was more than just a single act. Genocide, he said, was "a coordinated plan of different actions aiming at the destruction of essential foundations of the life of national groups, with the aim of annihilating the groups themselves." *Génocidaires*, as they would be called in Rwanda five decades after Lemkin's epiphany, were bent on the destruction of the essential elements that bound groups together. They sought to destroy political and social institutions, culture, language, and the very livelihoods of their victims. "Genocide can destroy a culture instantly," Lemkin wrote, "like fire can destroy a building in an hour."

* * *

History tells us that the war crimes trials at Nuremberg were an American-inspired effort. In his last meeting with Stalin, Winston Churchill had remarked that the Nazi leaders should be shot. Stalin responded: "In the Soviet Union, we never execute anyone without a trial." Churchill agreed. "Of course, of course, we should give them a trial first."

In 1944, President Truman assigned his assistant secretary of war, John McCloy, one of the president's so-called wise men, to draw up a blueprint for an international court. There were no precedents, no existing bodies of law, not even a court from which lessons could be drawn, but the president was convinced that when the war was over, international justice would be needed. The Germans would have to be held accountable.

McCloy, still overworked with the day-to-day execution of the war, bucked the problem of justice to another office in the War Department, and it bumped and bounced its way down to the office of a three-man catchall unit called the Special Projects Branch. It was led by Colonel Murray Bernays.

Right away Bernays understood that he had to construct a system that allowed hundreds of thousands of ordinary Germans who joined the violence to slip through its net, while making the leadership—the men who delivered the orders but may not have had blood on their hands—responsible. He decided that the Nazi regime would have to be seen, legally, as a criminal conspiracy, an enormous plot to arm for war, seize other nations, plunder their wealth, and exterminate their people. If the Nazi movement was a criminal conspiracy, those who were behind it could be tried as criminals.

Bernays also decided that the court would have to declare that the organizations making up the Nazi regime—the party, the SS, the Gestapo—were criminal too. The logic was that if the Gestapo was a criminal organization, then there was no reason to have to prove its individual members were criminals. The court needed to show only that the men belonged to the Gestapo and then mete out the appropriate punishment. The only problem was that Anglo-Saxon law recognized criminal conspiracy, but the concept didn't exist in French, German, or Soviet courts. It was also unclear whether organizations could be deemed criminal all of a piece. It was precisely those issues that would come back to haunt the creators of Nuremberg and the international courts that followed it.

The twenty-two high-ranking German officials in the docket at Nuremberg included the men who would become the household names of Nazism: Adolf Hitler's number-two man, Hermann Göring; deputy Führer Rudolf Hess; the chief of staff and the operations chief of the German armed forces, Wilhelm Keitel and Alfred Jodl; Albert Speer, the Reich minister for armaments and war production; and one newspaperman, Julius Streicher, publisher of the anti-Semitic newspaper *Der Stürmer.*

In his opening argument, Nuremberg's chief prosecutor, U.S. Supreme Court Justice Robert Jackson, said the trial of Nazi leaders would emerge as the triumph of reason over revenge. "The wrongs which we seek to condemn and punish have been so calculated, so malignant, and so devastating that civilization cannot tolerate their being ignored because it cannot survive their being repeated. That four great nations, flushed with victory and stung with injury, stay the hand of vengeance and voluntarily submit their captive enemies to the judgment of the law is one of the most significant tributes that power has ever paid to reason."

Jackson said that the men would not be found guilty by the testimony of their enemies. Instead the men would be held responsible by a written record. The accused, he said, "shared the Teutonic passion for thoroughness in putting things to paper." The men, he said, had written themselves into a death sentence.

Prosecutors who would travel to Africa to try the leaders of the Rwanda genocide in an international court two generations later had a more difficult task: this genocide was conducted with few fingerprints. Written records had been destroyed, so, in many cases, men would be found guilty by the testimony of enemies. Rwanda's blurred history made it difficult to sift fact from fiction. At best, there was only the faintest trail from which lawyers could draw their conclusions and bring the masterminds of a modern massacre to justice.

4

"I Want a Big, American Lawyer"

Ferdinand Nahimana never had the opportunity to see the full force of what the presidential plane crash had ignited. By the second week in April, he had been whisked out of Rwanda with diplomats from the French embassy. The French evacuation plane was one of the first flights out of Kigali International Airport after the crash. Nahimana had been told, as the diplomats were escorted through the streets of the capital to their waiting plane, that they were going to Gisenyi or Cyangugu. Certainly they would be safe in one of the nation's far-flung western towns until this coup d'état, or whatever it was, ended. Instead, when the plane's hatch opened and Nahimana emerged with the others, they were blinking against the light of a Burundian sky. No one was more surprised than Nahimana. Suddenly, in his country's time of trial, the history professor found himself on the outside looking in.

He was greeted on the tarmac by the former Burundian ambassador to Kigali, Marc Nteturuye. The diplomat, clearly surprised to see Nahimana on the evacuation plane, met the professor with an admonition. "I hope you have not brought along your damned RTLM radio," he muttered, not bothering to extend a hand to shake.

Nahimana didn't miss a beat. "Your Excellency, why do you seem to be afraid of RTLM?" he asked.

The ambassador narrowed his eyes and was decidedly undiplomatic. "If it were brought to Burundi, I feel that Burundi would disappear the following day," he replied.

Nahimana would say later that the ambassador's reaction had pleased him. It proved that RTLM had been successful in waking up the majority people, so successful that it attracted the attention of neighboring countries.

"My name is Ferdinand Nahimana and I am one of the founders of RTLM radio station, which is now very well known in the country," Nahimana said in an interview on Radio Rwanda at the end of April just days after his return from Burundi. "The war resumed by our enemy—the Inkotanyi—has devastated Kigali City. This has forced us to leave our homes, running away from the bullets."

But the majority people have stood up, he continued. That was why he had returned so quickly to Rwanda. He was wanted to help his brothers fight the enemy. RTLM and Radio Rwanda had called up reservists as the RPF began its march toward the capital.

"You must have known that the populations in virtually all corners of the country have stood up to assist the military in defending our country," the broadcaster told Nahimana. "How do you view the zeal demonstrated?"

Nahimana responded, with a smile in his voice, "We were satisfied with both radio stations, Radio Rwanda and RTLM radio, because they informed us on how the population from all corners of the country had stood up and worked together with our armed forces with a view to halting the enemy." The words would come back to haunt him.

In fact, the only enemies RTLM succeeded in stopping were the unarmed ones, the civilians making their way toward the Burundian border. Against the real enemy, the RPF army, the radio was no match. Kagame beat back the Rwandan government army with an invasion force of 4,000. Nearly all his troops were veterans in the Ugandan army and their discipline prevailed. Kagame would claim later that he had purposely fought a protracted battle so the rebel casualties would be low. The RPF strategy was to hit government positions with mortar fire relentlessly, day after day, so their morale would crumble. He said RPF forces encouraged them to flee, rather than fight, by leaving a front line corridor through which they could pass. When the last of the government forces slipped into Zaire, Kagame declared victory. It was mid-July 1994.

He vowed to set up a coalition government, with Hutu and Tutsi, and end Rwanda's cycle of violence. Within weeks, two Hutu moderates emerged with top administration positions. Faustin Twagiramungu was made prime minister. Pasteur Bizimungu emerged as president. Paul Kagame had become vice president and minister of defense. The newspapers lauded Kagame's brilliant military campaign. They called him the Napoleon of Africa. What they didn't say was his decision to fight a protracted war probably cost tens of thousands of Rwandan civilians their lives. While he tried to limit RPF casualties, the genocide raged around them.

* * *

John Shattuck noticed the vultures first. They barely moved their wings but somehow they climbed above Kigali, riding the rising columns of air until they became dashes against the blue sky. The genocide had ended only a month earlier and Shattuck, assistant secretary of state for human rights, had been sent by the Clinton administration to convince General Paul Kagame, now vice president and defense minister of Rwanda, to embrace an international criminal tribunal that would hold the masterminds of the genocide responsible for what they had done.

The security situation in Rwanda was still fragile. The piles of bodies that had once littered the streets had been shoved into mass graves. A musky smell remained. The vultures were looking for the bodies the RPF soldiers had missed. So many of them were circling, they made Shattuck slightly dizzy. They were, he said later, the classic symbol of where things were in August 1994 for Rwanda.

A fleet of beaten-up Land Rovers met Shattuck at Kigali International Airport. There were RPF troops every hundred feet. They were the only moving things in the streets. The Land Rovers moved quickly up into the hills above the city center. The red clay roads were rutted and the trip was hard going. Shattuck met the hero of the Rwandan genocide, the man who managed to end the killing, in a small villa. It was part of a complex of buildings that used to belong to a tea plantation, a graceful house with a huge veranda overlooking what once might have been a formal garden.

Paul Kagame stood when Shattuck entered, and shook his hand. Given that the United States had done little during the genocide, Shattuck saw the gesture as a good sign.

Shattuck was immediately struck by how ascetic Kagame was. He was painfully thin—six-two but only 128 pounds. He spoke precisely, and slowly. "He struck me as a cross between a monk and a king," Shattuck said. Kagame's message for the envoy was clear and simple. He was not convinced any U.N. court would be helpful to Rwanda. When Rwanda needed assistance stopping the genocide, the United Nations did nothing. "We have done this entirely by ourselves," he said.

It was difficult to argue. But Shattuck pressed on and presented Kagame with a proposal to create a tribunal. The court would arrest individuals accused of involvement in genocide, lay down principles of international law that would serve as precedents for other international criminal tribunals and courts all over the world, and pioneer advocacy for victim-oriented, restitutive justice. He urged Kagame to send a letter to the Security Council calling for the creation of a tribunal. Kagame was not enthusiastic. The United Nations would be too slow, he said. It would take a long time to launch an international tribunal, and "we need early and viable justice," he told Shattuck. "We need the people of Rwanda to see this justice for themselves."

What Shattuck didn't say that day, as the vultures and buzzards circled, was that the United Nations was adamant about not having the tribunal take place in Rwanda. Any trial in Rwanda of a high-level *génocidaire*, or genocide mastermind, would be, by definition, unfair. The International Criminal Tribunal for the Former Yugoslavia was in The Hague, and, the international officials reasoned, the tribunal for Rwanda could be there too. Twagiramungu, from the safety of Belgium, had asked for a tribunal in May 1994, three months earlier, with a question that sent eyes to shoe tops. "Is what is happening different from what happened in Nazi Germany?" he asked reporters at a press conference. "Is it because we're African that a court has not been set up?"

Part of the problem was that just six months earlier, a U.S. Blackhawk helicopter had been shot out of the sky by rebels in Mogadishu, Somalia. Americans watched their television sets in horror as news channels showed footage of a dead U.S. soldier dragged through the streets of Somalia: "The Pentagon could not have been more hunkered down than that," said Shattuck. "They were unwilling to do anything. And I was one of the people trying to change that. I just couldn't do it fast enough."

It wasn't until June, when the massacres began to slow, that the United States finally called the killing a genocide. "The first and most important step to reconciliation in Rwanda is justice," Shattuck told reporters after his meeting with Kagame. "The principal movers in the genocide must be identified and then prosecuted so that the cloud of collective guilt and confusion hanging over Rwanda can be lifted." The fact that the same cloud hung over an international community went without saying.

The Clinton administration offered $3 million in cash assistance to help set up the war crimes tribunal—the same amount it had pledged to help establish the Yugoslavian criminal court months earlier. There was a $4 million offer to help rebuild the Rwandan justice system. Washington had offered the intelligence it had gathered concerning genocide and crimes against humanity in Rwanda so the leaders would be better prosecuted. (The offer meant, of course, that the United States knew precisely what was unfolding during those hundred days of chaos—and chose to do nothing to stop it.)

"These are important elements in the ongoing and very difficult effort to end impunity and restore justice in Rwanda so the process of national reconciliation can begin," Shattuck told reporters. Days later Kagame announced plans to prosecute, and possibly execute, the masterminds of the genocide in Rwanda itself. The U.N. vowed to come up with a solution everyone could live with.

The world body picked at the issue for months. It began by pushing for a Rwandan tribunal in The Hague, and the debate deteriorated from there. No detail was too trivial for extended discussion. Diplomats argued over where the court should be located and whether it should include any crimes the RPF might have committed as it marched toward Kigali. They argued about jurisdiction and whether the sentences could include the death penalty. It was this last point, in particular, that caused the most consternation. The RPF wanted the ability to put the *génocidaires* to death, as Rwandan law allowed. Most of the U.N. member states had collectively decided in 1968 to work toward ending capital punishment once and for all. The United Nations could not, therefore, mete out such a penalty, no matter how terrible the crime.

The eventual compromise was that those sentenced to life imprisonment would have to serve their terms in African jails, instead of European ones. Three months of discussion later, a resolution finally went before the Security Council for a vote. The new tribunal would be in Africa and the chief prosecutor would be in The Hague, overseeing the Yugoslavian and Rwandan courts. Richard Goldstone, the man designated to hold that job, would travel between the two continents.

The jurisdiction of the court would be very limited: it would focus on the discrete period between January 1, 1994, and December 31, 1994. That meant, technically, that the genocide would be viewed in a historical vacuum. What came before—the Hutu Revolution of 1959, Tutsi incursions in the 1990s, the Burundian coup—was not admissible.

Seven months after the genocide had begun, in November 1994, the Security Council voted overwhelmingly in favor of the tribunal plan, with the exception of one of its temporary members: Rwanda voted no. Without the possibility of a death penalty, the Rwandan ambassador said, his nation couldn't support it. It was not the last protest the U.N. tribunal would hear from Rwanda.

After much to-ing and fro-ing, the International Criminal Tribunal for Rwanda (ICTR) landed in Arusha, Tanzania—the same place where the failed peace accords had been forged. It was a compromise solution. No nation in Africa, aside from Tanzania, was willing to welcome the court. There were excuses of instability, or security, or political turmoil. The truth was, African leaders were wary of being too closely associated with the world's Band-Aid solution. What was to be gained domestically in helping the international community to absolve itself for having done nothing while Rwandans killed one another?

The countries that did support the tribunal saw the whole enterprise through a different lens. The court was meant to be a testament to Africa that the rest of the world would not allow the genocide in Rwanda to go unpunished. The world needed to find the masterminds of the 1994 massacres guilty so that Rwandans, and Africans more generally, would believe in the genuineness of the world's outrage. Judges would be flown in from the far corners of the planet. Police would round up suspects in faraway lands. And they would all descend on this small, dusty town in East Africa to make sure justice was served. What was unspoken was that Rwanda had suffered wrongs in 1994 for which no court could ever adequately compensate.

Making the tribunal effective and credible not only meant

establishing a historical record of what happened but also required judges to determine where justice lay. It meant testing the question of whether acts of genocide and crimes against humanity had consequences for the people responsible. Unlike the World Court, which judges nation-states, the ICTR would judge individuals—a new concept for Rwanda, which had a long history of letting individuals who orchestrated mass killings go free. For scholars of Rwanda who had watched the country struggle to make sense of its amorphous history, the court offered the promise of a definitive rendering of events. It would provide a coherent narrative of the conspiracy and how it unfolded. History with an agreed-upon narrative thread had eluded Rwanda since its inception. Now there was an international body that vowed to give the nation something it had never had. The tribunal had the potential to demystify Rwanda, to document for its future generations that the nation's tribalism was not about ancient hatreds but was really about modern tyranny. That wasn't an easy concept to explain.

"The international tribunal is meant for taking over when the national system fails," Judge Erik Møse, the future president of the ICTR, said soon after he arrived at the tribunal. "In many situations the national system is breaking down and you need something else instead. We understand that even if it is only one hour's flight from Kigali to Arusha, it is mentally quite a long distance between Arusha and the countryside in Rwanda. And we're trying to bridge that gap, so Rwandans know what we are doing. It isn't always easy to understand why things here seem slow to those outside, but we are trying."

Arusha, Tanzania, was better known as the base camp for the climbing of Mount Kilimanjaro—ground zero for rich Western adventurers seeking a thrill—than as a seat of international justice.

The tribunal was housed in a nondescript former conference center that managed to authentically reproduce the pale light and cement muskiness of a badly designed American high school. Attempts to convert the building into something resembling a courthouse fell short. The conference rooms were turned into a series of legal chambers with low ceilings and windows barely large enough to squeeze a cat through. The effort seemed rushed. The walls were cheaply constructed. The courtrooms were set off from spectator chambers with precarious looking-glass frames in cheap wood. Despite the U.N. team's best efforts, the building was more convention center than courtroom.

The hollowness of the tribunal was in stark contrast to the majesty of the courtrooms of Nuremburg. Nuremberg's Palace of Justice was chosen to try Nazi war criminals precisely because it provided a Hollywood backdrop, an epic ending to World War II. Justice was the epilogue everyone needed to put the war behind them.

A battalion of engineers doubled the size of the main courtroom in the building, both vertically and horizontally. A rear wall was removed and the attic over the courtroom was made into a visitors' gallery. Fancy chandeliers and gingerbread molding were torn out. There was office space for six hundred people and cabinetmakers were brought in to build the furniture. Glass for the windows was flown in specially from Belgium. Seats for the visitors' gallery came from an ornate theater in Ansbach, Germany. The Nuremberg trials convened in a place of greatness. In comparison, the Arusha tribunal seemed third-rate.

The ICTR opened its doors in May 1995. Its first accused criminal, Georges Rutaganda, an Interahamwe leader, was put behind bars in Arusha almost exactly a year later. The process, it was clear, was going to be slow in spite of the fact that this was a court running against the clock. There was a deadline on this tribunal. It would meet until 2006 and then its money would run out, the United Nations had said. It was as if on that date all the justice available for Rwanda would be dispensed and when the appointed hour struck, everyone would go home. All this seemed to be summed up by a makeshift sign by the front gate, which appeared to be painted by hand. It read: ARUSHA, THE GENEVA OF AFRICA. The comparison came from remarks that President Clinton made during his belated presidential visit to Rwanda, though few could remember his trip (he never left the airport) or the remarks he made. In March 1998, Clinton apologized to Rwandans for failing to come to their rescue. He said it took the world too long to call the massacres what they were, genocide. While Rwandans appreciated the sentiment, and genuinely believed President Clinton felt bad, it didn't bring their families back. The tribunal couldn't do that either.

Those working with the court felt they were doing the next best thing. They were holding people responsible for the deaths of eight hundred thousand people. It was, they believed, a start. They put the best face on a difficult situation. The tribunal maintained a decorum of the highest order. Judges wore satin robes, and British attorneys wore powdered wigs. The corridors rang with the staccato beats of African languages and the mellifluous sounds of French and English. As in courthouses everywhere, there was an odd camaraderie in the cafeteria in the back of the building. Defense lawyers sat with prosecutors. Journalists sat with diplomats. And the conversation belied the gravity of what was taking place all around them. The waitresses and waiters were nonchalant and a little slow. The menu was decidedly American: meat loaf specials, grilled ham and cheese with fries, pasta with tomato sauce—all washed down with Fanta Orange or Coke in big returnable glass bottles.

After lunch, staffers repaired to the tribunal's small library to scramble for one of the six computers set up there. Instant messages stacked up on the screens, Walkmans hissed something concussive into ears. Librarians shushed, or moved staffers along so that others could have their turn at the computer screens and make their evening plans for dinner dates or dance parties. And while all this activity buzzed down below, in the three tribunal chambers above, judges weighed the fates of men as witnesses relived crimes against humanity. Africans who looked too young to shave stood guard, holding rifles that looked too old to shoot.

For the visitors who wanted to watch history unfold, there were rules, but they were not so much written down as learned by trial and error. Judges, for example, had no designated elevators, so whenever he or she got into one, anyone who was in it was supposed to step out and allow a judge to ride up or down alone. Frequently, spotting a judge was not easy. They were not always in their robes and often, in the morning, arrived in fine suits, looking every bit like any other distinguished visitor to the proceedings. It was only the regulars who knew to scurry out of the elevators when the judges approached. Newcomers to the tribunal blithely rode up with sitting judges, wondering to themselves why, suddenly, everyone else had left the car. Judges, in good humor, managed a smile for the uninitiated.

* * *

The world hardly noticed when the Rwanda tribunal began its first case in January 1997. The U.N. court in The Hague, where the leaders of the ethnic cleansing in the former Yugoslavia would be tried, garnered greater interest. That conflict was more tangible. It was in Bosnia that the shot that ignited World War I was fired. A young Bosnian Serb nationalist, Gavrilo Princip, a member of a group that wanted Austria-Hungary to relinquish its hold on Bosnia, had killed Hapsburg archduke Franz Ferdinand and his wife in Sarajevo on June 28, 1914. Within six weeks Austria-Hungary had declared war on Serbia, and Germany invaded France. It was the stuff of high school social studies. Rwanda's wars were not in the curriculum.

High schoolers know that at the end of the war, in 1918, the Bosnians, Serbs, Croats, and Slovenes finally had the kingdom they sought: they were ruled by the Serbian royal family. They know, too, that that did little to ease tensions. The Croats and Serbs, divided for centuries by religion and culture, were at each other's throats. World War II only added to their divisions, turning the fighting into fratricide. Josip Broz (Tito) decided the only way to settle scores was to pretend they didn't exist. Little or no mention of who sided with whom was allowed.

Tito, the son of a Croat father and a Slovene mother, decided to do away with ethnic identity and enforce a national one. Under Tito there were no Croats, Serbs, and Macedonians. Instead they were all Yugoslavs. Ethnic pasts were to be forgotten. There was only one religion, he decreed: Titoism.

As a result, Serbs, Croats, and Muslims in Yugoslavia were forced to work together in every walk of life just as Rwandans did under Belgian rule.

Many Yugoslavs didn't know that those who lived beside them were Serb or Muslim—that is, until 1991, when Serbian nationalist Slobodan Milosevic decided to move vast numbers of Bosnia's Muslims and Croats out of key parts of Bosnia so the areas could be populated by Serbs. The same thing had happened in Rwanda when Hutu migrated north and Tutsi went south.

Between 1991 to 1995 close to three hundred thousand people were killed in the former Yugoslavia because they were from one ethnic group or the other. By the early summer of 1992, nearly 90 percent of the atrocities in Bosnia and Croatia had been carried out by Serbs in the name of Milosevic's dream of a "greater Serbia." Rwandans would do the same in their support of Hutu power just two years later.

In both cases the world seemed unable to muster a military response. It offered a judicial one instead. The United Nations Security Council took the unprecedented step of creating a war crimes tribunal for Yugoslavia, the first since Nuremberg, to stop the killing. The idea was to bring tyrants to justice, uphold the rule of law, and help reconcile war-torn countries. The International Criminal Tribunal for the Former Yugoslavia opened its doors in The Hague in 1993—two years after the killing in Bosnia had started and a full year after the term "ethnic cleansing" had become part of the world's lexicon.

At the time there was a widespread belief that Yugoslavia's killing fields were somehow preordained by history. Rebecca West's *Black Lamb and Grey Falcon,* first published in 1941, declared that there was nothing that could be done by outsiders in a region so steeped in ethnic hatred, with enemies that went back hundreds of years. Then, in 1993, President Clinton was given a copy of Robert Kaplan's best seller *Balkan Ghosts: A Journey Through History*, which left most of its readers, including the president, with the sense Yugoslavia was lost until the different ethnic groups got tired of killing one another. (It was a lesson that the president would apply in Rwanda a year later.)

In fact, there was nothing preordained about the slaughter at all. It took a war crimes tribunal, and hindsight, to conclude that Yugoslavia's killing was the product of bad, even criminal, political leaders, who had encouraged ethnic confrontation for personal, political, and financial gain. Rwanda was similarly cursed—ruled by men who dressed up politics in the gown of ethnic hatred.

Yugoslavia was a cautionary tale about how much history can matter to a country's sense of itself. And just as it had in Yugoslavia, history in Rwanda had routinely been forged into a political tool to justify current interests. The heat generated by those forces, its citizens' long years of antsiness, predictably lead to explosion.

* * *

For RTLM founders Ferdinand Nahimana and Jean-Bosco Barayagwiza, their long tangle with the International Criminal Tribunal for Rwanda began when their names appeared on a list of criminals tagged by the Rwandan government as masterminds of the genocide. The list had been used as a guide for lawyers and investigators at the ICTR. Individuals who they determined could be caught and successfully tried were put on a separate roster, known internally as the Gamma List. The tribunal also focused on individuals who represented different strata of Rwandan society. Prosecutors wanted clergymen and politicians and military men and media executives to be tried. If they focused their efforts that way, they felt, it could never be

said that the ICTR was picking on just a small subsection of the *génocidaires*. Instead, they would prosecute the worst offenders from every walk of life.

The tribunal came into the lives of Ferdinand Nahimana and Jean-Bosco Barayagwiza in 1996 when the president of Cameroon, Paul Biya, bowed to international pressure and promised to extradite the duo. Nahimana, one of the hundreds of people on the Rwandan government list and the subsequent Gamma List, was formally indicted by the ICTR in July 1996 for his role in founding Rwanda's best-known hate radio station.

Jean-Bosco Barayagwiza's arrival at the tribunal was more difficult. The ICTR prosecution team battled for his extradition from Cameroon for ten months. While the Cameroon government stalled for time, Barayagwiza remained behind bars. When he finally arrived in Arusha, he cried foul. He had been in jail in Cameroon for nearly a year without an indictment, he said, which was against international law and the bylaws of the ICTR. The former jurist demanded his own release. Sputtering about his unfair detention, he called the tribunal a farce.

Hassan Ngeze's capture, like the man, was somewhat more dramatic. He was a late addition to the Rwandan government's most-wanted list. Two years after the genocide, Ngeze ran into Rwanda's vice president, Paul Kagame, at a conference in Egypt. Seeing Ngeze in Egypt evidently reminded Kagame of his role in the genocide. Within hours of their exchange of glances, Egyptian police swarmed the conference center and arrested Ngeze as one of the co-conspirators of the 1994 massacre.

When Egyptian authorities called Richard Goldstone, the first prosecutor of both the Yugoslavian and Rwandan tribunals, however, he had never heard of Ngeze. He told the Egyptians to release him. They did. Kagame was furious.

A year later, Ngeze was drinking tea at his house in Nairobi when there was a knock at the door. He opened it to find a handful of Kenyan police and investigators from the ICTR. His name had been added to the Rwandan government's most-wanted list.

As the officers swarmed into the room, they told Ngeze he was under arrest. They began seizing papers, stacks of past *Kangura* issues, over two hundred passports, and $20,000 in cash. They seized his bank passbook, which showed he had $247,000 in savings. "I know who assassinated the president of Rwanda," Ngeze kept telling the officers as they handcuffed him. "I have proof of who killed him." That, the policemen told him, was of no immediate concern. They asked about the passports. Ngeze said he was helping Rwandan refugees get out of Kenya. Those who could afford it paid him, he said. Those who could not, he added, he sometimes helped for free. He tried to explain how helpful he was to Rwandans still trying to escape the horrors of the genocide. He apparently wasn't very convincing. By nightfall, Ngeze was on a plane to Arusha. It was July 18, 1997. The three men who would come to be known as the media trio were behind bars.

* * *

Defense attorney John Floyd had arrived at that point in his life when long-held habits had graduated to rituals. There were favorite coffee cups, lucky ties, meals that corresponded as much to days of the week (if it is Friday, it must be fish) as with an internal hankering set off by having done the same thing the same way for so long. Life had fallen into a comfortable rhythm of early mornings at the computer, early evenings at the desk opening the day's mail with a datebook open and a pen at the ready.

Floyd was a big man, with hands like hams and wrists so wide it was difficult to see where his hands ended and his arms began. Bespectacled, with big, wide-framed glasses that intensely magnified all that was around him, he had the look of an enormous dusky owl, and one expected his face to make a full owl-like rotation at any moment. His gait was a lumbering one and he moved as big men do, with deliberation rather than deftness.

And it was with deliberation that he sat down at his desk in August 1999 and began to go through his mail, transferring court notices into his date book and carefully placing the letters, one by

one, into a box for filing. Then he stumbled upon an envelope with a postmark from Arusha, Tanzania. "I remember getting the letter because of the stamps and because of the Arabic writing that was on the letterhead of the stationery," he said later. "There are lots of guys who are Islamic who write me from prison, and it might be some African-American who changed his name from Leroy Jones to Mohammed. They write to tell me they are innocent and that they need some help. But this one, this one was different."

The letter was from Hassan Ngeze.

"I get used to a lot of letters that say, 'I am innocent, I am on death row,'" Floyd said. "But this one was from Tanzania, and when he told his story about being unfairly locked up in a U.N. detention center awaiting trial, it made me think. I didn't think of the U.N. as a lawyer."

Floyd switched on his computer, called up a search engine, and typed "Hassan Ngeze" into the search field. The screen filled with entries. The headline on the first one showed that Ngeze had tried to commit suicide. He had been unsuccessful. Floyd narrowed his eyes and thought that Hassan Ngeze was desperate. He put the letter in his box for filing and thought nothing more of it.

A few days later a second letter arrived. And then another. And another. The letters were all neatly typed, and were written in the broken, ungrammatical English of those who study a language but rarely have occasion to use it. As the days passed, the letters kept on coming. Some arrived with photographs, others with newspaper clippings about Ngeze. They all carried the same message: "I want a big, American lawyer," Ngeze wrote. "Not a little, African lawyer."

After a dozen letters had arrived, Floyd wrote Ngeze back saying he would like to help, but he wasn't sure how.

"It wasn't about him particularly," Floyd said later. "It was really about me, wanting to get someone out of trouble. What I couldn't understand was how he could be locked up for years without a lawyer and without a trial. I didn't want to believe that could happen in 1999."

To be sure, by the time Hassan Ngeze had contacted John Floyd he was beyond desperate. He was talking to himself in the U.N. Detention Facility and suffered what the doctors had decided was a psychotic episode. He was wandering around naked in the middle of the night. He was paranoid, and doctors initially diagnosed him as schizophrenic. What was certain was that he had a personality disorder that required medication. Ngeze refused to take it.

For all his craziness, Ngeze had enough of his wits about him to find out about John Floyd in much the same way John Floyd had learned about him: the Internet. While it is not clear how Ngeze managed to get access to the Internet while he was in a U.N. Detention Facility, what is certain is that he had enough access to the Web to do his own legal sleuthing. He found John Floyd's name because Floyd was the chairman of the criminal section and the juvenile justice section of the National Bar Association. That seemed a good credential for the fix in which Ngeze found himself. He carefully typed the letters to Floyd and had a friend smuggle them out to the post office. He was sure he could convince the American to get him out of jail in Africa.

John Floyd had grown up in the mean streets of south-central Los Angeles, where violence in his neighborhood, even in his home, had emitted an inky cloud over any aspirations he might have held. He hadn't thought about traveling, or college, or the future. He was more concerned about survival.

Floyd's father was a waiter who spent more time drunk than sober. His mother picked up work when she could find it. She was a maid, then a waitress, then a clerk typist. Money was tight and the Floyds had little to spend on their only son. The younger Floyd figured this out for himself early on, and he found ways to make cash on his own. "I would leave in the morning and I would make sure I would come back after my dad left for work as a waiter," Floyd said. "It was better for everybody that way."

A good student at Holy Name Grammar School in south-central L.A., Floyd managed to make himself an indispensable part of a gang known as the Kings Men. The gang would play basketball every afternoon in the playground at Holy Name, and Floyd, eight years old at the time, would ride his bicycle down to the school yard and watch the games. Floyd began running errands for the older boys. He would buy them tacos and cigarettes and hamburgers and make nickels and dimes for his trouble.

"I was their mascot," he said. "I was reliable, I got them hamburgers for twenty cents and they'd give me a quarter and let me keep the change."

The boys called him Major Jahoopie, after a comic strip character in *Beetle Bailey* who had an unusually large head. "The guy who headed the gang was known as Mile Away," Floyd said later, recalling those early days in L.A., "because when the police showed up, he was a mile away."

The Kings Men mascot status protected Floyd through grammar school and his early years in high school. When he became too old to hang around with the Kings Men, he joined other gangs, for protection, in south-central L.A. "I learned early on not to be a leader, but to be a member," he said. "Leaders always get killed."

Floyd managed to make it through Los Angeles's Loyola High School unscathed and then enrolled in East Los Angeles Junior College, before he transferred to Los Angeles State (now known as California State University, Los Angeles), to study English. After graduation, he began to teach in the neighborhood at a Catholic high school. After the first Watts riots in 1965, Floyd got a teaching post in Watts. "It was then that I really saw the dividing line between haves and have-nots," he said.

So he went to law school to see if he could do anything about it.

"What I really liked was tax law," Floyd said. "I thought it was interesting how it was used to develop social policy, and I was all set to become a tax attorney, and then I ended up helping out Jerry Brown's gubernatorial campaign, and that was it. I was bitten by the political bug and decided as soon as I finished law school, I was going to Washington."

Floyd didn't have to wait long. He graduated from law school in 1972 and four years later went to Washington to work in the Legal Services Corporation as an assistant of field services. That led to criminal law. "I didn't find criminal law," he said. "It found me."

5

When Two Elephants Fight, It Is the Grass That Suffers

John Floyd arrived in Arusha, Tanzania, on January 15, 2000, wondering what he had gotten himself into. His flight on Ethiopian Airlines into Kilimanjaro International Airport had been largely uneventful. The service was good, as was the food, and just as he was beginning to convince himself a case in Africa wouldn't be too bad, he landed in Arusha. He spent the entirety of the flight reading Philip Gourevitch's *We Wish to Inform You That Tomorrow We Will Be Killed with Our Families*, the award-winning book about the Rwandan genocide. It was all Floyd knew at the time about the massacres. And now he was about to delve into their aftermath.

"I was expecting a city," he said later. "I remember looking out the plane window and all I could see was darkness and I kept wondering where they had put the city."

A U.N. van arrived on the tarmac and Floyd climbed in next to some other tribunal employees, who sat in silence for the hour-long trip. The group bounced along unpaved roads and unlit streets, and finally Floyd was deposited at the Impala Hotel. It was, he thought, a dump. The building was under construction. Its swimming pool was just a hole in the ground. There was no television. Power surges were common. And after the first night, Floyd got so many mosquito bites he was ready to fly back to America. This whole enterprise, he thought, was a terrible mistake.

The next morning didn't bode much better. Floyd caught a taxi to the United Nations Detention Facility, only to find that his client, Hassan Ngeze, hardly seemed to speak English. Floyd didn't speak French. Even without the language barrier, Floyd felt his client was evasive. He wouldn't answer questions and kept giving Floyd sidelong glances. After an hour, Floyd gave up. Inexplicably, the next day, Floyd found a different Ngeze. Overnight, Ngeze had apparently decided that Floyd was his best chance for acquittal. For eight hours Ngeze spoke nonstop. On that first trip, Floyd was in Arusha for three weeks. He said that it felt like three months.

"On the way home I just got angry," Floyd said. "I was angry that I couldn't seem to get any straight answers. I couldn't get information out of the Office of the Prosecutor. I couldn't get exhibits that were supposed to be used against my client. I couldn't get any answers out of the government in Kigali. I thought Ngeze was being railroaded. Something wasn't right. And I had about a month before the trial would start to find out what exactly that was."

Floyd worried aloud and often about the United Nations meddling in media affairs. "The United Nations has no business messing in this area," he said. "This isn't just a press freedom issue. This is an intellectual freedom issue. This is dangerous, dangerous stuff. People don't realize what they are wanting to decide here, and someone has to stop it."

Doing so, however, wasn't going to be easy. Floyd saw bureaucratic obstacles at every turn and groused that he didn't have the resources to defend his client properly. *Kangura,* for example, was written in Kinyarwanda but the U.N. said that it would pay for only a handful of translations. "Ngeze is being denied due process and fundamental fairness," Floyd began during one of his rants before the chamber. "The 1994 genocide was caused not by the media, or my client, but by rebels who invaded Rwanda and assassinated Habyarimana. *Kangura* wasn't even published during the genocide, so how can my client be guilty of inciting it?"

* * *

Floyd wasn't alone in his concern about a U.N. court setting the bar on press freedom. For free speech advocates in the United States, it was an equally frightening prospect. Could words kill? Could judges hold editors at a radio station and newspaper accountable for something other journalists did? Could Hassan Ngeze be responsible for incitement if back copies of his newspaper were circulating in Rwanda but he stopped publishing *Kangura* before the violence began?

Prosecutors at the tribunal had decided to try Barayagwiza, Nahimana, and Ngeze together, to group them thematically in order to create a media trial. All three had been linked to RTLM, though Barayagwiza and Nahimana more directly so. Ngeze's newspaper had had a symbiotic, if not direct, relationship with the radio station. *Kangura* and RTLM traded advertisements and co-sponsored contests. And they were both anti-Tutsi. That was enough for the prosecution. The concern among free speech advocates was that the facts surrounding RTLM and *Kangura* were so bad, a verdict could end up criminalizing responsible journalists when they reported the truth, because sometimes the truth can incite an audience.

Prosecutors forged ahead anyway. They drew up the indictments based on the Genocide Convention of 1948, which calls for the punishment of "direct and public incitement to commit genocide."

When the United Nations initially debated the 1948 provision, the American delegation protested that incitement was "too remote" from the actual crime of genocide. It would be too difficult to trace mass murders back to a single source, to particular words spoken or phrases written that inspired mass killing. There had to be a more direct link, a concrete cause and effect to make such a provision palatable, the United States said. America was alone in this view. Its view was defeated by other countries in a roll-call vote.

The Supreme Court of the United States hasn't upheld a conviction for hate speech since 1951. The Court's view of protected speech is a broad one. The First Amendment could even safeguard cross burning, the Court has ruled. The 1992 case of *R.A.V. v. the City of St. Paul* was an example of the Court's reasoning. Robert Victoria was charged with illegally burning a cross in the yard of an African-American family, under a city ordinance that banned speech or symbols that could "arouse anger, alarm, or resentment in others on the basis of race, color, creed, religion or gender." Striking down the law as unconstitutional, the Supreme Court overturned Victoria's conviction. The justices concluded that the ordinance was too broad because it criminalized forms of expression that deserved free speech protection.

Denmark outlaws racial slurs. Britain and Switzerland have similar prohibitions. And Germany has gone so far as to convict right-wing leaders of inciting racial hatred: Gunther Deckert hosted a 1991 speech by a man named Fred Leuchter, who presented "research" denying the existence of the Auschwitz gas chambers. Deckert, the man who had invited Leuchter to speak, was convicted of incitement and sentenced to five years in prison. Such precedents boded ill for Barayagwiza, Nahimana, and Ngeze. Though their voices seldom were heard over the airwaves of RTLM and Ngeze rarely signed his editorials, Barayagwiza and Nahimana were directors at the radio station and Ngeze was the force behind *Kangura*. If the tribunal were to take its cues from Germany in deciding their case, the trio would almost certainly be found guilty.

In Europe, where memories of the Holocaust have particular force and resonance, lawmakers have concluded that it is safer to curb some speech than to provide the hate movement with a chance to gain any momentum. It became clear that the media trial would revolve around the crucial aspect of competing American and European views: would prosecutors have to show that the calls to defend the motherland against the Tutsi that blasted from RTLM's transmitters and the pages of *Kangura* were linked to particular killings—or would judges demand a less vigorous standard and be satisfied with the idea that the media outlets incited Rwandans more generally with their racist talk?

If the trio were found guilty, the war crimes tribunal for Rwanda—of all places—could decide for the world at what point political propaganda or journalism became criminal. The bad facts of the Radio Mille Collines case might well end up making for bad law. One of the prosecutors at Nuremberg, Telford Taylor, warned about the dangers of targeting journalists for such grave crimes. He worried about the ripple effect the verdict against anti-semitic newspaperman Julius Streicher would have on freedom of speech. "Publication of a newspaper, however maddening and unconscionable it may be, should be touched with criminal accusations only with the greatest caution," he said. Streicher went to the gallows for what he wrote.

Others, like Norwegian judge Erik Møse, had a different view. "Some people have said that this could be seen as a freedom of the press issue and that is dangerous ground for the United Nations to tread on," he said after the ICTR gave him the media case. "I say that perhaps it is time for the U.N. to make a decision on this sort of thing, to set a standard. It has been more than fifty years since an international court has attempted to do so, and it is about time that someone set those limits."

* * *

"Do people dig in America?"

Simone Monasebian had just arrived in Kigali and was walking toward her new U.N. office when the question was fired at her from across the parking lot. It came from a Rwandan man leaning against a taxi parked outside the tribunal offices. Monasebian smiled and wondered if she had heard him wrong.

"I hear you are American," he began again. "Do people dig in America?"

She hadn't misunderstood.

He waved an arm. "The worst job in Rwanda is to be a digger," he explained. "I have always wanted to go to America, I hear life is much easier there. So I expect that people in America don't have to dig."

Monasebian assured him that even in America, some people dig.

He looked a little disappointed.

Monasebian had come to her new job hoping to make a difference, so she accepted the difficult Rwanda assignment as she did most everything: with vigor. She worked at the scene of the crime, Rwanda, for three months before she was transferred to Arusha. By that time Monasebian had spent weeks meeting with victims of the violence. She interviewed witnesses and visited villages. She emerged with a very real sense of the psychic damage the genocide had caused. Rwanda was a wounded country. Monasebian walked through the gates of the ICTR six years, almost to the day, after the genocide began, determined to help Rwanda break its cycle of violence. While she wasn't sure which trial team she would join, she was certain which case she wanted to give a wide berth: the media trial of Barayagwiza, Nahimana, and Ngeze. She had been a journalist, she had been involved in the hip-hop scene, and she certainly didn't want to get into the business of muzzling expression. "I always believed the First Amendment protections were the most important thing about American society," she said. "I always thought the cure for hate speech was more speech, not less." It was a uniquely American view.

Almost as soon as she arrived, Monasebian found herself the target of intense wooing. A variety of cases at the tribunal were about to start and various teams were eager to bring another lawyer on board. Monasebian already had her eye on a favorite case. She wanted to try Elizaphan Ntakirutimana, a pastor who had helped kill a Tutsi who had run to his church for refuge. It was a clear-cut case of good against evil—a solid place to start. During her time in Rwanda, Monasebian had befriended a personable Kenyan lawyer named Charity Kagwi. The two had worked on a bill of particulars for defendant Hassan Ngeze. The bill of particulars is familiar fare to American lawyers. It is filed in civil or criminal cases to get details on charges from the other side. Monasebian had answered dozens of similar bills in New York. What Monasebian didn't know was that the bill of particulars work was the beginning of Kagwi's effort to get Monasebian assigned to the media trial.

She discovered her fate when she was summoned to a conference room on the seventh floor of the tribunal in the fall of 2000. Monasebian hurried down the corridors wondering why she had been called. She burst into the conference room to find the deputy prosecutor, Bernard Muna, and her friend Charity Kagwi sitting at a long table with a handful of other lawyers. Muna smiled widely. "Welcome to the media case," he said. "You are with us now."

Monasebian was too surprised to argue.

* * *

For the people of Taba commune, a rural farming community just west of Kigali, the change in Mayor Jean-Paul Akayesu was evident when he appeared before them in a camouflage military jacket instead of the dark blazer he usually favored. Until that point, in the third week of April 1994, residents of Taba knew their mayor as a man who was staunchly against the violence flaring throughout the country. He tried to keep the peace. The words he used were meant to calm. And then his jacket changed. And so, too, did he. Compassion gave way to violence. Peacemaker became executioner.

Had anyone inquired about Mr. Akayesu's character before the killing began, they would have received a glowing report. A forty-one-year-old father of five, he had been a schoolteacher by training and had all the requisite standing in the community that went with that sort of job. He was friendly, well educated, and articulate. He was a Hutu, but he had always been fair and impartial when it came to the administration of Taba. When citizens arrived on his doorstep bearing complaints, he was helpful, empathetic. He was, by all accounts, everything anyone would want in a community leader. And then he changed jackets, and priorities—and life in Taba as people knew it changed.

The genocidal violence in communes like Taba appeared, at first, to show just how thoroughly the state had failed. Certainly no mayor would permit his residents to be killed and raped by criminals in their midst. But in Rwanda, the ruthlessness grew out of the efficient organization of communes and villages like Taba. The communities were so successfully hierarchical, so parsed and divided and subdivided again, that they were easily mobilized. The men in communes like Taba were of the herd: they listened to those in authority with bovine obedience. What Akayesu desired, they did.

When Akayesu went on trial at the ICTR, in May 1997, he was not accused of being a mastermind of the genocide. He was, in many ways, something worse: he was the link between instigators and their followers. He was the highly effective middle management of the genocide. Without him, people in Taba said later, the massacres would not have happened. When he ordered them to kill, they did. When he ordered them to rape, they did that as well.

The municipal headquarters—referred to as the *bureau communal*—in Taba was a small concrete building with a courtyard before it and the community cultural center behind. The offices were small and dark, the phone service spotty. In late April 1994, when the killing had moved from Kigali to other parts of Rwanda, the fear in Taba was palpable. Citizens had always seen Jean-Paul Akayesu as a man of his word, an upstanding citizen. He had stood against the killing in Taba in the first two weeks of April, so citizens descended on the *bureau communal* looking for shelter. When one woman, who would later testify as Witness JJ, arrived in the *bureau*'s courtyard, she found sixty refugees already there, squatting in the mud outside the building. Most of the assembled were women and children. She noticed they were moving haltingly. When she got closer she realized something more horrifying: they had all been beaten. It was Akayesu, she said later, who had given the order. "Beat them," he shouted to the young men with their knives and clubs and small hoes. "They are wicked, wicked people who no longer have a right to shelter."

Akayesu was also a party to something worse, the systematic rape of Taba's Tutsi women. The Interahamwe took young girls and women from the refuge near the *bureau communal* into the forest and ravaged them. It happened day after day. There were single rapes and gang rapes and violations of the most unspeakable kind. And while JJ never saw Akayesu rape anyone, she believed, as others did, that he could have prevented the rapes but never tried to do so.

The second time she was taken to the forest to be raped, she remembered seeing Akayesu standing at the entrance of the cultural center and hearing him say loudly to the Interahamwe, "Never ask me again what a Tutsi woman tastes like." Then he grunted and said, "Tomorrow they will be killed." The Interahamwe stopped before Akayesu and told him they were taking girls away to "sleep with them," and he nodded approvingly. "Take them," he said.

Later, before judges at the international tribunal, Akayesu would say he was surprised to hear there were any allegations about rapes in Taba. "Anyone who says that even a single woman was raped at the *bureau communal* was lying," he told the courtroom defiantly. He never saw rapes and never heard from policemen that there had been any in Taba, he continued. "These women have worked up to agree that they have been raped," he said. The tales were pure fiction.

The judges disagreed.

For his part in the killings, the International Criminal Tribunal for Rwanda found him guilty on nine counts of genocide, torture, rape, murder, and crimes against humanity. Jean-Paul Akayesu became the first defendant ever to be convicted for the crime of genocide by an international court. It took the judges more than an hour to read the summary of their three-hundred-page judgment against him. And he made history not only as the first to be found guilty at the ICTR. The ICTR established the international definition of the crime of rape with the Akayesu verdict. "Sexual violence, including rape, is not limited to physical invasion of the human body and may include acts which do not involve penetration or even physical contact," the judges said in their judgment. "Threats, intimidation, extortion, and other forms of duress which prey on fear or desperation could be coercion." The judges also declared that rape and sexual violence constituted genocide when they were intended to destroy a particular targeted group. And in the case of Taba, they said, "The rape of Tutsi women was systematic and was perpetrated against all Tutsi women and solely against Tutsi women." Rape, so long considered a weapon of war, had been redefined as a war crime. The instances in Rwanda were so rife that the judges decided that they were part of the violence, not an offshoot of it as courts had held previously.

Navanethem Pillay, a former South African Supreme Court jurist, was one of the three judges presiding over the Akayesu trial. The only female judge at the tribunal, she came from a law career that had made her a standard-bearer for women's rights in South Africa. At a time when most women in South Africa would never even think of going to college, she was attending Natal University with an eye toward the law. She graduated at the top of her class and traveled to the United States to get her law degree from Harvard University. She opened her law practice—the first woman to do so in Natal province—in 1967. As a senior partner in the firm, she represented many opponents of apartheid, and became such a threat to the sitting regime she was denied a passport for many years.

Her focus had always been on human rights: on precedent-setting cases that established the effects of solitary confinement,

on the rights of political prisoners to due process, and on family violence syndrome as a defense. By 1995, she had become the first black woman attorney to be appointed acting judge of the Supreme Court of South Africa. A short time later she was elected by the United Nations to serve as a judge on the tribunal for Rwanda. With Akayesu, Pillay had made history again. "Rape had always been regarded as one of the spoils of war," she said in a statement after the verdict. "Now it is a war crime, no longer a trophy."

The ruling would have meant more if the thousands of women in Rwanda who had been victims of rape during the genocide had known it even occurred. This, too, was one of the problems with the ICTR. It meted out justice and Rwandans were never informed.

* * *

The media trial trio had been in the United Nations Detention Facility (UNDF), three miles outside of downtown Arusha, for three years by the time their attorneys had finished their investigations and depositions and were ready to go to trial. The men sat in their small cells with long hours to kill and little to distract them from the lengthy proceedings that lay ahead. There had been rumors in Rwanda that the UNDF was a prisoner's paradise: officials in the Kigali government had taken to calling it the Arusha Hilton. There were stories about lobster and shrimp dinners, beer for the inmates, warm croissants for breakfast, and AIDS drugs for those who had been diagnosed with the disease.

The stories only reinforced the general feeling in Rwanda that those who held political power never suffered as much as the people who toiled below them. When two elephants fight, the saying went, it is the grass that suffers. Kagame and the *génocidaires* were the elephants. Ordinary Rwandans were the grass.

While the situation at the UNDF was far superior to the difficult conditions in Rwandan prisons, it was hardly the Hilton. The facility was inside the compound of a Tanzanian high-security

prison. It had fifty-six cells, a gas-powered kitchen, a dispensary and hospital, classrooms for language instruction, and a gym. The cells where the trio sat were about nine feet long and fifteen feet high. Each had only a small bed and a toilet area with commode and sink. The detainees were allowed to make one outgoing telephone call a week, but they could receive unlimited incoming calls. The phones were in a common hall and inmates had to talk standing up. The compounds also had a computer room where detainees were permitted to work on their cases. Some detainees had their own laptops. The tribunal also provided the prisoners with two suits of clothing for their courtroom appearances. Families were also permitted to provide clothes. Meals, while they were better than anything most people were eating in Rwanda, were plain: fried fish, vegetables, yogurt, fresh milk.

Rwandans heard that inmates were complaining because the food was too rich. Those who were eating their one bowl of gruel a day in Rwanda's prisons were having a difficult time feeling sorry for them. Mastermind a genocide, they said, and get three square meals a day. Follow orders, and you end up eating corn porridge once a day with 120,000 other prisoners.

Had Jean-Bosco Barayagwiza been captured in Rwanda, he likely would have been among the *génocidaires* who were shot in a public execution in a Kigali stadium months after the killing ended. Pasteur Bizimungu, a member of the RPF executive committee, was the president of the reconciliation government. Kagame was ostensibly second in command. He was vice president and also was in charge of the army, as minister of defense. Both men set the tone for the traumatized nation, and it was a tough one. While some Hutu, like Faustin Twagiramungu, were brought into the government to prove that this was not a Tutsi autocracy, there was still a great deal of conflict in Rwanda, often along ethnic lines.

Barayagwiza was fortunate that he was in Arusha, fighting for his release by filing motions on legal technicalities. According to Rule 40 of the International Criminal Tribunal for Rwanda, pris-

oners could not be detained for more than ninety days without a signed arrest warrant and an indictment. Barayagwiza was in detention in Cameroon for ten months before he was transferred to Arusha. Under the rules of the tribunal, procedural delays in Cameroon had violated his rights, international judges said in November 1999, and for that reason Barayagwiza should be set free.

The fallout from the decision was swift. Rwanda's vice president, Paul Kagame, cried foul. If Barayagwiza were to go free, he warned, there would be consequences. Any cooperation with Kigali for the ICTR would cease if Barayagwiza won release. There would be no help for investigators, no visas for witnesses, no turning over of documents. It was the first of many episodes in which the Rwandan government made clear that it held the success or failure of the ICTR in the palm of its hands. Though officials of ICTR emphatically denied it, politics was at the heart of the court.

Knowing that, chief prosecutor Carla Del Ponte decided that she needed to handle the appeal that would keep Barayagwiza behind bars herself. "I have eight hundred thousand to one million corpses crying out for justice," she told the Appeals Court judges in a special session. "Whether we like it or not, we must come to terms with the fact that we depend on the government of Rwanda. Either Barayagwiza has to be tried or he should be handed over to Rwanda. Otherwise, I think we will have to open the doors of the prison."

Barayagwiza's initial ten-month detention in Cameroon was delayed because the authorities there were examining an extradition request from the government of Rwanda, she argued. It was the slow-moving Cameroon justice system, not the foot dragging of the ICTR Prosecutor's Office, which had kept Barayagwiza in prison longer than the prescribed ninety days. "Who decides the moment of transfer?" she asked. "It is not the tribunal but the national authorities."

In September 2000, a week after Del Ponte's argument, the Appeals Court reversed the decision. While there were some procedural problems for which the Prosecutor's Office was to blame, the long delay for an indictment was laid at the feet of the Cameroon government. Should Barayagwiza be found innocent he would be financially compensated for the delay, the judges said. If he should be found guilty, then the sentence would be appropriately reduced.

The Prosecutor's Office said the tribunal had dodged a bullet. Barayagwiza, for his part, started a boycott of the chamber. Soon after the decision he wrote a letter to the court saying he was ready to contest the allegations against him and prove his innocence before any independent and impartial tribunal in any democratic state. The U.N. tribunal was too dependent on what he called "the dictatorial anti-Hutu regime in Kigali" to provide him with anything approximating a fair trial.

"I challenge the ability of the ICTR to render an independent and impartial justice," he wrote in a letter to the court in October 2000, vowing not to attend the proceedings or even be a party to them. He asked that the court allow him to fire his lawyers. "I will never accept to give support to a mockery of justice by this tribunal."

* * *

When *The Prosecutor v. Jean-Bosco Barayagwiza, Ferdinand Nahimana, and Hassan Ngeze* finally opened, in early 2001, the world was looking the other way. In *USA Today*, political columnist Walter Shapiro was focused on the lack of idealism in America. Students at Harvard University were attending a forum on hate crimes, but the issue of the Rwandan genocide never came up. President Bush's proposal for required testing in schools was filling editorial pages, and on Capitol Hill, Democrats in Congress offered up a $900 billion tax-cut plan they said would be easier on the economy than President Bush's $1.6 trillion proposal.

The prosecutors rolled out an eighty-page list of charges against the trio. Indictments are usually just three or four pages long. In retrospect, the lawyers said the document could have used some editing. It was more of a narrative than a recitation of crimes. The indictment began—rather oddly, given that the jurisdiction of the court was limited to 1994—with the history of Rwanda. It opened with the 1959 uprising, chewed through the nation's bloody cycle of massacres, and ended up accusing the three men of a litany of crimes: incitement, conspiracy, crimes against humanity, murder, and genocide. The media trio, the prosecutors said, had infected people's minds with ethnic hatred and persecution.

The indictment said Barayagwiza had presided over several meetings called to plan the murder of Tutsi and moderate Hutu in Mutura commune, in Gisenyi prefecture, in northwest Rwanda. Prosecutors also alleged that he had distributed weapons and money to Interahamwe militia. It was on his orders, the indictment said, that Interahamwe youth began to kill Tutsi. Barayagwiza, as a leader of the Coalition pour la Défense de la République, or CDR party, knew that its members were preparing a genocide, but he did nothing to stop it. He was also accused of conspiring with Nahimana and his friend Rwandan businessman Félicien Kabuga to set up RTLM expressly to promote Hutu extremism. What the indictment didn't say was that there was scant evidence to link Barayagwiza to radio station RTLM. Barayagwiza pleaded not guilty.

Ferdinand Nahimana, small and compact to begin with, shrank even further into his suit when the charges were read against him. He was accused of having broadcast messages on national radio that were meant to incite ethnic hatred and the murder of Tutsi. Prosecutors said he joined forces with Hassan Ngeze and Barayagwiza to wipe out Tutsi and their moderate Hutu supporters. There was also proof, they said, that Nahimana had encouraged unemployed Rwandan youth to form self-defense groups to oppose the RPF. Those who took up his call became the core of the Interahamwe. Prosecutors went further. Nahimana had chaired meetings in which top officials of the Mouvement Républicain National pour la Démocratie et le Développement, or MRNDD party, plotted to eliminate the Tutsi. He, too, ordered the murder of Tutsi and helped get arms to the Interahamwe, the prosecution said. His Ph.D. thesis had provided the ideological basis for the 1994 genocide, the lawyers continued. They didn't mention that his voice had come over the airwaves only a handful of times or that he was out of the country soon after the genocide began or that his thesis was twenty years old.

Hassan Ngeze's work at *Kangura* was the focus of the charges against him. Prosecutors said he had consented to the publication of material in the newspaper that promoted ethnic hatred and incited mass killings of the Tutsi. Editorials, guest journalist articles, political and social cartoons, and the names of individuals targeted for assassination were found in the pages of *Kangura*. The tribunal's mandate to try crimes committed from January 1, 1994, to the end of that year meant, technically, that few *Kangura* issues would be admissible since the newspaper stopped publishing before the genocide began. Prosecutors used the RTLM contest as a way to get more issues of the newspapers entered into evidence.

Provisos aside, prosecutors said they intended to prove that Nahimana, Barayagwiza, and Ngeze were men who used words to kill.

The counts and charges rang through the tribunal courtroom like chimes, and the accused sat emotionless as history was made: the three became the first journalists since the self-proclaimed "number-one Nazi," Julius Streicher, to stand trial in an international court for such grave crimes.

"Every count in the indictment will be proved by credible evidence and is supported by hundreds of hours of taped radio broadcasts and newspapers generated by the prisoners themselves," the media trial's first prosecutor, Bernard Muna, said in his opening statement. He called Nahimana the "intellectual high priest of Hutu Supremacy." Barayagwiza was the "master manipulator of the truth both at home and abroad." Ngeze was not spared from his own superlatives. Muna called him "the venomous vulgarian and purveyor of racial libel and slander."

"Your Honors, this case has been popularly known as the media trial," Muna said. "In fact, the media is not on trial here. It is the trial of three prisoners who used, or rather misused, the media.

When people who speak on radio are people in political leadership and when such broadcasts are seemingly approved or sanctioned by a government, I can only leave it to the imagination of any reasonable person to estimate the influence that such broadcasts can have on the ordinary citizens on the hills."

The trial, Muna went on, was to prove that the trio were principally responsible for what was broadcast or appeared in print and that the genocide was part of an overall strategy and plan. "The conspiracy to commit genocide in Rwanda can be likened to a moving train," said Muna. "The train would stop at the prefecture and the prefect and his assistants would be invited to join the conspiracy."

The strategy, working through a grassroots campaign, explains why the genocide that took place in Rwanda is considered to have been the most efficient killing in human history, Muna said, adding that in Germany the targeting of the Jews went through four stages. There was classification as a Jew, the expropriation of property, banishment to the ghettos, and then transportation to the camps and eventual extermination. "The whole process took nine years," Muna said. "By comparison, the Hutu leaders went from stage one to stage four within a few weeks."

Muna, who until that point had made a compelling case, then veered inexplicably into a tamping down of expectations. "I cannot assure Your Honors that this case will not suffer from incomplete research," he said. "We are but human and are not infallible. What I can assure you is that the best professional efforts have been made by us in preparation of this case and are completely adequate."

Muna's prosecution team held their heads in their hands as he read these last words. Certainly, they could try for something better than adequate. Monasebian knew they could do better. The head of prosecution at the tribunal must have thought so too. Within weeks, Muna was reassigned. Three more prosecutors would fill his shoes until the arrival of a politically savvy prosecutor from Iowa. His name was Stephen Rapp.

Soon after accepting a job in the Prosecutor's Office at the ICTR, Rapp became a student of Nuremberg, going so far as to offer to play videos of the Allied trial during potluck dinners. Rapp, his colleagues in Arusha said with amusement, was a bit of a Nuremberg geek. And while Rapp seemed a bit homespun, all soft smiles and quiet ways, his exterior belied tremendous ambition. This was one of the secrets of his success. Being underestimated is a great weapon, in or out of the courtroom. He was passionate about the tribunal's work. "The great crimes of the modern world happened in Rwanda, and I want to prosecute them," he said. "What happened there has no real parallel in history. Terrible crimes took place during the genocide, far worse than what happened in the former Yugoslavia. As far as I am concerned, this is our Nuremberg."

Prosecutors had testimony from many survivors who described radio broadcasts that were followed by attacks. But very few witnesses could explain what happened cogently, in a narrative, so that it would be easy to see cause and effect. Complicating the problem was the difficult task of trying to match broadcasts with victims. Prosecutors had less than 10 percent of RTLM's broadcasts on tape, and the names of individual victims had rarely been included in the transcripts themselves.

Akayesu's conviction in 1998 provided some help there. He was found guilty of incitement partly because of a speech he gave in which he urged Taba residents to kill Tutsi. The tribunal had said that Akayesu's speech was effectively an order because he had been mayor and he had standing. The prosecution needed to prove that RTLM and *Kangura* held that same sort of authority. They had to prove that Rwandans would obey orders over the airwaves with the same alacrity with which they obeyed orders spoken by their leaders. The only problem, prosecutors thought, was that in the process they could be setting an international standard for prosecuting incitement that was far wider than the one in Akayesu's case.

6

"We Had No Control"

Damien Nzabakira startled awake. His eyes scanned the people around him, landing first on one sleeping face and then another. In the haze of sleep his first thought was to look for the children. Then he realized he was no longer at the orphanage. He listened to the wheezing, humming snores, and breathed in the strong, dank smells around him. The room smelled of sour sweat and unwashed bodies and wet leaves. The closeness of the men, the loud rhythm of unhealthy breathing, seemed to suck the air right out of the room. There were no windows, so there was no light. Damien waited for his eyes to adjust.

Yellow plastic jerry cans were tied to the ceiling above him. The men had constructed makeshift bunks, cubbyholes really, where they slept in shifts because there was not room enough for them all. Those who were waiting their turn stood outside in the prison yard, covering themselves against rain with thin plastic sheeting. Damien stretched as best he could without waking the men on either side of him and smoothed out his uniform.

Damien was behind bars, accused of killing forty children and some of his colleagues at the Red Cross orphanage in a bloody rampage on April 29, 1994. Of course, he hadn't acted alone, his accuser, an assistant director of the orphanage where Damien worked, told authorities. But when Rwandan army soldiers arrived in Butare, it was Damien who helped them, she said. Never mind that she could not provide details on the killings he committed; she knew only that he joined with military officers in killing all the Tutsi and moderate Hutu hiding out at the school. He killed the children, too, she said. And he killed her husband. It didn't seem to matter to police that with Damien out of the way, his accuser would get his job at the orphanage and possibly, if she worked it out just right, his house and his land. What mattered then, a little more than a year after the genocide, when she came forward, was that she was pointing a long finger in Damien's general direction. That was enough to call for his arrest.

The policemen came to his house bearing nothing but her accusations. There were no warrants, no written charges, just the wisp of an idea that he had done something wrong. Damien was in his living room with his child, a new baby girl, when the knock sounded. The officers took the child, handed her to her mother, and led Damien outside.

"You need to come with us," they told him. "You have been accused."

Damien's heart raced as he climbed into the back of their pickup truck. Accused of what? He was certain there must be some mistake. He had killed no one during the genocide. He had not joined in. He was a God-fearing man. God-fearing men didn't kill their neighbors. As the truck sputtered to life, he looked back at his wife and his daughter. This was all a terrible misunderstanding. Two hours later Damien arrived at the gates of Prison 1930, in the capital city of Kigali. It was July 15, 1995.

The central prison is known among Rwandans simply as "1930." The numbers are carved in stone above the prison gates as if they were keeping count of the number of prisons built around the country. In fact, the prison was built in that year. Rather incongruously, from a distance 1930 looks like a castle. There are turrets, and the walls are a great eruption of brick, rising thirty feet in the air from the red clay. The exterior of 1930 belies what lies inside. It was built to accommodate 750 prisoners. By 1995, when Damien began his incarceration there, it held more than seven thousand. Two years later, ten times that number of Rwandans were in prison nationwide.

As a result, Prison 1930 was a zoo of humanity. Once inside, a visitor saw an undulating wave of pink rising and falling, like rose-colored chips at sea. President Habyarimana, before he died, had decided the nation's prisoners ought to wear pink. Previously, they had been dressed in black, but that uniform, Habyarimana said, sent a gloomy message. It suggested there could be no redemption, and in a country as Catholic as Rwanda there was always the distant possibility of forgiveness. So the president opted for what he saw as a redemptive color: bright pink. Years after his edict, years after he was assassinated, Habyarimana's color choice meant crowded knots of men accused of murdering in the worst way were dressed in the soft hues of infants. They wore pink knee-length safari shorts and pink pressed shirts with oversized pockets on the front. On their heads were pink ball caps, with the bills curved in half circles.

After 1994, Rwandan prisons arguably became the most crowded, most dangerous, and most inhumane prisons in the world. There was, if one was lucky, one meal a day. It was a bowl of a corn gruel that prison cooks, stripped to the waist, stirred in enormous caldrons over open fires set off from the main building. There were no fences around the kitchen. No one would dare escape. In a country as small as Rwanda there was nowhere to run, nowhere to go where one wouldn't be recognized by a neighbor and summarily returned to the authorities. Because of this, security was light. Guards were relaxed. The prisoners were tied to their prison by a feeling of hopelessness, making the stay that much worse.

As bad as 1930 was, Damien knew that in some ways he had been relatively lucky to be taken there. There were hundreds of thousands of makeshift prisons sprouting up around the country.

Some Rwandans, usually Hutu, were held in truck containers or disused factories. Anything that showed promise of confinement was turned into a modern-day dungeon. Citizens would vanish for months at a time, only to emerge with spirits crushed, limbs missing, memories seared.

Damien, ever the optimist, focused on his weekly visits from his wife. She would wake at dawn on those Saturdays, leave their daughter at a neighbor's, and walk from their home outside Kigali up the hill to Prison 1930. She would get there around 9 a.m. and join the queue of wives and mothers and sisters who had come to the prison to deliver food to their men. Sometimes the guards asked for money, a little pourboire for producing husbands in a timely fashion. Inside, the women in their brightly colored Sunday dresses turned the monotone prison yard into a riot of African colors: pinks were punctuated with yellows and greens as couples sat side by side on long benches in the dusty prison yard. Then, in late afternoon, a whistle would blow. Visitors and prisoners would all rise in unison, and the women would file out, returning the prison yard once again to its uniform pinkish hue.

The prisons, filled mostly with men, sprinkled with a handful of women, housed those who were accused but not yet tried. They were a repository of bitterness and resentment. It was hard not to notice that the only people locked up were Hutu. Prisoners and human rights groups began to suggest that the ultimate objective of Rwanda's prison system had nothing to do with rehabilitation. It might be ethnic cleansing against the Hutu. The lives of the Hutu elite—the educated, the professionals, businesspeople, teachers like Damien—were stopped dead by summary arrests and the long prison stays without trial that followed. Families with men in jail ended up trading property for food or for money to bribe the police. By the time a husband finally perished behind bars the family had lost everything.

"They are exterminating us," said one prisoner at 1930. "All the Hutu will disappear and it will be because they were killed off by the prison system. The war between the Hutu and the Tutsi hasn't stopped, it has just changed. Now it is dressed up as an attempt to mete out justice. But look around. Were Hutu the only people in Rwanda to ever commit a crime? Is that why there are only Hutu in prison?"

Part of the problem was that Rwanda's court system had died with the genocide. Most of the nation's judges and lawyers had been killed. Law books had been burned, courthouses destroyed. As a result the nation had to start, literally, from scratch. It had to find judges and draw up laws. It had to round up lawyers willing to defend those accused of mass murder. Furthermore, there were few, if any, written records of crimes committed during those hundred days of killing. So many people took part in the frenzied killing that it was difficult to tell who had done what. Accusations were based on hearsay or fuzzy recollections from a time when the world appeared to have gone mad. Imprisoning people, holding them accountable, was one way to bring a semblance of order. Accusers told themselves that even if they had not denounced the right person, more than likely this Hutu or that Hutu had committed some atrocity no one had seen, so putting them in prison was the right thing to do.

Slowly, the gathering of prisoners broadened the destruction of the genocide. Now it was not just Tutsi and moderate Hutu who had lost loved ones. Hutu families were suffering their own casualties. With fathers, brothers, sisters, and mothers behind bars, Hutu families experienced loss as well. And any hope of freedom, of a trial that would allow the evidence to show that the accusations had all been a huge misunderstanding or a case of mistaken identity, was vanquished as the prisons filled to bursting. By the end of 1996, only fifty-three hundred persons had been judged, fewer than 5 percent of the detained. It was a lack of personnel and resources, the government said. It was politics and corruption, the prisoners grumbled.

Experts said that even the American legal system, with its half million lawyers, would collapse under the numbers Rwanda was dealing with. The Bizimungu government passed a genocide law in 1996 to add some order to the chaos. Capital punishment was reserved for those who planned, organized, incited, or supervised the genocide, it said. Ordinary murderers, rapists, and lesser criminals could receive reduced sentences by admitting their crimes.

Damien tried to calculate how long he would be in prison if he waited his turn. It would take, he figured conservatively, somewhere close to a hundred years. Even if Damien got his day in court, the fight didn't appear to be a fair one. Most defendants did not get lawyers. Defense witnesses rarely appeared in court. Defendants were refused the opportunity to question witnesses. Witnesses and judges expressed fear for their personal safety. The safest route, it became clear, was to accept guilt and hope for mercy. Damien did not want to give up so easily.

His wife had contacted a lawyer, but he wanted a million Rwandan francs, or about $2,000, up front, to take Damien's case. "People owed me money and I might have been able to come up with at least some of that," Damien said later. "But those I had lent money to suddenly decided they didn't need to pay up. God gave me the strength not to see them as bad. I just accepted that all these people who had been my friends had changed."

* * *

While the transitional government promised to bring Hutu who killed Tutsi to justice, any discussion about holding RPF soldiers responsible for reprisal killings against Hutu was scuttled. Killing during a war, in self-defense, is entirely different from a genocide, the argument went. And nowhere was this attitude more evident than in the weekly sessions President Bizimungu called in the presidential offices in Urugwiro Village, just outside of Kigali. Pasteur Bizimungu, appointed president in July 1995, was the Rwandan government's highest-ranking Hutu member and, as such, was integral to maintaining the nation's delicate balance of power. While most Rwandans believed it was Vice President Kagame who actually ran the country, Bizimungu's presence in the presidential palace symbolized Rwanda's postgenocide reconciliation. Bizimungu met with a handful of Rwanda's best and brightest every Saturday to discuss the nation's struggle for redemption. Former diplomat Bonaventure Ubalijoro was among the wise men asked for counsel.

While it was said in these meetings that candor was encouraged, in fact it was not. Ubalijoro, a man who had always spoken his mind, managed to anger a great many of the attendees by calling for an investigation into the RPF. Certainly launching a discussion and deciding, definitively, what took place would help lead to national reconciliation, he argued. Everyone knew there were some rogue officers who killed in the heat of the moment. Admitting as much would only strengthen the current regime's hand and show this was not a Tutsi coup, but a legitimate government that represented all Rwandans.

President Bizimungu would not hear of it.

Meeting after weekly meeting the two men clashed. Angry words were exchanged. Accusations flew. The debate became so tense that Ubalijoro's friends suggested the former ambassador stop attending the meetings for fear he would find himself on the wrong end of a political reprisal. Ubalijoro reluctantly agreed.

One night not long after he stopped attending the meetings, Ubalijoro was finishing dinner with his wife, just taking the last sip of his carefully rationed beer with supper, when a knock sounded on the door. Ubalijoro looked through the glass. A soldier stood outside. The prefect of Kigali needed to see the ambassador urgently, the soldier said politely. He motioned toward his car. "We'll drive you."

Ubalijoro peered out into the night. He could make out a Toyota 4Runner full of armed soldiers. Ubalijoro was alarmed but managed to keep his composure before the military man who stood before him.

"I have my own car," he said slowly. "I will follow along behind you."

"No, you need to come with us," the soldier said. There would be no argument.

Ubalijoro's wife, Madeleine, watched as the taillights of the SUV disappeared down the hilly driveway into the darkness. She began to pack her purse and pulled on her coat. She was certain that Bonaventure Ubalijoro was not urgently wanted by the prefect. Something else was afoot. Her sense was correct. By the end of the night, Ubalijoro was in a Kigali prison, though it wasn't clear, exactly, what he had done. He was told he was in "preventive detention." Ubalijoro was certain it was connected to his battle with Bizimungu.

The former ambassador soon learned that he had become an unwitting part of the fifth anniversary commemoration of the genocide. During a ceremony to mark the beginning of the killing, the Bizimungu government staged the reburial of twenty thousand genocide victims. It was there that President Bizimungu announced that Rwanda had rounded up five high-level *génocidaires* who would be tried for their crimes. Bonaventure Ubalijoro, the president said, had been arrested for committing genocide against the Tutsi when he was an intelligence chief in the 1960s. More worrisome, Bizimungu said, was the former ambassador's recent secret campaign to sow the seeds of divisionism throughout the country.

"In 1963, Belgian soldiers shot people from helicopters in Kibeho, Kigali, Bugesera, and Ruhengeri," Bizimungu told the crowd. "They killed with the assistance of Bonaventure Ubalijoro, who at that time headed the secret police. We shall try to arrest those we can." The next day the local newspapers picked up the story. The articles helpfully provided a list of those whom Ubalijoro had allegedly killed. The minister of justice was the source of the story. Ubalijoro's defense was nowhere to be found.

While Ubalijoro assumed his imprisonment was related to his many tête-à-têtes with President Bizimungu, he may have just been a casualty in a wider purge of moderate Hutu figures from the Kigali government. With each passing month the list got longer. The first prime minister of the new postgenocidal Rwanda, Faustin Twagiramungu, was forced to resign amid allegations that he played a role in the genocide. His replacement, Hutu Prime Minister Pierre-Celestin Rwigyema, resigned in February 2000 following accusations of corruption. President Bizimungu stepped down a month later citing differences with hard-liners in the RPF. Kagame became acting president.

As he took the oath of office at the Amahoro Stadium in Kigali, he urged Rwandans to shun the ethnic divisions that divided them. "It is the first time in the history of Rwanda that a change of power has taken place without bloodshed," Kagame said at the time. "Peace and security have been established in the whole country."

Ubalijoro heard the speech from his jail cell.

* * *

Barayagwiza, Nahimana, and Ngeze would tell anyone who would listen that the charges against them were also politically motivated. While they had indeed started RTLM, or Radio Mille Collines, and published *Kangura,* their motives were more innocent than the prosecutors alleged. The tribunal was seeking to take all their actions out of context. Rwanda was a country at odds with itself when Radio Mille Collines got its start. It wasn't a matter of whipping up the Hutu to kill Tutsi; to focus on that missed the point entirely. Instead it was important to understand that Tutsi exiles, particularly those in Uganda, had organized themselves into bands intent on seizing power in Kigali. Not to have been frightened by such a threat would have been naive.

Not only had the Tutsi launched incursions into Rwandan territory, they had also set up a political organization, known as the Rwandan Patriotic Front, in anticipation of returning to Rwanda from exile. President Habyarimana had told them there wasn't enough food in Rwanda to feed all the Tutsi who wanted to return. In response, the rebels made clear they intended to overthrow Habyarimana. They wanted to use the Arusha Accords under negotiation in Tanzania as a way to gain a toehold on power. The coalition government it laid out would give them the base they needed to overthrow the Hutu government. Power had been their objective since 1990, Nahimana would testify. Not to understand that Rwanda was in the throes of a slow-simmering civil war in the run-up to the president's plane crash was to not understand Rwanda.

Radio Mille Collines began for a very simple reason—to counter the broadcasts of an RPF station called Radio Muhabura—the defense later explained. Radio Muhabura was insidious. It supported the Arusha Accords, it whipped up opposition to President Habyarimana, it sought to recruit young Tutsi into the RPF so they could overthrow the government. Radio Mille Collines, as they saw it, was merely fighting fire with fire, presenting the opposing view, the contrarian interpretation of the Arusha Accords. This made the media trial not about incitement at all, they argued. This was an issue of free speech. And until April 6, when the president's plane was shot down, that's all Radio Mille Collines offered. After April 6, the defense said, Nahimana and Barayagwiza had lost all control over the radio station. It was taken over by the military. After that, the motivations of the radio station ceased to be their responsibility. It was out of their hands.

The problem for Barayagwiza and Nahimana was that the broadcasts on RTLM were problematic before April 6. That's why, the prosecution said, the minister of information had called in the duo on at least two separate occasions to warn them that RTLM was dancing perilously close to the line of incitement. The prosecution planned to introduce minutes and tapes of those meetings, and in the case of Nahimana, the minutes repeatedly referred to him as one of the directors of RTLM—the man in charge of Radio Hate.

"The press had become a weapon which was more dangerous than a machete," one witness said later. "This weapon kills more people than a machete."

* * *

It was never clear how Hassan Ngeze raised the money to start his own newspaper. Those who would testify against him said that

Habyarimana's intelligence service provided the initial seed capital. One of Ngeze's fellow journalists said that an Interahamwe leader had told him that there had been a Hutu Power meeting organized to find ways to support *Kangura* and it had helped raise 2 million Rwandan francs to get it off the ground. But that was rumor and innuendo. There was no concrete proof of any of this. John Floyd would say later that his client, Ngeze, had started the paper with his own money and was chronically indebted to publishing houses throughout Rwanda as a consequence.

"He never paid those bills," Floyd said. "If the government was really backing him, why did he leave all these bills unpaid? It doesn't make sense"—unless, of course, Ngeze did get the money from the intelligence agency and simply spent the money on something else.

Ngeze was not a person one would describe as a good credit risk. Even so, Ngeze was taken seriously enough that the state publishing house agreed to print *Kangura* on a regular basis. At its most popular, as many as fifteen hundred to three thousand copies rolled off the presses at any one time, sometimes as often as weekly, sometime less regularly than that. It was not a giant publication, but respectably sized in a largely illiterate nation.

"It was not an ordinary newspaper," Witness AHA, a former journalist at *Kangura,* would testify. "It was different from the other newspapers in the country. *Kangura* was one of the few newspapers in Rwanda that was independent, or at least private, and 'independent' with a question mark. There was a certain freedom of expression in *Kangura* and a certain extravagance due probably to the lack of knowledge of our profession."

Kangura used sensationalism to ensure it sold. "It exaggerated the facts," said AHA. "It was sensational to trigger some sort of reaction. Everyone wanted to read it and everyone wanted to give his or her opinion on the information."

In an early issue, Ngeze had published an investigation of *Kanguka,* his former employer. The publisher of the competing paper had Machiavellian plans to destabilize the country, Ngeze wrote.

"Ngeze said he was a patriot, and as a patriot he had to decided call on other patriots to join him," AHA testified, adding that the call to arms was different because Rwandans were used to official statements, official inaugurations, and official decrees in their newspapers. "Hassan Ngeze came in with something new, something extraordinary. The veracity of such information was not the concern of Rwandans at the time."

Subsequent issues of *Kangura* reported on Tutsi coming in from Uganda. They launched sizable attacks and were gathering accomplices across the country for their ultimate strike. Ngeze began to publish the names of the suspects. He threw his editorial weight behind the Coalition for the Defense of the Republic, or CDR party. He called for a coalition of all the world's Hutu so they would stand as a united front against the Tutsi. He said the Tutsi had a plan to govern all the countries in Central Africa. Rwanda would fall, he predicted, followed by Tanzania, unless the Hutu fought back. Ngeze suggested Hutu submit ideas to *Kangura* on how they might defend the republic as it teetered on the edge of a Tutsi-led apocalypse.

Years later, when people talked about *Kangura* and what it really had or had not been trying to do, they focused on *Kangura* number 6. Published in December 1990, it included an article that appealed to the conscience of the Hutu and ended with what became known as the Hutu Ten Commandments. The article had been published elsewhere in Rwanda, but its resurrection in *Kangura* in 1990, when ordinary residents were rattled by the RPF, made it resonate more than it might have otherwise. The commandments were pure racial hatred, reminiscent of the most extreme Nazi anti-Semitism or Klan black vilification. It was incendiary and dangerous.

> 1. Every Hutu male should know that Tutsi women, wherever they may be, are working in the pay of their Tutsi ethnic group. Consequently, shall be deemed a traitor any Hutu male who marries a Tutsi women, any Hutu male who keeps

a Tutsi concubine; any Hutu male who makes Tutsi women his secretary or protégée.
2. Every Hutu male must know that our Hutu daughters are more dignified and conscientious in the role of woman, wife and mother. Are they not pretty, good secretaries and most honest!
3. Hutu women, be vigilant and bring your husbands, brothers, sons back to their senses.
4. Every Hutu male must know that all Tutsis are dishonest in their business dealings. They are only seeking ethnic supremacy.
5. Strategic positions in the political, administrative, economic, military and security domain should, to a large extent, be entrusted to Hutus.
6. In the education sector, it must be in the majority Hutu.
7. The Rwandan Armed Forces should be exclusively Hutu. That is the lesson we learned from the October 1990 war. No soldier must marry a Tutsi woman.
8. Hutus must cease having any pity for the Tutsi.
9. Hutu males, wherever they may be, should be united in solidarity, and be concerned about the fate of their Hutu brothers.
10. The 1959 revolution, the 1961 revolution, and the Hutu ideology must be taught to Hutus at all levels. Every Hutu must propagate the present ideology widely. Any Hutu who persecutes his brother having read, disseminated, and taught this ideology shall be deemed a traitor.

It was a manifesto, the prosecution said later, meant to prepare the ground for the 1994 killings. Hutu were supposed to start seeing the Tutsi as enemies, not citizens, and by the same token, the Tutsi started seeing the Hutu as a threat. The defense would claim later that *Kangura* wasn't the first place the Ten Commandments appeared. They had been widely disseminated in Rwanda for years. The difference: this time the commandments went out to a receptive audience. This question of audience, of how regular Rwandans reacted to news reports, would be key in the discussion of the trio's guilt or innocence.

Several months later Ngeze decided his front page needed a banner, a motto so that everyone knew where he stood. It sent a stark message. In a mass of vowels and crashing consonants it read: *IJWI RIGAMIJE GUKANGURA NO KURENGERA RUBANDA NYAMWINSHI*—"The Voice That Awakens and Defends the Majority People."

As the paper grew in size and stature, contributors grew too. Instead of Ngeze and a team of interns writing all the copy, the newspaper began advertising for submissions. National political figures, radio personalities, and some well-known journalists began to appear in its pages. Ngeze began calling editorial team meetings. He hired employees. He set up editorial pages.

Defense attorney John Floyd saw that as a key to the whole case. Hassan Ngeze wasn't a journalist, he was an opportunist. He wasn't trying to incite the masses. He was trying to make money. He was certain Ngeze would be found innocent as long as the judges required proof that the *Kangura* articles directly caused acts of genocide. Any objectionable content in *Kangura*, the defense lawyer insisted, should be seen as the product of bad taste or the bad judgment of inexperienced writers at the newspaper.

* * *

While Hassan Ngeze was cutting his teeth in journalism, Nahimana was working to train the Rwandan press corps. He held conferences, met with the leaders of the country's first private press organizations, and as time went on, decided to do something that no one had done before in Rwanda: create guidelines that would govern the press.

"In 1991, multiparty ideas were just becoming fashionable," Nahimana said later in court, adding that everyone agreed that the media had to change in order to give the various political parties their due. "The conclusion was, and this was what I was hoping for, that ORINFOR [the Rwandan Bureau of Information] had to put aside for recognized parties columns of the newspapers for these parties to express themselves. As for radio, they were supposed to allow airtime for these parties. We decided each political party would be allotted twelve minutes a week on air in Radio Rwanda, and during those twelve minutes, the party was going to publicize its platform, what it stood for, and so on. This was implemented from November 1991."

He was also brought aboard, it was said, to clean house. ORINFOR and the biggest government radio station, Radio Rwanda, were seen as bloated and inefficient. There were too many operators, too many drivers, too many hangers-on. Nahimana came in determined to cut the ranks. He fired sixty out of four hundred people almost at the start. That, apparently, wasn't enough for his superiors. Unable to decide who should be given the axe next, he began, witnesses testified later, firing Tutsis.

"I don't think there was a definitive list," said a Radio Rwanda journalist later in testimony, but Nahimana was definitely working on the basis of ethnicity and not incompetence or competence. "It stopped after he was told by someone in the president's office he had to stop or there would be serious political consequences."

Nahimana later denied he fired anyone because he was Tutsi. The sackings, he said, were based on ability. "I'm not here to give a lecture on how to manage a company," he told judges later. "But when one conducts an exercise of retrenchment due to budgetary reasons, you don't look at individuals, you look at posts. When accusations are made here, everything is done to talk about Tutsis. As far as I'm concerned it was a reduction in the number of members of staff, and that concerned Hutus, Tutsis, and even Burundians and other foreigners. I never drew up a list of Tutsi to be dismissed. Ethnicity and one's region of origin were never taken into consideration."

* * *

Damien had already been in prison for six years by the time the media trial began on October 23, 2000. Unlike the defendants in

Arusha, Damien did not have a dossier of evidence gathered against him. There was no file full of witness testimony. Instead there were still only the vague allegations from a woman who had once worked with Damien at the orphanage. It was her word against his and for six years his claims of innocence hardly seemed to matter. Ironically, the one helpful thing about her accusations was that she accused Damien of having worked alongside military personnel. That entitled Damien to a transfer from Prison 1930 to a military prison, where conditions were markedly better. In February 2002, he changed from the bright pink uniform of a regular inmate to the luminous bottle green prison garb of a military captive. After more than six years of regular beatings and living virtually on top of thousands of other men, Damien suddenly had a mattress, just three cell mates, and television. There were two meals a day and an atmosphere of respect that was nonexistent in the regular prison. "It is hard to explain it, but when the transfer came I was so happy," he said. "I was in prison, yes. I still had a case to prove, yes. But at least now I could live."

Security at the military prison was light. A single guard without a gun sat in a grass-and-wood shack at the end of the prison's dirt driveway. On Saturdays, prisoners and their families gathered under a large tarp, pulled tight between trees for shade. There were bottled sodas and cookies for sale. And there were long, low benches, row upon row, for the visitors and prisoners to sit in huddled groups. From a distance it looked like a company picnic. The children hung on their fathers and then skipped away to play with friends on the grass. There were baskets of food shared. Wives and mothers didn't shed tears. Instead they simply held hands with their loved ones and talked in low voices. Anyone was permitted to visit. All it took was a moment to check in with the guard, and then one was admitted to the grounds to find his or her prisoner and spend the day.

Damien spent these visits with his wife and daughter planning his defense. Some of those around him said they had been ordered to kill. Others said they were told they would be murdered unless they killed Tutsi. And then there were those, like Damien, who said they were unjustly accused. They claimed not to have killed anyone. But genocide is a conformist crime. Those who said they had killed no one were the hardest to believe. Certainly there was no one, or almost no one, left in Rwanda whose hands were clean.

Another year had passed, seven in all, when a prison guard told Damien that the Rwandan authorities were preparing to convene a military tribunal to look into his case. The trial would take place not far from the prison, he was told, and the government would appoint a lawyer to defend him. His accuser, they said, would have to provide proof in court of the atrocities he allegedly committed. The military tribunals, run by military judges of the Rwandan Patriotic Front, found 85 percent of the defendants who came before them guilty. Many cases ended with firing squads. From prison, Damien knew he was going to have to find a way to convince a handful of judges and a dubious courtroom audience that when Rwanda went mad, somehow he did not.

7

Merci, Génocide

Sammy Bahati Weza was an investigator for the International Criminal Tribunal for Rwanda and would probably have lived his days as an anonymous face in the bureaucracy of the court had it not been for one thing: he was not who he said he was.

When he was hired by the ICTR he appeared to be another African who wanted to help Rwanda emerge from its hunkered-down, self-imposed wartime state and make a sizable United Nations salary doing so. He was taken on as a defense investigator, which meant his job was to find evidence to exonerate defendants and, in many cases, at least work on the assumption that the massacres were spontaneous, not planned.

Weza had told the tribunal that he was Congolese, but that wasn't true. Instead of being a disinterested party, the tribunal discovered quite by accident, Weza was the deputy prosecutor of Cyangugu during the genocide. According to witnesses who recognized him in the corridors of the ICTR, he had supervised roadblocks and ordered the killing of Tutsi who tried to pass through them. The witnesses said he had helped herd people into a local stadium, where some of them died for lack of food, water, and sanitation.

In early 2002, the forty-one-year-old defense investigator was before a panel of judges pleading not guilty to charges of genocide and crimes against humanity. His arrest was followed by the dismissal or suspension of four other defense investigators also suspected of killing Tutsi. It was a black eye the already beleaguered tribunal didn't need. Suddenly, the ICTR was having to explain how it had managed to allow the equivalent of Gestapo officer Klaus Barbie to work for the U.N., investigating crimes that he had himself committed.

While the discovery was bad enough, it particularly rattled the Prosecutor's Office. Investigators often received confidential information about survivors who were testifying at the tribunal, including their real names before their alphabetical pseudonyms were assigned. A genocide suspect who could identify a survivor poised to give incriminating testimony in Arusha could easily encourage colleagues in Rwanda to intimidate or kill the witness. Already there were rumors that it had happened.

An organization representing survivors of the genocide, Ibuka—literally "Remember" in Kinyarwanda—said one or two genocide survivors were killed every month, some in connection with the ICTR tribunal, others for daring to say they would testify in separate, lower-level, Rwandan courts. The scandal at the ICTR with the investigator confirmed Ibuka's worst fears, and the Rwandan government and Ibuka responded by suspending cooperation with the tribunal. For six months, potential witnesses refused to work with tribunal investigators. The government suddenly required Rwandans to have special papers to travel to Arusha. Those who wanted to testify were required to obtain birth details from their administrative units and then apply for the official documents. This made the process of being a witness, bleak to begin with, that much more difficult. An already glacial judicial process became that much more so.

Friction between the Kigali government and the tribunal had been a burden for everyone. The Rwandan government's ire could wreak havoc on any case without warning. Ngeze's lawyer,

John Floyd, had asked for two U.N. officers to be brought to the tribunal as witnesses. The men had known Ngeze in 1993 and 1994. Floyd wanted them to testify about Ngeze's relationship with the U.N. contingent. He had been a reliable informant, Floyd said. They would have testified that Ngeze wasn't killing Tutsi. He was trying to save them. Floyd was certain the Rwandan government had threatened to stop its cooperation with the tribunal if the U.N. helped in Ngeze's defense. Floyd found that any witnesses he sought to bring to Arusha for Ngeze's defense either recanted their testimony before they arrived, couldn't get the necessary paperwork from the Rwandan government, or, he said, went missing when he traveled to Rwanda to interview them.

"The Rwandan government did everything it could to prevent us, to prevent the truth from coming out," Floyd said. "They didn't want Ngeze to have a fair trial."

Trying to get full excerpts from RTLM recordings was also difficult. There were ninety recordings on file, but only nine were from April, when the genocide began. The Rwandan government provided the excerpts, so it was unclear whether they were edited to put the trio and the radio station in their worst light or fairly represented what had taken place.

About the same time the news about Sammy Weza broke, the tribunal's chief prosecutor, Carla Del Ponte, rankled Kigali by suggesting that she would begin to seek indictments of RPF members suspected of war crimes. President Kagame was furious. Witness organizations such as Ibuka threatened to break ties with the tribunal altogether. When Del Ponte traveled to Kigali to discuss the matter with the government in June 2002, three thousand protesters greeted her outside the court's offices in the Rwandan capital. "Go home, you are worse than Interahamwe," shouted one demonstrator. Diplomats said the Kagame government, which usually brooked no dissent, had to have been behind the outburst. Discussion of RPF indictments evaporated.

Even without the issue of suspects in the ranks, the Kagame government wondered aloud why the United Nations decided justice could be done only from outside Rwanda. If Rwandans wanted to visit the tribunal where justice was being sought in their name, they would have to bus through four countries—across Rwanda through Uganda to Kenya before finally arriving in Tanzania. It was a two-day journey. The fare was $40 and the transit visa in Kenya would set any visitor back another $20. All told, watching a trial would set the average Rwandan back nearly a month's pay. When the United Nations set up the tribunal, Rwanda was never really considered as a venue. It was too unstable, organizers said. John Shattuck had hinted as much when he met with Kagame in Kigali just weeks after the genocide ended. Defense witnesses would be too frightened to stand up and tell their account out of fear of reprisals from the Tutsi-led government, U.N. officials reasoned. What they hadn't counted on was the efficiency with which Kigali could manage to work its will from hundreds of miles away.

The Kagame government made their displeasure with the tribunal more tangible by making sure the Rwandan people saw the tribunal as they saw it. They had learned the lessons of RTLM: if they controlled the perception of the tribunal, they essentially controlled the tribunal itself. So the Rwandan people became the targets of a high-saturation ad campaign that felt, at times, like an overly friendly stranger putting his arm around you in a bar and giving you advice you weren't comfortable following.

Knowing they were on the wrong end of a Kagame offensive, tribunal officials had toyed with transferring parts of the major trials to Kigali, where the local people could have an opportunity to see leading *génocidaires* penned behind bulletproof glass. But there was a very real fear that the Rwandan government would never let the defendants leave. Officials floated the idea of televising the trials in Rwandan stadiums so citizens could watch leaders of the killing get their due. Rwandan authorities abandoned that idea for its insensitivity: thousands of Rwandans had been called to the stadiums by the authorities in 1994 and had never left. Eventually, Radio Rwanda was selected as the vehicle for updating Rwandans on the progress at the ICTR. Officials saw no irony in the fact that they were updating Rwandans on the fates of Barayagwiza, Nahimana, and Ngeze via the same medium the defendants were charged with abusing.

* * *

The Soros Foundation, backed by billionaire financier George Soros, provided another solution. It began funding a series of film documentaries aimed at reaching Rwandans in the hinterlands and showing them that, contrary to much of the evidence around them, justice was being done. Known as the *Arusha Tapes*, the Kinyarwanda language films focused on cases being decided at the tribunal so those who could not visit could glimpse the justice being done in their stead. The films were shown in Rwandan churches, schools, and prisons.

In May 2002, Cyangugu prison's six thousand inmates had gathered in the central courtyard to see just such a Soros feature. They jostled and elbowed for space on low-slung benches before a makeshift screen—a giant sheet duct-taped to a wall. This audience was, by its very nature, a hostile one. Small, dark, compact men in bright pink safari suits sat fifty to a row. In every cranny of the yard there was a tightly packed knot of humanity.

These were the people that Rwanda had thrown away, the people who might have committed crimes. They were Hutu who, by their sheer Hutuness, lost any ability to enjoy the benefit of the doubt. They were victims of the aftershock. In the early days and months after the genocide, there was hope of a trial, a clearing up of the misunderstanding, the righting of mistaken identity. But as the years dragged on, the expectation of justice withered and quietly died.

In the meantime, their lives in prison took on some of the hallmarks of polite society. The prisoners had, for example, worked out their own hierarchies and ranks. While they all wore pink, some had embroidery on their collars. They were not chevrons exactly, just the badly executed woven stitches of men who sewed out of necessity, not training. Black dashes and dots telegraphed status on one collar. Red sunbursts stood out on another. Trusties, if one could call them that, wore red scarves, knotted at the neck. They were supposed to keep order in this tangled mass of bodies and they did this with whistles and sticks so thin they would not have inspired trained behavior from a small dog, much less a strapping prisoner. The handful of guards were dressed in pale blue. There were no guns to be seen.

The prisoners were almost giddy at the prospect of a break in their day. Trusties whistled and tapped prisoners on the shoulder with their sticks to get the men to settle down. The program would run as follows, the warden told the assembly through a karaoke microphone: there would be the movie, then the question-and-answer session; and then the guests who had come to screen the film would be escorted out while the men remained on their benches. The pink sea undulated in agreement.

Ferdinand Nahimana's face appeared on the screen. The crowd roared. The voice-over provided the commentary. Nahimana, it said, was on trial with Jean-Bosco Barayagwiza and Hassan Ngeze for his role in Radio Mille Collines and incitement to genocide. The crowd growled. "He is on trial at the United Nations International Criminal Tribunal for Rwanda," the sound track continued, "and he is being held at the United Nations Detention Facility in Tanzania." The camera cut to the prison and the catcalls began. The sea of pink rolled and roiled. These men who were packed into Rwanda's prisons hissed at the pristine empty corridors. They saw the shiny, roomy cells, prisoners speaking on the telephone, a state-of-the-art kitchen. Trusties blew whistles. Multiple sticks tapped multiple shoulders. The masters of the genocide were being treated like royalty, the prisoners grumbled.

When the movie ended and the gospel music swelled and the credits rolled, the warden entertained questions. One man in the back stood up and asked for the microphone. "Why do the people who started the genocide enjoy such privilege? We heard they have even refused food because it is too rich. And we are here, with one bowl of porridge a day?"

The crowd alternately stood and sat and applauded to indicate their approval or physically register their displeasure. Guards whistled for calm. "It is the difference between law in Rwanda and international law," said the warden quietly. "They are enjoying the standards of an international prison. That's how that works. That's why their facilities are so good. But they don't have their freedom, let me assure you." A man stood up and yelled, "I'd rather be in their prison." The crowd roared its approval. "Their prison is better than our lives of freedom," he added. "Our politicians used us. They told us to kill and we did. And now look where that brought us. How could that possibly be fair?"

The warden didn't have an answer. The guards blew their whistles for calm. The men in pink rose and crashed down on the benches in waves.

* * *

Weeks gave way to months as Bonaventure Ubalijoro languished in a Kigali prison. It was difficult to follow the charges leveled against him, they changed so often. The government had started by declaring that the former ambassador had run amok while he was the leader of Rwanda's intelligence agency in the 1960s. He had killed many people, the government said. When allegations from thirty years earlier were too difficult to prove, the investigation turned to Ubalijoro's work at the state petrochemical company, Petrorwanda. Money was missing, newspaper reports said. Exactly how much money Ubalijoro had embezzled was unclear. On occasion there were hundreds of thousands of dollars unaccounted for. At other times, it was millions. What was certain, as old charges faded and new charges appeared to take their place, was that Ubalijoro was a victim of political infighting.

The former diplomat decided his only course of action was to wait out his foes, to ride the current political wave until it shifted, again, in his favor. The government information agency, still

nning in November 1981. She had
e genocidal dangers that lay ahead. B
't understand, her message.
umented by the Vatican, described an
en people claimed to have seen the
ber 1981, the Vatican officially certified
en because they appeared to have pre-
een years before it occurred. The three
eir eyes to a chilling scene. They de-
a massacre, abandoned bodies that lay
s aflame, open chasms, a monster of
ecapitated heads lying on a tangle of
, thousands of Tutsi who sought refuge
npound were killed there, on the very
aries said they saw the Virgin Mary.
en so carefully documented before the
found it hard to deny that the three
mething miraculous.
a, where an unshakable faith in God
wise chaotic and difficult life, miracles
ope, an indication that things would
nsine Mumureke, seventeen, Nathalie
nd Marie-Claire Mukangango, twent
ned Virgin Mary. The first appariti
n November 28, 1981. Alphon
g room of the local Catholic
voice call out to her. "My da
ed the voice into the corrid
an awaiting her. The fi
white veil. He hand
her finger the gir

sked.
ion said. "am
u because I

number of months, begi
to warn Rwandans of th
they didn't listen, or didr

The 1981 visions, do
apocalypse. Though se
Blessed Virgin in Novem
the vision of three wom
viewed the genocide thir
young women closed th
scribed a river of blood,
unburied. They saw tree
some description, and d
limbs. Thirteen years late
at the Kibeho church co
ground where the vision
Because the visions had be
killing began, Rwandans
young women had seen so

In a nation like Rwand
provided order to an other
were seen as a beacon of h
eventually improve. Alpho
Mukamazimpaka, twenty, a
one, had all seen a dark-ski
took place at lunchtime
Mumureke was in the dini
in Kibeho when she heard a
it began. Mumureke follow
find a very beautiful wom
seamless white dress and a
together on her breast, and
pointed to the sky.

"Who are you?" Mum

"Ndi Nyina Wa Jam
the Word and I have

prayers. I would like your friends to have faith, because they do not believe strongly enough."

And then the Virgin Mary disappeared.

She returned to Kibeho two months later, in January 1982, to appear before Nathalie Mukamazimpaka; these apparitions continued through December 3, 1983. On March 2, 1982, it was Marie-Claire Mukangango's turn. The apparitions lasted six months in her case, until September 15, 1982.

Mumureke saw the Virgin Mary one last time, on November 28, 1989, exactly eight years after her first vision. For outsiders, the question was why the Virgin Mary had chosen Kibeho. For Rwandans it was just further proof that their nation was special.

RTLM's Valerie Bemeriki said as much in one broadcast in May 1994. The Virgin Mary had appeared to her as well, she told listeners. The Virgin Mary had told her that the victims of the genocide were paying for their part in killing Habyarimana on April 6, 1994. The massacres, she suggested, had been sanctioned from the highest power.

More than six years later, long after the genocide was over, Bonaventure Ubalijoro found himself counting on a similar sign from the heavens. His prayers for divine intervention, for some path out of jail, were answered in June 2000. The former ambassador was told that the charges against him had all been dropped. He had been incarcerated for fourteen months without ever facing trial.

* * *

Hassan Ngeze may have been expecting a miracle himself when he decided to send Simone Monasebian a letter. It did not seem to matter to him that Monasebian was the most aggressive prosecutor on the media trial team or that they had hardly exchanged two words. It appeared Ngeze had fallen in love with her. The note was neither ugly nor explicit. Instead, it inquired in an almost schoolboy way whether Monasebian could find it in her heart to love him too. At first Monasebian thought this was just the latest in a series of crazy Ngeze stunts. Instead of interrupting judges or staging outbursts in chambers, now Ngeze had decided he was smitten. While the initial note was harmless, Ngeze's ability to have someone drop a note in Monasebian's mailbox was worrisome. Did that mean that Ngeze also had contacts outside the U.N. Detention Facility that he could mobilize when necessary? Could he intimidate witnesses from behind bars? Could he have those prepared to testify against him harmed?

While Monasebian was subject to good-natured teasing from her colleagues on the prosecution team, Ngeze's ability to send her notes, and later flowers and small presents, was symptomatic of the same sorts of problems the tribunal fought in the case of Sammy Weza, the Congolese investigator who wasn't. Was there a guard in the chambers or someone in the detention facility who had been previously allied with Ngeze in Rwanda and was now at the ICTR helping prisoners?

Ngeze, ever resourceful, also had managed to set up a Web site: hassanngeze.com. He had posted photographs of himself and published a long legalistic treatise he said provided all the proof anyone needed to see he was innocent. He encouraged any and all fans to write to his e-mail address. The fact that he was behind bars hardly seemed to matter. An e-mail sent to the imprisoned newspaper editor was usually answered, in passable English, in twenty-four hours. There were no phone lines in the cells, though prisoners had access to computers. Defense attorney John Floyd figured Ngeze had managed to get a guard or a visitor to sneak a cell phone into the prison. Whatever it was, Ngeze had few problems maintaining and even stepping up his contact with the outside world.

* * *

The billboards appeared on all the main thoroughfares in Rwanda. At first glance, the advertisements looked like they could have been pitching a soft drink or new shampoo. But on closer inspection the billboards were trying to sell something more fundamental: justice. They were an attempt to convince Rwandans to embrace the resurrection of *gacaca*, or literally, "justice on the grass." *UKURI KURAKIZA*, the *gacaca* billboard read: "The truth heals."

Originally *gacaca* (pronounced *ga-cha-cha*) was the name of a type of grass that grew in Rwanda, but the word came to refer to a tribal system of justice dispensed on patches of grass. *Gacaca* was a kind of informal small claims court in which wise men of the village would bring parties to a dispute together in the open air and mediate. Generally, the case involved cows or land or water and could be remedied by reparations or a heartfelt apology. The elders' decisions were final and neighborly battles were supposed to end with their sage and equitable judgments. *Gacaca* faded to black in the 1930s before Kagame sanctioned its return. While the idea may have first appeared as a profound and brilliant instrument of justice and forgiveness, the motivation was more craven than that: it was a last-ditch effort to empty the nation's prisons without declaring a general amnesty.

Publicly, President Kagame said the success of the new tribal courts would be a good way to measure how well Rwanda had managed to put the genocide behind it. The courts could act as a barometer of whether Rwanda would continue to be a nation of recycling violence or a country that had risen above vengeance. We can forgive, the public service announcements said on the radio, but not forget. The government held a national competition for the best song promoting *gacaca*. (A prison group in Butare, in southern Rwanda, won first prize.)

When the wave of billboards and radio commercials extolling the virtues of *gacaca* didn't produce the expected groundswell of support, Kagame tried television. The government produced a movie and then a television series that was the Rwandan equivalent of Perry Mason. Just as the Raymond Burr character always triumphed in the end, after twists and turns in the plot, so do did the *gacaca* process on television. The story lines were simple and repetitive.

Opening credits flash on the screen with a swell of music. The camera cuts to a Hutu man. Despairing after years in a Rwandan prison, the prisoner decides to confess and go through the *gacaca* process. He applies for *gacaca* with an essay in which he lays out his crimes and asks for forgiveness. The sincerity of his remorse moves the people of his village and he is taken, still in his pink prisoner garb, to his home village, where a council of elders have convened a court. The *gacaca* is set up near the intersection of two unpaved roads—presumably there are two paths to be chosen: one leads down the path of righteousness and redemption, the other leads back to prison.

In the clearing there is a table, a megaphone, and benches for spectators and witnesses. The Hutu prisoner, sorry for what he did in 1994, admits to killing his neighbor. He asks for forgiveness, and after some tense moments, the *gacaca* court sentences him to work in the village for several years—manual penance in exchange for redemption. The show invariably closes with a Tutsi and a Hutu walking into the sunset, arm in arm, reconciled, friends and neighbors once more. The show's theme music was a top-twenty hit on Radio Rwanda.

The government organized elections for *gacaca* judges. They created prisoner dossiers and set up sentencing guidelines. Half of any sentence imposed by the *gacaca* judges would be served within the community. It was expected that because most of the nation's accused had been in jail for more than seven years, most would be released to serve the remainder of their terms at home.

A cynical audience might have said *gacaca* was motivated by President Kagame's political ambitions. He had held out the possibility of national elections, and families were much more likely to support the incumbent at the ballot box if the relatives they were visiting in prison had at least a distant hope of release. More fundamentally, Rwanda didn't have the money to feed the prisoners. Foreign donors, who had been helping pay the bill, were losing patience and warned that their donations would soon run out. The Rwandan government, they said, would have to assume reduction he or she would receive. Joseph's problem, he said later, was that he hadn't done anything during the genocide. It was unclear what, precisely, he was accused of doing. To plead innocent meant that there was a good chance that the *gacaca* judges would decide he wasn't repentant enough for whatever he had done and therefore would need to return to prison to reflect on his intransigence.

"There were lots of people who claimed they had nothing to do with the genocide, and they had killed alongside the Interahamwe," said Joseph. "But what do you do if you really didn't kill someone, and people in your community claim you did? Do you lie? Do you confess just so you can get out of prison?"

Theoretically, in the pre-*gacaca* screening process the authorities gathered testimony that linked the suspect to the crime. When nobody came forward to offer evidence against a suspect at the *gacaca*, he or she was released. That is what happened to Joseph. When the authorities finally turned to his case, after he had spent seven years in prison, they determined there was no evidence against him. He was released before his *gacaca* even started.

"I was before a crowd and they asked if anyone had any evidence against me," he said. "I was standing before all these people from my community and then a voice spoke up from behind some villagers and said, 'Joseph didn't take part, he was always a good boy.' Other people nodded and said they had always known me to be helpful and polite. Five minutes after my *gacaca* started it ended, just like that, and I was free. But you can't help wondering, couldn't they have decided this before I spent seven years of my life in prison just for being Hutu?"

Joseph watched as the prisoners around him, dressed in their pink uniforms, each came before their accusers in the clearing.

"Who knows this man?" one of the elders began. A sudden hush fell over the crowd. A Tutsi survivor stepped forward. "I know him," said one woman in a brightly colored skirt, turning her back on the accused and facing the crowd instead. "He killed

an increasing share of the cost of feeding the 120,000 men and women behind bars. From a purely practical perspective, *gacaca* offered an opportunity to winnow the nation's prison population. With so many jurisdictions operating simultaneously throughout the country, tens of thousands of Rwandans who had been wondering about their fate would suddenly have resolution.

While on the surface the plans for *gacaca* seemed dispassionate and balanced, the reality was more complex. Rwanda did not have the resources it needed to adequately prepare the country for what was to come. In South Africa, counselors went into the townships months before launching an amnesty program for those who fully confessed and apologized for crimes committed during apartheid. The Truth and Reconciliation Commission made a point of explaining to black South Africans why such an amnesty process was important. Certified lawyers ran the hearings. Witnesses were called and deposed. And history shows that a large tranche of the South African population followed the commission's work carefully. Human rights experts say that the participation of ordinary South Africans was the key to the commission's success. An entire nation watched a rational process unfold to deal with the past trauma of apartheid. The Truth and Reconciliation Commission also provided a definitive public record of the crimes and atrocities committed so everyone could agree on what happened.

Rwanda's *gacaca* remedy was more ragtag. In October 2001, each of Rwanda's eleven thousand voting districts elected nineteen "persons of integrity" to serve as unpaid *gacaca* judges. Many of the more than 200,000 chosen were illiterate. Others were rejected for having possibly taken part in the genocide themselves. Those left standing took a thirty-six-hour crash course in *gacaca*, and then, upon graduation, launched investigations, summoned Rwandans to court, pronounced sentences, and confiscated property.

The problem was that, as with the Truth and Reconciliation Commission in South Africa, *gacaca*'s success depended on the quantity and quality of the confessions it elicited. Those seeking redemption had to be what the Rwandan government called Category Two killers, a type of petty murderer. They may have killed during the genocide but they were caught in the moment. Category One killers were the planners, those who murdered with "excessive zeal" or "wickedness." (Ferdinand Nahimana, Jean-Bosco Barayagwiza, and Hassan Ngeze had been classified as Category One killers.)

The November 2002 *gacaca* outside Gikondo prison in Kigali began with entertainment. A dozen *Intore*, or warrior dancers, wearing cotton cloth and a strip of leopard skin over their prison uniforms, put on headdresses meant to look like lion manes. They had beads around their necks and had attached bells to their ankles and wrists. They carried ceremonial spears and shields. They leapt lightly into the air, staying aloft for moments at a time, twisting their bodies in midair, and then landed softly on the pads of their bare feet. They ended the performance by presenting their weapons to the crowd.

The prison director, Faustin Murigo, decided that because this was one of the first *gacaca* held in Kigali, some instruction was in order. He had chosen a handful of the six thousand prisoners incarcerated at Gikondo to provide *gacaca* lessons to the assembled. Prison guards had come out early in the morning to pour lines of sand on the red clay ground outside the main prison building. Behind one line of sand stood the families and villagers of Gikondo prefecture. Behind the other, twenty yards away, the prisoners stood with a bullhorn in hand. Their task, the prison director said, was to teach the villagers about the *gacaca* process. The people who stood across from them were, in their own way, also a captive audience. The government had decreed attendance at local *gacaca* compulsory after early trials were sparsely attended.

"The public isn't convinced *gacaca* is a good idea," Murigo said. "The prisoners will explain to them why it is so important and why it is good for Rwanda." In actual fact, the warden seemed completely unaware of the irony of having a handful of prisoners

accused of genocide explain to their victims how the legal system would prevail. He was more concerned with the fact that Rwandans in general believed that those who were in jail probably deserved to stay there. The Hutu had, after all, wiped out hundreds of thousands of Tutsi in a matter of days. To have been so efficient, Tutsi said, shaking their heads, hundreds of thousands of Hutu had to have been involved. The way the Tutsi saw it, with only 120,000 Hutu in prison, there were many who escaped justice. The Tutsi felt little motivation to exonerate anyone.

Joseph N. was one of the men who was chosen to go through the process at the *gacaca* level. A former student in Kibuye, a verdant suburb of Kigali, Joseph had been picked up by authorities in Kigali weeks after the genocide began. He had come to the capital to make sure his parents were safe, but an ill-timed stop at a sidewalk restaurant for a snack ended with soldiers pushing him into a truck and Joseph finding himself at Prison 1930, accused of taking part in the genocide. "I was in the wrong place at the wrong time," he said later. "Just because I was Hutu, they assumed I had killed people. They accused me of killing people in Kibuye and then escaping to Kigali." Joseph was assured by the soldiers that if his story checked out and they could prove that he had indeed simply come to Kigali to find his parents, he woul be released. At most, they said, it would take a month to do th investigation. A month came and went. And then three more.

Joseph was in prison for six years before he was able to get a l ter to the mayor of Kibuye asking for help. The *gacaca* proc the mayor and Joseph agreed, was his best chance to clear name. Joseph was nineteen when he was taken from the res rant. He was twenty-six when he was taken to Kibuye to be sented" to a *gacaca* court.

Gacaca is all about confessions. Those who admit to and who are thought to have recounted all the details of th in the genocide with sufficient remorse could see se slashed in half or even to time served. The later a prison fession came in the process, however, the less of a my brother with a machete." The inmate shook his head. "It wasn't me, I did not kill," he said. "I wasn't even in Kibuye during the killings."

Another man stepped out of the brightly colored crowd and shuffled to the center of the courtyard. "He was at the roadblocks," he said. "I saw him checking for identification cards."

The prisoner looked uncomfortable as the accuser provided times and details that placed the accused at the roadblocks in town. "I was only seeing a friend at the roadblocks," he began weakly. "But it wasn't when you said. It was before the killing started." The crowd growled as another Tutsi citizen stepped forward, trembling, and provided details of the death of a young Tutsi boy whom another resident had seen walking with the accused a short time before his death.

The prisoner was asked if he wanted to add anything to his plea. "I saw the boy," he said. "But I didn't kill him. A gang of Interahamwe did. I tried to protect him, but I could not." The judges added his words and those of his accusers to his file and told him to sit down. His recitation of the events, it appeared, was too weak and too late in coming. Joseph was one of ten prisoners who had their sentences commuted that day. Fifty more climbed back in the truck and returned to prison. Usually, about a quarter of those prisoners who stood before the *gacaca* judges ended up going free. Either they seemed repentant enough or no one stood up to testify against them.

In spite of his release, Joseph said the *gacaca* process was patently unfair. The discussion was confined to the genocide, preventing Hutu from testifying against Tutsi soldiers who committed their own war crimes. "This process doesn't work because only the Hutu are guilty," Joseph muttered. "Everyone knows that there were reprisal killings by the Tutsi army. Do people think they walked into Kigali in 1994 without harming any Rwandans? That they were unopposed? How can we possibly have reconciliation if the only people who have to admit to anything are the Hutu?"

As he saw it, all the fear that spread across Rwanda in the days leading up to the genocide was realized. What Radio Mille Collines had said would happen had come to pass. It reported that the RPF was going to come into Rwanda and restore power to the Tutsi. Once they had succeeded, the Hutu would become second-class citizens in a land where all the power would go to the minority.

He pointed out mansions on the hills around Kigali. They looked more Beverly Hills than Africa with their white stucco walls, tile roofs, and air-conditioning. "Hutu prisoners built those houses," he said. "Do you know who lives in them? Tutsi officials. We call those mansions *merci, génocide* houses. Thanks to the genocide, the Tutsi live like kings."

If Rwanda returned to Tutsi rule, the best schools, the best jobs, the best houses would be reserved for them, *Kangura* had said. The RPF can't be trusted, Hassan Ngeze had added; their leaders won't stop until they reverse all the gains the Hutu made in the 1959 revolution. The chorus of fear emanating from Jean-Bosco Barayagwiza, Ferdinand Nahimana, and Hassan Ngeze had, in the opinion of many Rwandans like Joseph, verged on the clairvoyant.

"*Gacaca* is a farce," he said. "There is no justice on this grass."

8

The Rape Babies Arrived in the Spring

He was known at the ICTR as Witness FW. A man who not only could testify as to what he heard come across the airwaves of RTLM during the genocide, but could also describe what unfolded as he and countless others listened. A young man in his twenties during the massacres, when he arrived at the tribunal in Arusha to testify against the media trio seven years later he looked like an old man.

The witnesses' waiting room at the ICTR was sparse. There was no television, no coffee brewer, not even magazines to while away the hours. One might think that everything had been stripped from the room on purpose, so its inhabitants would be required to think only about what they were about to say in the chamber. Even the furniture was ascetic. There was only a small bench, two chairs, and a table.

The morning FW arrived to testify, the room was bare but for a French tabloid magazine that had been left by a previous occupant. It was sitting by itself on the table. FW flipped it open and found himself staring at a centerfold of Monica Lewinsky. She was in shorts, all flesh and creamy white thighs. Certainly the American president could do better than that, he said to Simone

Monasebian when she came in to check on him. She laughed and offered to get him something else to read.

"I have a stack of *Kanguras* next door," she began, sure he wouldn't take her up on it. In fact, he said, he was keen to see them. She left a stack of the newspapers in front of him and when she returned sometime later, FW's mischievousness had disappeared.

"How can anyone defend this?" he demanded, shaking the copies of the newspaper. What he had read in them seven years before had obviously softened in his mind over the years. Seeing them again awakened a rage. "This is genocide in black-and-white," he yelled. "You don't need to call witnesses, just show these to the judges." Monasebian took the *Kanguras* away, making a mental note not to make them available to Rwandan witnesses ever again.

FW had his radio tuned to RTLM when Habyarimana's plane went down. Seven years later, he could still recall the broadcast in exquisite detail. "We were told there was bad news, sad news, that the head of state—the plane of the head of state had been shot down by evildoers," he told the court. "Then RTLM radio announced that no one should leave his or her home."

The screams began a short time later. One neighbor ran to FW's house to tell him that her husband had just been killed. There was twelve-year-old Muhammed, who appeared in the doorway with his shirt covered in blood; the army had just cut off his father's hands.

It was clear at that moment, FW said later, that the only chance for survival was to hide. "We did not have any specific objective, we did not have any specific destination because everywhere we went we realized people had been killed," he testified. He took several of his neighbors, and Muhammed, and fled.

One of the oddities of instinct is how predictable it can be. When thousands of people rush headlong to hide themselves, they go through the same thought process, they hit upon the same places to secret themselves. FW and his neighbors learned this firsthand when they arrived at a nearby school. Others had already taken their places there. Men, women, and children filled every classroom. There were too many who had thought of the sanctuary first. "We were so many that we could not all fit in," FW said. "We stayed there on the tenth of April. People in the neighborhood who worked with the Interahamwe came to spy—to see where people of the neighborhood had taken refuge. So we stayed there in this environment of fear. On the eleventh of April, I remember it was around three-thirty p.m., we heard an RTLM broadcast saying that all Tutsis who had fled their houses should return home because there was a search for arms and that if these people did not go back home, their houses were going to be destroyed."

The news divided the crowd, he said. Could RTLM be trusted? After months of listening to the station's anti-Tutsi screeds, could the call to return to home be a trap? Those who left, FW testified, were killed when they returned to their houses. "On that day I had lost all hope because of these events, and there were bullets that fell close to where we were hiding, there was war, and when the soldiers were shooting, we were very scared."

The group decided it was only a matter of time before the Interahamwe discovered them, so they decamped to the nearby Islamic Cultural Center. They dressed themselves as militiamen, with T-shirts and banana leaves, and marched down the street to their new hiding place. They saw a Caterpillar tractor by the roadside. They heard the grinding of gears and saw smoke from the engine. It was digging an enormous trench. Amid all this chaos it was hard at work, taking great shovelfuls of clay from the earth and setting them to the side. Bright yellow trucks from the Ministry of Public Works arrived. They pulled up beside the trench and unloaded their cargo. "It looked like they were dumping beans, bags of beans, into the holes," FW said. He realized only later that they were corpses.

Kigali's Islamic Cultural Center was a major institution. It was a compound surrounded by several buildings, which included offices, a school, dormitories, and a mosque. By the time FW and his friends arrived, the dormitories were already full of refugees. There was no running water and hundreds of people crowded into every spare inch of space. "You can imagine a similar place with such a number of people without any running water with toilets inside, what we call modern toilets," FW told the court. "And the people were very afraid. They were asking themselves many questions." They were asking, among other things, about the U.N. peacekeepers. Where had they gone? Why weren't they out in force to stop the killing? Many of the refugees at the mosque would have headed for Burundi, but they had this deep-seated belief that the U.N. would come to their rescue.

FW moved into the mosque, where hundreds of refugees had already gathered. Some were wounded. Others were close to death. Many had been stopped by bands of Interahamwe and wore the scars of their encounter: machete gashes crisscrossed their bodies. Their low moans were muffled by the mass of humanity crammed into such a small space. There were no doctors to provide treatment, so the injured resigned themselves to quiet suffering. Most of the crowd had arrived nearly a week before.

The story would have been just another account of a terrible episode during the genocide were it not for one thing: FW's recollection, in all its vivid detail, unequivocally linked RTLM to specific killings. FW tied specific broadcasts to specific murders. The prosecution needed that to prove incitement.

"Could you tell us what you saw that afternoon?" Simone Monasebian asked from behind the prosecutor's lectern. Gone was the lighthearted banter about Monica Lewinsky in the French tabloid. She knew what FW had to say was compelling. Her strategy was to guide FW gently and stay out of the way of the narrative. That, she decided, would be more powerful.

"Outside I saw Noël Hitimana," FW continued. "At that time, he was working with the RTLM. I don't where he was going or what he was doing at that particular moment. I heard him ask

[Photos courtesy of the International Criminal Tribunal for Rwanda]

The media trio included history professor Ferdinand Nahimana (top left), editor Hassan Ngeze (top right), and extremist CDR party chief Jean-Bosco Barayagwiza (above). They became the first media executives to stand trial in an international court for crimes against humanity since Nuremberg. The three founded a radio station and a tabloid newspaper accused of helping to incite the 1994 genocide.

Nº

IJWI RIGAMIJE GUKANGURA NO KURENGERA RUBANDA NYAMWINSHI.

SPECIAL

BATUTSI BWOKO BW'IMANA !

NI IZIHE NTWARO TUZAKORESHA KUGIRA NGO DUTSINDE INYENZI BURUNDU ??

Twamenye icyo NZIRORERA apfa n'Abatutsi.

Uwagarura Revolisiyo y'1959 y'abahutu kugirango dutsinde inyenzi-Ntutsi.

[Courtesy of the International Criminal Tribunal for Rwanda]

Prosecutors said *Kangura* used cartoons and editorials to get its anti-Tutsi message across. One early banner headline, pictured on the left, read: "How about relaunching the 1959 BaHutu revolution so we can conquer the Inyenzi-BaTutsi?" Adding: "What weapons shall we use to conquer the Inyenzi once and for all?" A drawing of a machete supplied the answer.

Hassan Ngeze spent long hours in this small kiosk in downtown Gisenyi collecting gossip and fodder for his fledgling newspaper.

[D. S. Temple-Raston]

[Courtesy of Monique Mujawamariya]

Monique Mujawamariya, Rwanda's most famous homegrown human rights activist, met with President Clinton in the White House just months before the genocide.

Damien Nzabakira, a young school teacher, was jailed for eight years for a crime he didn't commit. His neighbors accused him of killing forty school children. The Rwandan army was implicated in the murder. Damien (right) is pictured with his daughter shortly after his release from prison.

[D. S. Temple-Raston]

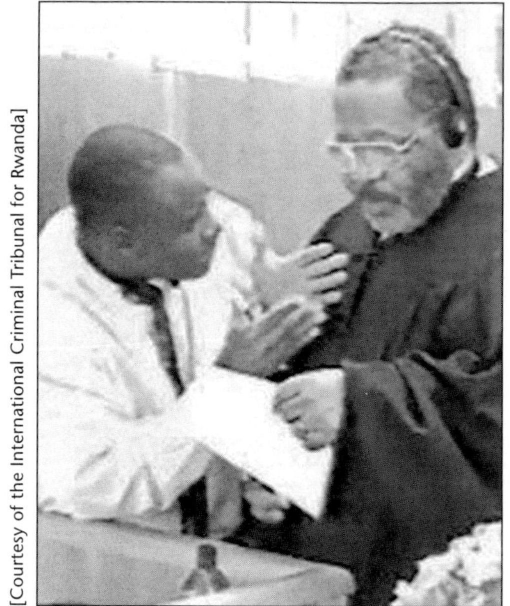

[Courtesy of the International Criminal Tribunal for Rwanda]

Defendant Hassan Ngeze (left) found his lawyer, John Floyd (right) on the Internet. Floyd worried the trial would set a dangerous precedent. "The United Nations has no business setting the standard for press freedom," he said.

The media trial was considered the most complicated and difficult of the cases underway at the International Criminal Tribunal for Rwanda. Many lawyers came and went during the proceedings. The final team, pictured below, included (from the left) William Egbe, deputy prosecutor Simone Monasebian, senior prosecutor Stephen Rapp, and Charity Kagwi (inset).

[Photos by D. S. Temple-Raston]

[Courtesy of the International Criminal Tribunal for Rwanda]

Navanethem Pillay, a former South African Supreme Court judge, was one of the three judges presiding over the media trial. In 1995, she became the first black woman to be appointed to the Supreme Court of South Africa.

Erik Møse, a Norwegian judge renowned for his work on human rights, also presided. Forty years after Nuremberg, he believed it was time to revisit the issue of press freedom. The media trial provided the opportunity.

[Courtesy of the International Criminal Tribunal for Rwanda]

[Courtesy of Bonaventure Ubalijoro]

Bonaventure Ubalijoro was part of the Rwandan elite. He went to the best schools, headed Rwanda's intelligence agency, was the nation's ambassador to Paris and the United States and, at one point, was the leader of the moderate wing of the MDR party. He was a target of the Hutu Power forces in the early days of the genocide, and then found himself on the receiving end of reprisals by the transition government. He spent nearly two years in jail though actual charges against him were never formally filed.

ISHYIRAHAMWE
FPR
DUTERANINKUNGA
RY'ABASEZEREWE-MU-
NGABO N'ABATURAGE-B'UMUGI-WA
RUHANGO-DUSHYIGIKIYE-
UMUKANDIDA WACU → 100%
PAUL KAGAME

[Photos by D. S. Temple-Raston]

Although the first democratic multiparty election in Rwanda in August 2003 was a joyous event, there was some uneasiness as well. It could have been the armed soldiers who stood with their guns at the ready before a Kagame election rally or the plain clothes police officials stationed within the crowd to ensure President Kagame would witness nothing less than unmitigated adulation when his campaign convoy arrived. The children grouped themselves together about fifty feet from the stage to catch their first glimpse of the president. They were held back at gunpoint too.

[Photos by D. S. Temple-Raston]

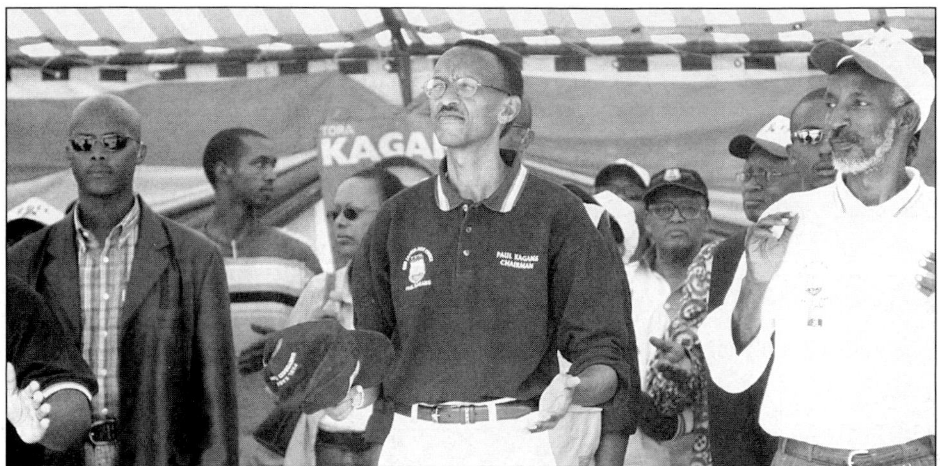

There was never any doubt that Paul Kagame (above center) would win re-election. The only suspense was by how much. In the end, he won 98 percent of the vote.

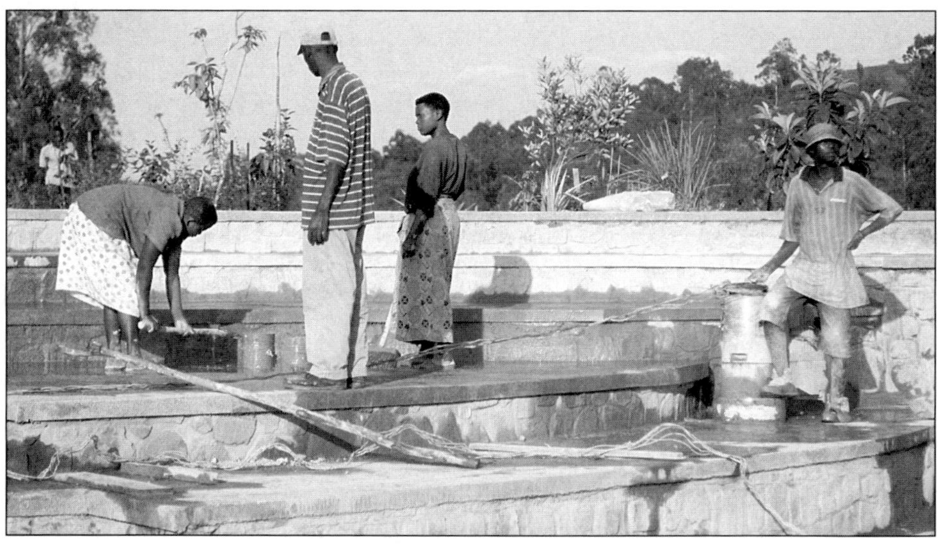

On the tenth anniversary of the genocide, President Kagame and dignitaries laid a wreath at a mass gravesite outside a memorial center in Kigali. These were neat, sanitized concrete crypts—eight feet deep, each filled floor to ceiling with coffins containing the unidentified remains of fifty Rwandans found in shallow makeshift graves throughout the capital. Ten years after the killing stopped, Rwandans were still discovering new burial sites.

these people why they were bringing food to the Inyenzi who were in the Islamic Cultural Center."

FW knew Noël Hitimana. They had been friends, and he couldn't believe what he was hearing. "These people that you are now calling Inyenzi, are they not your neighbors, people with whom you were living, people with whom you shared everything, you would share a drink with them, you shared everything, why are you now calling them Inyenzi?"

Hitimana didn't respond. Instead he looked right through FW and went on his way. About an hour later, as FW was monitoring a broadcast on RTLM, he heard Kantano Habimana, one of the broadcasters, announce that there were Inyenzi and Inyenzi soldiers hiding out in the Islamic Cultural Center.

"Kantano was a very famous person," FW told the court. "His voice was well known. He used to say a lot of things jokingly, and even when he spoke about killing, he said it jokingly and everybody knew him. I remember that I turned on my radio and I heard one of Simon Bikindi's songs. Bikindi was a singer who composed songs inciting people to kill. And after that the song was interrupted, and I heard Kantano's voice. He was saying, you should know, ha-ha, he was laughing that in the Islamic Cultural Center, there are armed Inyenzi who are hiding there. The Rwandan armed forces must be made aware of this fact."

It was, FW said, like hearing a death sentence. The next day, the apocalypse arrived.

With those words, FW began to visibly shake on the stand. He couldn't catch his breath. Silence descended on the chamber. The judges decided to adjourn for lunch so FW could regain his composure. Ngeze and Nahimana smirked and then laughed as the witness crumbled on the stand. Pillay exchanged a look with the two other judges on the bench. All rose when they left the room.

The people at the Islamic center were resigned to their fate, FW said after lunch. The younger people had drifted outside. The elderly and children had stayed inside. There was a panic

when gunfire erupted. "People who had gone outside to warm themselves in the sun, they came back shouting and saying, 'They are coming back, they are coming back. We are finished, we are going to perish.'"

FW had anticipated the Interahamwe offensive so he had prepared his own hiding place under an abandoned VW Bus in the yard. It was old and covered with weeds and, FW was to discover, full of snakes. But it offered sanctuary away from the center and a hope that the attacking bands wouldn't bother to look under a car for a hiding Tutsi.

"Given the arrangement of the place I could see everything," FW told the court. "The soldiers and Interahamwe came in and circled the dormitory. That place was locked with a big chain and the Interahamwe armed with grenades and clubs got orders from the soldiers to break the chain and to go and kill the refugees. Then they broke the door."

Once the door was open the soldiers paused, FW said. Some of the young militiamen balked. They didn't want to kill the refugees in a mosque, a place of worship. The refugees, they said, would have to be driven outside and killed there. The Interahamwe swarmed the entrances and drove the refugees out into the yard. Little children who could walk, elderly ladies who could not tumbled out into the compound, shoved and dragged out at gunpoint.

FW slipped out of his hiding place to get a better view.

"Sometime after that I heard gunfire," he said. The next morning he found only three refugees alive. The rest, he said, had been killed. The Interahamwe and soldiers had taken some of their victims to houses close to the compound. They locked them inside and then threw grenades into the buildings.

FW circulated between a number of hiding places—a shed, his VW Bus, empty rooms at the mosque—until June 10. He emerged when the RPF arrived to free the neighborhood. "We came out very hungry and ready to die," he said, weeping again. "We were very, very thin, we had lost several kilos, you yourself

can imagine, spending two months in such a location. We had lost at least fifteen kilos. Our beards had grown, we looked like wild people.

"What RTLM did was pour petrol, to spread petrol throughout the country little by little, so that one day it would be able to set fire to the whole country," he said, gaining his composure once more.

It was as close as the prosecution team could get to causation. The radio had spoken and a massacre had occurred.

* * *

Georges Ruggiu had come to Rwanda seeking his fortune. Instead, eight years after he climbed into President Habyarimana's car to ask for a job at RTLM, he was cutting a deal for his life. Two years after his arrest, he called prosecutors to the detention facility and said he would testify against his old boss, Ferdinand Nahimana. He told them he could help prove that Nahimana was still in charge of RTLM after the genocide started. There was a hitch for the prosecution, though: Georges Ruggiu was a proven liar.

Chief among his problems was a book he had written while in exile in Kenya, entitled *In the Rwandan Torment*. The book tried to make the case that the RPF not only was behind the assassination of President Habyarimana but was also responsible for sparking a civil war that ended with the death of hundreds of thousands of Rwandans. Ruggiu maintained that the information he wrote in his book was "one hundred percent correct, except for one paragraph." The paragraph he disavowed was one in which he claimed that "pregnant women were disemboweled, pillaged, and eaten" by RPF soldiers. Georges Ruggiu said he may have "exaggerated" that.

The book also claimed that the Hutu had no intention of wiping out the Tutsi and that Ruggiu would have been "shocked" had such a thing been suggested.

There was also the small problem of Ruggiu's mental state. Georges Ruggiu had spent six months as an outpatient at a mental health center in Liège before coming to Rwanda, and while he was incarcerated, he was under medical surveillance. He was taking medication "to help [him] cope with stress."

He was not the type of witness one builds a case on, but Ruggiu was one of just a handful of people who had worked at RTLM and survived the genocide. Most of the radio's leaders, save the three men on trial, were presumed dead. Ruggiu could fill in the details about the day-to-day operations at the radio station while at the same time shedding light on Nahimana's role there.

"We knew he was problematic. You have to work with the hand you are dealt," Prosecutor Stephen Rapp said later. "We needed to prove that Ferdinand Nahimana was in charge after the genocide began, that the army hadn't suddenly taken the reins of power at RTLM after April 6. Ruggiu worked there and was one of the few people who could describe RTLM from the inside. We didn't have much choice but to use him."

The only outward sign of Ruggiu's nervousness on the stand came from his incessant fiddling with a blue pen. It never stopped moving during his entire testimony. If one listened carefully, one could hear the soft clicking of the pen against his knuckles, speeding up when he spoke and slowing down when he listened. Much to the chagrin of the prosecution team, Ruggiu also tended to turn systematically to look over at the prosecutors' bench after each reply, as if looking for approval. If ever there would be witness testimony ripe for rebuttal, Ruggiu's was it.

"RTLM obeyed only two people," Ruggiu had told lawyers in an initial interview. He had said then, before changing his story, that Ferdinand Nahimana was not at the radio station often once the genocide began. "The two people whom RTLM obeyed were Phocas Habimana and Gaspard Gahigi," the director and editor-in-chief at the station. The statement would have given the defense some ammunition if Ruggiu had stayed with his story. Instead, he reversed himself and told prosecutors that he hadn't told the truth. He then painted Nahimana as a key figure at the radio station.

When defense attorneys asked Ruggiu about the change he claimed that, at the time, he had not wanted to make incriminating statements. So why mention Gahigi and Habimana? "To my knowledge, they were no longer alive. So I could incriminate the dead," he told the chamber. He also admitted that he was unsure whether his two ex-bosses were indeed dead or not, so his explanation was weak.

Even so, Ruggiu seemed important to the prosecution's case. Since Nahimana rarely spoke on RTLM and there was the thinnest of paper trails placing him squarely at the helm of the radio station once the genocide began, the young Belgian filled in vital details. Ruggiu had also spent time in prison with the trio. He claimed to have had a prison cell conversation with Ferdinand Nahimana in which the history professor took him aside and asked him what he had already told the Office of the Prosecutor. "He asked me if I had told the Office of the Prosecutor that he visited RTLM before the new government was in place. I told him that I hadn't said anything yet."

The prosecution decided to keep Ruggiu on a short leash and keep him focused on the handful of episodes that showed Nahimana was in control at RTLM between April and July and, therefore, was responsible for the radio station's incendiary broadcasts.

Ferdinand Nahimana came to the radio station on foot, emerging from the French embassy, where he had been hiding right after the plane crash, Ruggiu testified. "We asked Ferdinand Nahimana where he had been. He told us that he had taken refuge at the embassy and that he had paid the security guard to let him leave. He said that he had come to find out if everything was all right."

When did he hear from Nahimana again? prosecutors asked, trying to prevent Ruggiu from careening off the subject.

It had come in writing, the former journalist said. He was in a military camp in Kigali several weeks after the genocide began and received a letter from Nahimana. A military helicopter pilot had delivered it, he said. The letter had said Nahimana was in Cyangugu and couldn't get to Kigali. "The letter also encouraged us at RTLM to continue," he said. The letter, which would have made a stellar exhibit had Ruggiu actually possessed it, had gone the same way many things in Rwanda had. It had been lost. Conveniently it provided precisely the kind of information the prosecution was seeking, but it could have just as easily originated in Ruggiu's head. It was hard to make Ruggiu sound convincing. The pen in his hand spun at warp speed around his fingers.

Ruggiu said he saw Nahimana again in May 1994 in Murambi, the headquarters for the interim government. Ferdinand Nahimana was there with all the members of the Rwandan government who had fled Kigali. Ruggiu, who had had to get the president to get Nahimana to give him a job, said the former history professor welcomed him warmly and gave him a hug. "He even told the others that he was very happy, that we worked well together," he said. Ruggiu claimed there were two other meetings with Nahimana. There was a meeting that allegedly took place in Kigali in June, in the RTLM offices. Ferdinand Nahimana arrived late in the morning, he said, and left that evening with Phocas Habimana. Ruggiu also recalled having seen Nahimana in July 1994 at the Hôtel Méridien in Gisenyi.

The defense cried foul. Ruggiu wasn't a man who could be trusted. He began cooperating with the prosecution when they threatened to add four new counts against him, John Floyd bellowed from the far side of the chamber. Ruggiu denied that the new charges had prompted him to change his story.

Ferdinand Nahimana's defense was led by a tenacious but soft-spoken Frenchman named Jean-Marie Biju-Duval. A handsome man in his early forties, Biju-Duval had a hard time disguising his contempt for the hearsay evidence that appeared to be accepted as gospel in the courtroom. He was unequivocally convinced his client was innocent. Nahimana was being railroaded by the tribunal because he was one of the few individuals linked to RTLM who was still alive. That was a theme the Frenchman would revisit again and again as the trial dragged on for more than three years.

Ruggiu's testimony was aimed at breaking down Biju-Duval's main argument. Biju-Duval was trying to prove that while Ferdinand Nahimana had indeed started RTLM, he had done so with the intention of providing a different point of view. Nahimana and his investors had been against the Arusha Accords and were trying to explain to regular Rwandans why the peace pact was ill-advised. Nahimana was similarly concerned about civil war. He distrusted the Tutsi and felt his countrymen should be on alert for a Tutsi offensive. There had been small incursions into Rwanda by the RPF for years. Nahimana wasn't being paranoid, Biju-Duval argued, he was being prudent. The radio station's broadcasts before April 6 were not stoking a fire, they were warning a nation of a very real peril. For that, Ferdinand Nahimana did not deserve to spend the rest of his life in jail. The argument flew in the face of Ruggiu's testimony. He claimed Nahimana was running RTLM when the station's most incendiary broadcasts were aired, and he had encouraged them.

After April 6, the Ministry of Defense organized a briefing for RTLM and Radio Rwanda. "It covered two things: the daily military situation and instructions about how soldiers should be referred to at RTLM and on air," Ruggiu said.

The instructions were not surprising: when the news was good, report it at length; when it was bad, play it down. For Ruggiu, broadcasting "descriptions of wanted persons" was when the radio stations began to go too far. "These people were identified by their type of car, its color or registration plate. Information was given out about which road they were traveling on and who they were with," he said. The details were supplied by the soldiers or the Interahamwe, he said.

Between April and July, RTLM had "a relationship of mutual support" with the Rwandan army. The headquarters of RTLM "were protected by the presidential guard." RTLM journalists were given armed escorts, and petrol for their cars. Several of them were given rooms at the Hôtel des Diplomates. One of the founders of the station, Phocas Habimana, had "frequent" telephone conversations with General Augustin Bizimungu, the chief of staff of the Rwandan army. RTLM journalists were also armed, but not by the Rwandan army itself. Georges Ruggiu owned a nine-millimeter pistol, "of the Spanish make Star." Chief editor Gaspard Gahigi "wore an Uzi machine gun" before trading up to an R4 rifle, Ruggiu said.

From April to July, the government paid the staff's wages, "with fresh notes from the national bank." RTLM also received support from the national radio. "RTLM used anything useful at Radio Rwanda and ignored anything that did not serve its ends," Ruggiu said.

Ruggiu apparently got in the spirit of things when the killing began. He decided to set up a blackboard at RTLM on which he wrote the names of political opposition leaders who had been assassinated and those who risked death. The board was meant only to be used to monitor events so as to give out correct information. "You cannot say that someone is dead when you know that this is not true," he explained. Faustin Twagiramungu, Rwanda's best-known moderate politician, was at the top of the list. He, according to the list at the time, was still alive.

In fact, about the time his name was scrawled on the blackboard, Twagiramungu had escaped to the safety of Belgium.

* * *

The crowd was unruly in the benign way that people are when they compete for space in an auditorium before a program officially begins. When their former mayor Jean-Paul Akayesu appeared on the screen, however, they were struck dumb. The room suddenly stilled. Six years after their mayor had been arrested and put on trial, this clutch of Taba residents blinked in disbelief as Akayesu unexpectedly flickered back to life in a film during the spring of 2002.

In the intervening years, the man who had once stood among

them had made a name for himself by becoming the first person ever to be convicted of rape as a crime of genocide. The International Criminal Tribunal for Rwanda, a courtroom too remote for anyone in Taba to have given it much thought until now, had found their mayor guilty of crimes against humanity.

Many people in Taba had heard about a verdict in Tanzania, but seeing Akayesu on the screen, in a movie about the tribunal, made it real. The film, another in the Soros series, was meant to spark conversation. It was meant to show that an orderly process was at last bringing the perpetrators of the genocide to justice. When the last of the credits rolled up the screen, a moderator from Internews appeared with a microphone, asking for comment.

Many in the audience focused on conditions at the United Nations Detention Facility and the fact that those found guilty by the tribunal, like Akayesu, were not sentenced to death but instead to a life behind bars. "I was raped and now I have AIDS," one woman said after the film was over. "Why shouldn't those who killed and did this to me be killed as well?"

The moderator ran up and down the aisles of the auditorium like a Rwandan Phil Donahue, asking for comments. "Life in prison is not a light sentence," he told the audience. "Life in prison means that these men and women will have to live out their days thinking about their crimes. They have long hours to dwell on their sins."

And how about my sentence? one woman began. "I was gang raped during the genocide and now I am raising a child from that rape." She began to weep. "You come here with your movies and your promises of justice. I am raising a child whose father I don't even know. My neighbors look at me as if there is something wrong with me for having this child. But I didn't ask to be raped. But I am being sentenced too. Every time I look at my daughter I am reminded of what happened, I have to dwell on this sin. I did nothing wrong. I did not kill, yet I have to bear a heavier sentence than our mayor. What do you say to this?"

The moderator was quiet. What could he say?

* * *

The rape babies had arrived in the spring of 1995. The rapes were called *kubohoza*, which literally means, in Kinyarwanda, "to help liberate." The term was ironic and had its roots, like almost everything in Rwanda, in politics. When Rwanda first began its multiparty politics, political operatives used *kubohoza* to press people into changing their party affiliations. The term's meaning evolved. It came to describe the seizing of land, the robbing of cows or crops, and eventually it applied to the rape of women during the genocide. When people engaged in *kubohoza*, they often covered their faces in chalk, wore banana leaves, and attacked at the sound of a whistle—as the Interahamwe did throughout the genocide. The fact that *kubohoza* evolved into a term for rape was just more proof that in Rwanda violence was seen as a normal part of politics.

The offspring of the 1994 violence were known as the *enfants non-désirés* ("unwanted children"), or *enfants de mauvais souvenirs*, ("children of bad memories"). Others called them "children of hate" or "little Interahamwe." There are between three and five thousand children in Rwanda today who are the result of the genocide, and most of them don't know that they are children of the violence. Their mothers haven't told them.

Christine Uwamahoro was a proud woman with a square face and delicate hands. She sat ramrod straight and spoke in a slow voice as if she was weighing and measuring every word before she uttered it. Christine exuded strength and yet she harbored a secret. As she fled Kigali in the hours after the plane crash, she was captured by the Interahamwe and held captive. Her family had made it as far as Gisenyi, a beautiful town on the shores of Lake Kivu, in western Rwanda, when they were stopped at a military roadblock. "They pulled us out of the car and sat us down on the side of the road," she recalled. "They killed my mother and my brother immediately and just rolled them into a hole at the side of the road. We ran."

She lasted only several days on her own in the bush and was captured by Interahamwe before she could cross the border into the Congo. "It is more frightening than you can understand," she said. "It puts you out of your head. They put a gun on you and say, 'We'll kill you, remove your clothes, lie down.'" Sometimes her father was able to bribe the Interahamwe. If he gave them money, they left without raping his daughter. Sometimes even money didn't work. Christine found out two months after the rapes began that she was pregnant. She had been raped so many times, by so many different men, she had no idea who was the father.

When the genocide was over and the RPF took charge in Kigali, despair set in for Christine. She was sure she had contracted AIDS. The Interahamwe had purposely had those who were HIV-positive in their ranks rape the Tutsi women. And though she had returned to school and tried to resume her life, she couldn't concentrate. She was too depressed. Then her daughter was born.

"At first I hated the baby," she said. She sent the toddler to go live with her grandfather, Christine's father, in hopes that the memory of what had happened would fade. "The child just brings back bad memories," she said. "It is sad, my life was spoiled while I was still young."

The exact number of women who were raped during the genocide is still uncertain. Figures compiled at the University of Rwanda at Butare indicate that more than half the Tutsi women who survived the genocide had been raped during the violence. Survivors confirmed that rape was widespread and that thousands of women were individually raped, gang raped, raped with objects, held in sexual slavery, or sexually mutilated. Many women were killed immediately after they were raped so they could not accuse their captors after the genocide ended. The women who were allowed to live were told they were spared only so that they could, the Interahamwe said, "die of sadness," either because of the AIDS they had contracted or because they would be forced to raise a child conceived in a time of treachery.

Some observers said that nearly every woman and adolescent

girl who survived the genocide was raped. Statistically, one hundred cases of rape give rise to one pregnancy. The United Nations determined that would mean there were at least 250,000 rapes or, at the high end, 500,000. The number is particularly stark when one realizes that in the wake of the genocide Rwanda has become a country of women: females make up about 70 percent of the population and lead more than half the households. Many of those women had been left to "die of sadness."

Alphonsine, another survivor, sat in a mud hut ten years after the genocide. She held her head high and threw her shoulders back when she walked. But the proud demeanor collapsed when she began to talk about the events of 1994. She, too, had been gang raped by Interahamwe and found out a short time later that she would bear *un enfant de mauvais souvenirs.* "When I found out I was pregnant I felt I had to just accept the situation. I was sad, of course, and I even wanted to abort the child, but I didn't, because I felt that doing so would be a sin."

Life was difficult bringing up a child without a father. She was a sole survivor in her family but for a brother, and there were many occasions when she would look at her son, Jean de Dieu, or Jean of God, and wish he were dead.

When Jean was a toddler Alphonsine began dating another survivor, a man from her village. He shunned Jean. He beat the child, calling him a little Interahamwe, and beat Alphonsine when she defended him. "If you want to stay with me," the man told her, "then you must take the child away." Alphonsine tried to get her brother to take Jean in, but he refused. It was clear her son wasn't safe with her, so she began sending him on unnecessary errands to the houses of her friends. She instructed Jean to wait until dark and then knock on his uncle's door. His uncle, she said, would take him in. And for a while the ploy worked; her brother could not turn Jean away and send him back in the darkness. Her new husband was satisfied that Jean had been properly disposed of.

When Jean would see his mother in the market, he would run up to her and throw his arms around her, calling her "Maman."

She pushed him away. "Call me your aunt, not your mother," she would say. She wanted nothing to do with the little boy who was born of evil.

"We tried to convince her that the child was innocent," said Espérance Mukamana, a counselor at AVEGA, a government agency helping women like Alphonsine deal with the children of the genocide. "But these women are traumatized and can't care for the children. In the beginning, many don't even like these children." Because everyone has gone through so much, she said, perfect strangers have stepped up to help. It is this kindness of strangers that saved children like Jean de Dieu.

A woman named Primitiva was one of those strangers. Children gathered at her doorstep each night as soon as the sun began to slip behind the hills. Tugged from the outskirts of the village to a dimly lit cinder-block house, the tangle of children sat on grass mats in the courtyard waiting for Auntie Primitiva to feed them. It is difficult to say how the tangle of children was related. Some said they were cousins. Others were brothers and sisters. Most were orphans who gathered under the collective skirts of the community to find care and food among the women who lost children or sisters or brothers in the genocide. The women of Rwanda picked up the remains of other lives and wove them seamlessly into the threads of their own.

Such was the case with Primitiva. A mother in her early fifties with children who were working overseas, Primitiva lived alone in a blue-painted house of concrete blocks in Gitarama, just an hour's drive southwest of Kigali. By Rwandan standards, the home was enormous. There were a succession of bedrooms, a sitting room with velour couches, a dining room with a long wooden table, and a gated courtyard, where children from the village gathered, knowing that Primitiva would provide a large hot meal to anyone who asked.

Primitiva's dinner preparations were watched by an audience of children who sat as if attending a school assembly of great interest. Other women from the village helped start fires in one of the two concrete buildings behind the house. ("Kitchens are always separate from the rest of the house," Primitiva explained. "Why have a fire during dinner take your house down with it? Having a kitchen out here prevents tragedy.")

Primitiva had money enough from her children to provide the food. Two young mothers from the village offered labor. They peeled bananas and set them on a fire to boil. They washed beans and added twigs to a second fire. They shelled peanuts and ground them in a mortar for peanut soup. Their faces glowed by the orange of the cooking fires.

"She feeds all the children who come," Primitiva's daughter said. "Everyone knows that she will give food to anyone, so a lot of parents just send their children here. Sometimes she'll find fruit on the porch, or someone who buys a bag of beans or flour will drop some of it off. But they know that she has children who send money from abroad, so it is understood that she will help with the others. That's the way it works in Rwanda."

No one talks about Hutu or Tutsi. None of the children appear to be worried about such distinctions. They all have one thing in common: they are hungry, and this is the one place in the village where they know there is always food.

Because Rwanda is such a small place, everyone knows everyone else's sad stories. Primitiva had had five children. Her daughter was in school in Uganda during the genocide. Her eldest son was working in Kigali. He had walked for days when the violence broke out, to show up on his mother's doorstep. He hid there for the duration of the massacre out of concern that the Interahamwe would force him to kill. Her two younger sons, just teenagers, hid in the eucalyptus groves with the cobras and their cows. They climbed trees and slept under bushes. It was Primitiva's third son who no one talked about. He had joined Habyarimana's presidential guard in 1991. The family said later it was a rebellion of sorts.

"We always wondered what had gotten into his head," her daughter said. "Apparently he was killed by some of his own men.

That's what we heard anyway. It was never confirmed. Some of the soldiers had come to the house to kill Mum and my two youngest brothers but one of the Interahamwe had recognized them and said they should be spared because they had a serving soldier in the family. In a way my brother's rebellion ended up saving their lives. We never saw him again, so we don't really know how the story ends."

By 9 p.m. the meal is finally served. Some of the children have fallen asleep next to one another while waiting, in a tangle of limbs, but are roused with the rattle of metal bowls hitting the ground. The boiled bananas look, smell, and taste like potatoes. The peanut soup has become gravy, drizzled on top. Beans are piled high on the side. The children gobble up the meal with hardly a word. Two plastic tubs sit in the corner of the courtyard, one filled with warm soapy water, the other for the rinse. The children eat their fill and bring their metal bowls to the tub to wash. There is no splashing, no arguing, no whining. Instead, they wash their dishes and pile them neatly near the kitchen. They hug Primitiva and disappear into the night.

For outsiders it is difficult to square how a country that raged with such violence could find, simultaneously, room for such kindness.

9

Words Can Kill

Nearly a decade after the genocide, doubts still lingered about the degree to which the killings were planned. It was unclear whether they were part of a grand design or were improvised when chaos ensued. Was it a civil war, or something else altogether?

What was certain was that nearly all of those targeted were unarmed innocents. Tutsi and moderate Hutu were shot if they were lucky, macheted and left to die long, slow deaths if they were not. No one had ever come up with a satisfying explanation as to what was in the minds of the thousands who killed and what made them believe that the murder of neighbors was acceptable. Had Rwandans grown so used to seeing death, walking among the dead, sleeping among them, numbering themselves among the near dead, that after the fact it just didn't seem so wrong to have raised a machete against their own? The prosecution of Barayagwiza, Nahimana, Ngeze, and the others at the U.N. tribunal was meant to remind Rwandans that it was wrong. It sought to make something that had faded to gray return to black-and-white.

Human rights official and genocide survivor Monique Mujawamariya was part of the prosecution's plan to put a sharp focus on inchoate events. She knew Nahimana, she had met him on several occasions, and she was one of a handful of people who had been on the receiving end of RTLM's wrath and lived to tell of it.

"Do you know Ferdinand Nahimana?" the prosecution began.

"Ferdinand Nahimana is a major intellectual in Rwanda," Monique said. "I knew him when he was a lecturer in Rwanda, and when he was appointed director of ORINFOR. And I also know him as a member of the MRND party and the founder of RTLM."

The two had also locked horns. Monique had denounced Nahimana for broadcasting the fake communiqué on Radio Rwanda that said the RPF had been responsible for killing Tutsi in Bugesera. It was that same communiqué which eventually cost Nahimana his job at ORINFOR.

Monique said she had been traveling from the Kinihira region of Rwanda in June 1992, several months after Nahimana had decided to broadcast the communiqué. She was with two other human rights activists when they ran into Nahimana at a crossroads. The human rights officials had gone to Kinihira to check on refugees who had fled into Rwanda to escape an escalating war in Burundi. What worried Monique and her colleagues was the number of heavy weapons the displaced people seemed to be carrying. She worried the cache of weapons would fall into the wrong hands.

Nahimana had never been a fan of Monique's. He thought she found excuses to discredit the government and she seemed overtly pro-Tutsi. When they met outside Kinihira, his frustration boiled over. "You have just finished doing your dirty job, and you are going to spread these lies," he told her, referring to her trip to Kinihira and her report of heavy weapons. He said that he didn't believe the weapons were there.

Monique, never shy, told Nahimana to go and see for himself because the weapons stash was not far away. Nahimana scoffed, she said, and they parted.

They met again several months later. Nahimana informed her

then that he planned to start an independent radio station. "He said he was going to establish a radio station which would defend rights that we are not defending," she said.

Another year passed before Monique caught another sighting of the former professor. At the end of 1993, an RTLM shareholders' meeting was held at the Amahoro Hotel in Kigali. Monique went to investigate. "I was looking at the people who were waiting for the meeting to start. I happened to look into the meeting room, and the people who were close to the podium, and I realized I was in the middle of an Akazu meeting," she said. "Akazu is the name given to the presidential family and those close to the presidential family in Rwanda. And I said to myself that I shouldn't be there." Nahimana, she said, was near the podium.

The radio station was launched, she said, a short time later. In the beginning, she had liked it. The station played good music, the broadcasts were funny and lively. It provided relief from an otherwise mundane government broadcast. Her only criticism was that RTLM talked a lot about the 1959 revolution. "Particularly they said that one could not trust the Tutsis," she said. "I had a lot of worries after listening to the programs because in Rwandan culture, words kill more quickly, and more efficiently, than weapons. Our people are not very well educated, so I was afraid of how this propaganda would affect them."

In the weeks that followed, Monique began monitoring the broadcasts. She listened, she said, because members of Rwanda's human rights community knew that Barayagwiza's CDR party and the Interahamwe were up to something. The radio provided clues as to what they were planning. RTLM began mentioning individuals and neighborhoods over the air. RPF troops and sympathizers could be hiding there, they warned. Hours later the neighborhoods would be ransacked by the Interahamwe. Each time they heard a new neighborhood targeted, Monique's group tried to inform the foreign diplomats stationed in Rwanda.

Soon enough Monique herself was prey. Toward the end of December 1993, a presenter from RTLM mentioned her by

name. He played a popular song called "Monique"; it spoke of love. Monique Mujawamariya, he cooed into the microphone after the song ended, the Monique so well known in Rwanda, was "a pest." She had started to work for the enemy, the RTLM presenter said. "When I got to my house," she said, "the night watchman showed me a large stone which had been thrown into my compound by young militiamen wearing uniforms. A message was attached."

The message described the many ways the militia would kill Monique if given half a chance. "The message said they were going to crucify me, remove my skin, and leave me to be eaten by birds, hoping that before I died I will have understood that I was a traitor," she said.

RTLM began mentioning her name frequently, saying it was a shame such a little woman had decided to cause so much trouble. One afternoon, shortly after a broadcast, Monique was leaving the post office when three young men spotted her. "That's her," they said, rushing up to her. When they reached her one young man pulled his penis from his trousers and wagged it at her. "Is this enough to shut you up?" Two days later, her car was showered with stones. By this time, weeks before the genocide, every radio was turned to RTLM. Everyone was talking about the station. "The range of people who were listening had changed," she said. "RTLM was being listened to by individuals who felt they were threatened and wanted to know if there would be any information on themselves."

* * *

The key to proving that the genocide was a conspiracy, and not a sudden, unplanned explosion of violence, lay in the Bugesera massacre of 1992. In long talks with the man who had been in charge of Kigali's prosecutor's office during the genocide, François-Xavier Nsanzuwera, Simone Monasebian had come to believe that it was no coincidence that two of the men she was trying to convict in the media trial had had roles in what had gone on in

Bugesera. Nahimana had lost a job rewriting the history of the Bugesera killings. Ngeze was passing out newspapers, days before the massacre, that called on Hutu to kill Tutsi.

She also knew that a slow boil of harassment against the Tutsi made the 1994 genocide the most efficient massacre of modern times. The murderers used as modern a tool as they could find in 1994 Rwanda—the media—to air false reports, call Hutus to arms, and create a climate of fear in which reason gave way to revenge. The threats were veiled. RTLM journalists used code words and double entendres—not using the word Tutsi, but instead calling them *Inkotanyi*, or "cockroach" to send their messages. The trick was proving incitement and the intention to spark crimes against humanity with harrowing stories like those from Monique and FW, buttressed by experts like Human Rights Watch's Alison Des Forges and media analyst and former Nahimana mentor, Jean-Paul Chrétien.

Privately, Monasebian and the rest of the prosecution team were most concerned about their ability to prove there was a conspiracy. Planning, certainly—but a conspiracy, a vast web of individuals who together worked toward the extermination of the Tutsi? That would be more difficult.

Alison Des Forges, the woman who had tried to help Monique in 1994, did not harbor those same doubts. She was the author of *Leave None to Tell the Story*, a 789-page tome on the genocide that had become a textbook on Rwanda. The 1999 book provided everything from the historical context of the genocide to the organization of the military and militias that carried it out. She had facts, figures, receipts, and more than thirty years' experience in Rwanda. So when she spoke about the battles and skirmishes that led to the genocide, those assembled in the courtroom tended to lean forward to listen more intently. The defense attorneys objected to her inclusion in the trial. What did she know about the media? As Human Rights Watch's country expert, didn't she have an axe to grind? Certainly, much of what she was saying was conjecture, her impressions came after the

genocide. When the killing began she was in Buffalo, New York. But the defense team's objections were overruled.

The year 1993 had started badly for President Habyarimana and his cohorts, Des Forges began. The Rwandan Patriotic Front had been scoring victories in the north and south of Rwanda. The Arusha Accords, a pact that the president had been trying to derail for years, had taken shape in spite of his best efforts. It included provisions that were nettlesome to Habyarimana's followers. Officials, including the president, could be prosecuted for past abuses of power under the agreement. More worrisome was the fact that this was a power-sharing agreement. Hutu and Tutsi would have to find common ground and rule Rwanda together, equally, for the first time in the nation's history. For Habyarimana and his clique from northwestern Rwanda, the thought of sharing power was anathema.

Des Forges said it was clear that Habyarimana saw an opportunity to rally the Hutu majority by discrediting the Arusha Accords. The accords would return Rwanda to a time of injustices and Tutsi supremacy. Hutu would once again fall prey to the whims of the elite; everything they had strived for to this point would be lost. The refrain found resonance among Rwanda's Hutu. Habyarimana was finding that the ranks of his supporters were broadening. Instead of just a coterie of rich businessmen from his home province, Habyarimana's warnings were finding traction among a wide Hutu constituency. It was only a matter of time before the movement had a name: they called it Hutu Power.

The movement cut across party lines and brought Hutu together by virtue of their ethnicity. After Tutsi soldiers in neighboring Burundi murdered their freely elected Hutu president, Hutu Power not only had a base; it suddenly had a potent raison d'être. The RPF threat suddenly seemed very real. It was against that backdrop, Des Forges told the courtroom, that Habyarimana and his supporters began training the Interahamwe and a "civilian self-defense force."

The youth enrolled in the new militia were trained by soldiers in the Rwandan army. Unemployed, with little to occupy long, slow days, the young men folded into the militias had overnight importance and purpose. It was hardly a boot camp. Instead it was like a long fraternity party with banana beer and ganja and physical tests. The Hutu Power movement began gaining momentum. Colonel Théoneste Bagosora, one of the leaders of the Rwandan army, outlined the Hutu Power program in his appointment book, Des Forges said.

To hear Alison Des Forges tell it, the lessons of foreign intervention in Somalia were not lost on those planning the genocide in Rwanda. Kill a handful of foreign troops, was the instruction, and the world will turn tail. United Nations troops were in Rwanda in April 1993 as part of the peacekeeping component of the Arusha Accords. They were meant to ensure the smooth transition to the coalition government. When the killing began, however, they were immediately ordered back to the safety of their bases. After that, the Interahamwe strategy was straightforward: those who resisted were killed. Those who embraced their new work were rewarded.

"Zeal for killing took on more significance than formal rank," Des Forges said in her book. "Subordinates could prevail over their superiors, in both civilian and military spheres, if they showed greater commitment to the genocide. This flexibility encouraged ambition and initiative among those willing to trade human lives for personal advantage."

Des Forges was one of RTLM's biggest foes. In her interviews with citizens in Rwanda the subject of Radio Mille Collines came up again and again. The station's steady drumbeat of fear permeated Rwandan life in a way that Westerners could not fully understand, Des Forges said. "I'm not saying that any one broadcast or any one media was the determinant for people's behavior," Des Forges said. "I am not saying that RTLM acted alone to cause the genocide. But it was an integral component of efforts to encourage and bring about attacks on Tutsi with the intention of eliminating them as a group."

The authorities didn't stop RTLM because they were afraid, Des Forges explained to Monasebian as the assembly in the courtroom followed her every word. Des Forges remembered talking to a Rwandan official in Kigali in 1994 who told her that many officials gave up trying to restrict RTLM's broadcast because they were scared of its power.

In one broadcast, RTLM told its listeners to leave Information Minister Faustin Rucogoza alone "as he has now left us alone, realizing that shutting down the people's radio would bring him trouble. It was a cross too heavy to bear."

There were reams of evidence to suggest that Nahimana was in charge of Radio Mille Collines after the genocide began, Des Forges told the court. There were stock purchase receipts and receipts for financial transactions out of Nahimana's personal account. There was a letter from the then–Rwandan minister of defense authorizing RTLM to possess firearms. Nahimana shared his bank account with RTLM, and RTLM mingled its funds with his own. But by far the most damning evidence, Des Forges said, was that Nahimana never tried to stop RTLM's venomous broadcasts. He didn't distance himself from the radio station's work until he arrived at the tribunal.

"If he really did not agree with RTLM, he could have disassociated himself by resigning, but he never did," she said.

Defense attorney Biju-Duval stood up to dismantle Des Forges's testimony. Des Forges had said Nahimana's writings were proof of his prejudice against the Tutsi, Biju-Duval began. In particular, Des Forges had pointed to passages in Nahimana's work that said that the Tutsi were not indigenous to Rwanda but had migrated from Ethiopia. We agree that that version of history has since been disproved—correct? the defense attorney asked Des Forges. She nodded.

Biju-Duval opened a loose-leaf binder and began to read from Des Forges's own doctoral thesis, where she had said that the Tutsi were a race foreign to Rwanda. They had migrated, she wrote in her thirty-year-old paper, to Rwanda from Ethiopia.

"You are accusing Nahimana of being anti-Tutsi when he did the very same thing in his writings that you did in yours," Biju-Duval said.

Des Forges said the two works couldn't be compared. Her doctoral thesis was written in 1972, when the theory of emigrant Tutsi was widely believed and cited in historical texts. When the theory was eventually disproved, Des Forges said, her writing reflected that change. Nahimana's essays on the Tutsi were written in an entirely different context, she said. Nahimana was trying to resurrect "those discredited theories" years after they had been rejected.

Biju-Duval hoped he had put at least a dent in Des Forges's armor. He assured his client he was only getting started.

* * *

After months of testimony, it was difficult to doubt that RTLM had indeed fueled the genocide. Its broadcasts named names, provided license plate numbers for those targeted for killing, stirred up Rwandans who counted on the station to tell them what they should do next, where the Inkotanyi were now, or how they should keep their families safe.

The prosecution had yet to convince the tribunal that Nahimana, Barayagwiza, and Ngeze played an integral part in making that happen. Even with the testimony from Des Forges, the evidence linking the trio to the station was circumstantial: visits here, a signed check there, a sighting somewhere else. Records had been burned. Key players were dead or had simply vanished. One could be excused for thinking after two years of trial that the roles of Nahimana, Barayagwiza, and Ngeze in the day-to-day operations of RTLM were minor, maybe even tangential. But with an entire nation watching to see if three men known to be embroiled in the station would be brought to justice, there was a great deal of pressure to ensure that they were.

Nahimana testified in his own defense. He claimed he was afraid to defy RTLM once the genocide had started. The prosecution painted it another way: when Nahimana had the opportunity to close down the radio station, to stem the violence, he hadn't. In a rare on-air interview on April 25, 1994, three weeks after the genocide had started, Nahimana appeared very proud of his radio protégés and of how the people of Rwanda had responded to the broadcasts.

"The radio station informed us on how the population from all corners of the country had stood up and worked together with our armed forces, the armed forces of our country, with a view to halting the enemy," Nahimana said, adding, "Today's wars are not fought using bullets only. It is also a war of media, words, newspapers, and radio stations."

Two months later, government officials, pressured by the French, called on Nahimana to tone down the RTLM attacks on the head of the U.N. forces in Rwanda, the Canadian general Roméo Dallaire. Concerned that RTLM's focus on Dallaire would encourage Rwandans to murder him, which in turn would attract world attention at a time when it appeared the world's capitals were more content discussing what they ought to do than actually doing it, officials asked Nahimana to step in. The next day, Radio Mille Collines's tone regarding Dallaire changed.

* * *

Omar Serushago was a convicted *génocidaire*. He was an Interahamwe leader in Gisenyi, an admitted killer, and a man whom the tribunal sentenced to fifteen years in prison for crimes committed during the genocide. Even so, there he sat, not beside the accused but with the accusers, to testify against Barayagwiza, Nahimana, and Ngeze. There were objections all around, from Barayagwiza's Italian counsel, from Biju-Duval, and from John Floyd, who boomed his protest, sputtering with incredulity.

"Your Honors, this is a manufactured witness," Floyd said. "His evidence is preposterous, replete with dishonesty." One could imagine Floyd making similar motions in the defense of narcotics suspects in Washington, D.C. In many ways Serushago was a defense lawyer's nightmare. He was a survivor, a man who took part in the killing, who was willing to recount what he knew. As a resident of Gisenyi and an old friend and comrade of Ngeze and Barayagwiza, he could provide details on what he saw and heard in the months leading up to and following the April 1994 genocide.

Serushago's testimony went directly to the most contentious charges of the media trial in terms of historical proof, human rights, and legal precedent. He could help prosecutors prove conspiracy and incitement to genocide. Conspiracies are, by their very nature, difficult to pin down. As Serushago began to testify it was clear he offered—like Witness FW describing events at the mosque—a direct connection between RTLM and the genocide killings.

To understand what motivated Barayagwiza and Ngeze, one has to understand the Coalition for the Defense of the Republic, or CDR party. It was Rwanda's version of the Ku Klux Klan: extremists, in this case the Hutu, saw in the Tutsi all the ill that befell the nation. The party's ideology was blatantly fascist. Its bylaws called on Rwandans to return to the days of the 1959 Hutu revolution. Just as the Klan focused on extolling the virtues of the majority white race in America, the CDR was constantly reminding the majority Hutu that the Tutsi were invaders who did not belong in their land. CDR members donned ties and lapel pins like members of an exclusive country club: the telltale tricolors of the CDR flag stood for aggression. Red represented the blood spilled in the 1959 revolution. Black signified the republic that had thrown off the shackles of colonialism of 1961. Yellow signified the sun, and the unity of the majority. The prosecution entered several photographs of Ngeze, wearing a CDR tie, into evidence. But that was hardly necessary. He and Barayagwiza admitted that they had founded the CDR in 1992, and now their brother in arms, Serushago, was testifying against them.

Serushago's testimony was meant to shed light on the two men's role in the CDR, and by extension, their part in the conspiracy to commit genocide. On the stand, the convicted *géno-*

cidaire talked about standing in Ngeze's Gisenyi kiosk in February 1994, two months before the genocide began. The two men were gossiping, chewing the fat about nothing in particular, when Serushago noticed a fax from Jean-Bosco Barayagwiza on the table. Addressed to the leader of the youth wing of the CDR, it confirmed that Tutsi soldiers had been behind the recent murder of a former CDR chairman. Barayagwiza wrote in the fax that the CDR had to respond. He suggested that the youth wing militia find the Tutsi responsible and kill them. It was an early indication, two months before the downing of Habyarimana's plane, that the battle lines were already being drawn. The CDR was already preparing to hunt Tutsi and to blame Tutsi for the violence. The defense had said that the genocide was sparked in a great spontaneous outpouring of grief after the president's assassination. Instead, plans for reprisal killings against the Tutsi were being made two months before the crash. It suggested that the assassination was just a pretext for violence that had already been planned.

Serushago's story would have been devastating to the defense had a copy of the fax found its way to the tribunal. Instead, Serushago said it had been lost in the genocide.

The *génocidaire* also recalled seeing Ngeze and Barayagwiza at two CDR meetings in early 1994, before the genocide began. The CDR organized these gatherings in an attempt to galvanize the resolve of their Hutu Power followers and, at the same time, raise money for firearms and machetes, Serushago said. He distinctly remembered seeing Hassan Ngeze at both meetings. He heard Barayagwiza speak at the second. There was but one enemy, Barayagwiza had said, the Tutsi. The gatherings were the first of many that followed. From April to June 1994, Serushago added, such meetings were held every evening by leaders of the movement, including Ngeze and Barayagwiza. It was at these sessions during the genocide that community leaders reported on the number of Tutsi they had successfully slain.

* * *

Prisoners at the United Nations Detention Facility were given a great deal of freedom, and for a resourceful man like Hassan Ngeze, the facility provided a base from which he easily operated and carried on his day-to-day businesses. Telephone calls into the prison were neither limited nor monitored. It was not just attorneys who were able to get through. One needed only to dial the tribunal's switchboard (which had both a local, Tanzanian number and a New York one) and ask to be connected to the U.N. Detention Facility. There was but a momentary pause and then the phone in the prison rang. To talk to any of the prisoners one had only to claim to be a friend, and the prisoner would be called from his cell to pick up the line. The procedure was so routine that it was as if one were calling a neighbor whose spouse had slipped out back to take out the trash and would take a moment to come in and pick up the phone.

While the practice made it easier for lawyers to talk to their clients from abroad, it also made it child's play for those who were incarcerated to keep in contact with those from the outside. It became a problem for Serushago. Ngeze had made it a habit of contacting Simone Monasebian, to whom he had earlier professed his devotion from behind bars. To notes he added flowers and token gifts, all of which landed in her mailbox at the ICTR with startling regularity. There were e-mails, and Ngeze managed to upload photographs and update tracts on his Web site. He added candid photographs of John Floyd, action shots from the courtroom. All of this was orchestrated from what was said to be a maximum security facility.

Tribunal judges might have continued to look the other way were it not for the fact that Omar Serushago was on the receiving end of one of Ngeze's notes. An Islamic preacher employed by the ICTR made the delivery.

"I am writing to you this letter to remind you that our life on this earth is very short," the unsigned missive began. "I have read your statement which you gave to the Prosecutor on 9 July and 11 July. I was especially shocked by the way you created false evidence against me. Remember, even if we do not meet, our children will."

Floyd did his best, after the note came to light, to suggest that someone other than his client had written it. The language used in the letter suggests someone trained as an imam, not an ordinary person like Hassan Ngeze, Floyd declared. Serushago begged to differ. How could a preacher employed at the ICTR possibly have known the names of Ngeze and Serushago's neighbors? he said; those were in the note as well. And the letter mentioned dates on which the witness gave his testimony to the prosecution. The imam couldn't have known that.

"The imam does not speak Kinyarwanda," Serushago added. "These people are Rwandans and the imam is a Tanzanian. He could not have known these things."

Ignoring that, Floyd challenged Serushago again. Why hadn't he mentioned Ngeze in previous interviews with the prosecutor, before the trial began? Perhaps Serushago was paid in exchange for his testimony. He noted that Ngeze had been arrested in July 1997 with about $20,000 in a suitcase. That money had since disappeared. Perhaps it had found a way into Serushago's pocket?

Serushago laughed. "Ngeze had a lot of money he received from Rwandans he had promised to get to Europe using fake documents," he said. "The investigators are not bandits. They didn't need to seize Ngeze's money."

Serushago, it appeared, had won this round. The judges, as was their habit, listened to the testimony impassively

* * *

Ngeze, when it suited him, painted himself as an investigative journalist with incredible access but at the same time fostered the image of being someone who was willing to risk life and limb to get a story. His newspaper rankled authorities, he said, and he wore his frequent arrests as a badge of honor. He told friends, and the tribunal, that he'd been detained so many times he considered prison his second home. He said he would finish publishing and the day the newspaper went on sale he would pack his clothing because he knew the next day he would be in jail.

It wasn't because Ngeze was uncovering anything that he went to jail, one prosecutor explained. It was because he was forever trying to put himself in the spotlight. He angered those who backed his newspaper because they had put money in *Kangura* so it could be an anti-Tutsi vehicle, not a national platform for one man's shameless self-promotion. There were enormous centerfolds of Ngeze in the paper. There were articles extolling his virtues. Ngeze's moneymen had him thrown in jail, the prosecution said, to remind him that he was working for them, for a cause, not just for himself.

When asked about the genocide, Ngeze told tall tales of smuggling "thousands" of Tutsi out of Rwanda when the killing began. He would never talk about the killing. Asked to recall his most vivid memory of the genocide, Ngeze would say it was watching a Tutsi woman slip inside an oil drum outside his house to hide. Asked if there was any scene of a massacre, any moment during the killing that he could not erase from his memory, he shrugged.

No, I saved Tutsi, he said. I didn't see the killing.

For anyone in Rwanda during the genocide, and Ngeze had been in Rwanda, to have seen nothing, to have not been shattered by a single searing image, would have been impossible.

10

Hutu Blood, Is It Red?

By the summer of 2002, Rwandan justice had taken on various forms. For the masterminds of the genocide there was the international tribunal in Arusha. For the lower-level killers, those who committed individual murders, there was *gacaca*. For everyone else, the only available recourse was the Rwandan legal system. American lawyers arrived to help train local lawyers. Other nations sent experts to piece the nation's legal precedents back together. New judges were found and appointed. All this took time, and during this judicial reconstruction people like Damien Nzabakira waited behind bars. He was in prison nearly eight years before his trial began in late 2002.

Because he was accused of taking part in a massacre that involved soldiers, authorities decided to try Damien in a military court. He stood in the docket beside a line of uniformed codefendants in a dark room on the outskirts of Kigali. From the outside one would never have guessed that a trial was unfolding there. The building could easily have been mistaken for a middle school. It was in a low, hastily constructed structure that looked part academic, part Midwest ranch house. The makeshift courthouse sat a little more than a mile from Prison 1930 on a patch of red clay. When the wind shifted one could catch the sweet-and-sour smell of the garbage piles outside 1930. Clerks in the courtroom closed the windows, which managed to intensify the building's own smell of wet paper and old cement. There was only one guard in the room: a young soldier sat at the back with an old rifle on his lap. The casualness with which the tall, thin young man carried the firearm made one wonder whether it was even loaded.

The people gathered for the proceedings were relatives and friends from both sides of the case, and between them were sprinkled a goodly dose of anonymous members of the nearby Hutu and Tutsi communities. They had risen extra early to walk across the hills to see if justice would be done. They arrived at the courtroom armed with differing suppositions that led to the same conclusion: Damien, of course, was guilty. He either killed the children himself or failed to stop others from doing so. After the genocide the two crimes became one and the same thing. If courts, whether *gacaca* or the regular sort, could place someone at the scene of the killing, that was usually enough for a guilty verdict. Those who said they didn't kill were usually not believed.

The Hutu in the room were sure that Damien would be found guilty simply because he was Hutu. They were convinced the presumption of guilt overpowered any evidence to the contrary, that Tutsi would prevail, and the same patterns they had lived with all their lives—in which Hutu were given the short end of the stick—would predictably repeat themselves here. It was the word of a Tutsi, an assistant director at the school where Damien worked, against a Hutu. Everyone knew the way that kind of conflict played out in Rwanda. They had shown up to confirm their worst fears, to watch Damien's fruitless struggle against the power of the new Tutsi government.

The Tutsi who arrived in the courtroom were not altogether sure what force had drawn them there, aside from an odd feeling that bringing another Hutu to justice put the genocide that much farther behind them. Some just wanted a good look at Damien, to try to divine from watching him whatever it was that caused people like him to kill the innocent. His trial was going to reveal another facet of the conspiracy that fueled the genocide. This wasn't a civil war, this was a blatant attempt by the Hutu to erase Tutsi from the face of the earth. People like Damien, they thought, had nearly succeeded. Each trial reminded the Tutsi how close they had come to extinction.

The classroom disguised as a courtroom was too small to accommodate more than a small number of those who had lined up for admittance. Spectators squeezed onto benches, eschewing all sense of personal space. They sat thigh squeezed against thigh, somehow making room for just one more when it appeared the room was already filled to bursting. The conversation in the dirt courtyard as the spectators filed in was not about technical legal details but focused instead on the repetition of rumor.

"He killed forty children, one by one, with a machete," said one person inside the courtroom.

"He claims to have not been there when the killing happened. Does he really think we'll believe that?" said another.

"He deserves to be shot for what he did," said a third. "They say that he told the army officers where the children were hiding, led them right to them, and then helped with the killing himself."

Damien's supporters, members of his family, friends who had known him in prison and who themselves had since been absolved, sat quietly in the back, focusing their gaze on the judges before them, trying to discern, from the jurists' expressions, where they stood, whether Damien had a chance of acquittal.

Damien, for his part, stood at the front of the room facing a panel of five military judges with his back to the crowd. His accuser, who had taken Damien's old job at the orphanage when he was sent to prison, stood three feet away. Damien couldn't help but feel that his whole life was coming down to something he couldn't control. He would have to convince a court of law that he was an exception, one of those who did not get caught up in the swirl of violence. To Damien, the facts seemed simple. Why would he risk life and limb to spirit forty children out of Kigali only to kill them in Butare? It didn't make sense. That's what he needed to make the judges see.

Damien was aware that the way he measured time had changed: now events were all dated from the genocide. April 1994 cleaved lives in Rwanda into two halves: before and after. It marked the beginning of a profound sadness for those who lost friends and family in the massacres. It was the moment from which the accused, years later, would have to account for their whereabouts with enough precision to prove that they hadn't take part.

Five judges in military uniform sat behind a long table on a plywood platform at the front of the room. The wall behind them was dirty and pockmarked, and their uniforms had the tired look of clothes that had been laundered too often. Lawyers sat to the right of the defendants, where juries would normally sit in an American courtroom. They wore starched collars and black robes and looked strangely out of place in the dingy room. The desks in front of them were empty but for several dog-eared loose-leaf pages. Facing them, on the other side of the room, were the military prosecutors. These men wore full dress uniforms with shiny buttons and spit-polished boots.

"He was part of the Butare massacre," Damien's accuser, a large woman named Jacqueline, began. She was dressed as if for a Sunday service. She had on a silky black-and-gold blouse and a dark skirt. Her hair was tied in a scarf and she looked as though she had risen early, taken extra care to get ready for her court appearance, and found, to her surprise, the effort gave her a goodly amount of confidence. She spoke loudly as she addressed the judges, leaning on the table to emphasize each word. "He killed my husband in cold blood and then killed the children." Her husband, she said, had simply been at the wrong place at the wrong time, and Damien and the army soldiers had killed him. She didn't see the murder, but she found his body later.

Damien, in the forest green pajamas of a military prisoner, stood beside her, at a counter-height table. He managed only to look at the judges helplessly and shake his head.

"One of the officers came to my husband, asking for his identity card," she said. "My husband's card said he was a Tutsi so they took him away. Damien Nzabakira had been one of the directors of the school. He knew what had happened there and now he pretends he does not."

Why weren't you killed? one of the judges asked her from the dais.

She said she had given money to a soldier who had lied and said she was his sister.

Damien, she said, was the first to start separating Hutu from Tutsi in the village. "He had told my husband that if he gave him a hundred thousand Rwandan francs, he would be spared. My husband found the money and gave it to him. The next morning, they killed him anyway."

Is what she is saying true? the military officer said to Damien.

"No," he said. There was a titter in the crowd: half laughter, half disbelief. One of the officers glowered in the direction of the noise until it was silent.

"When I found her husband, he was already dead," Damien told the officers. The crowd giggled. It was, apparently, a common alibi among the accused. They admitted to being where the killing had taken place, but after the fact. They presented themselves as witnesses instead of murderers. "I had gone to the dormitory to find him. That is where everyone was hiding. And when I went there, he was already dead."

During the killing, Damien told the court, he had been in the dining hall with the students. He went to the dormitory to check on those who were hidden there and when he returned, the dining hall was empty. Soldiers had arrived and taken the children away.

"You were in charge of these students. You must have known about the killing," one of the judges said.

Damien shook his head. "I saw some of the killing," he said. "But it was so out of control. There was nothing anyone could have done. I had a friend from Cyangugu who was there and I watched as he was killed with a machete blow to the head." Damien tapped the back of his clean-shaven skull to illustrate.

Were there others in this room that you saw killing that day? another judge asked Jacqueline. She nodded and read names off a piece of paper in front of her. The judges scanned the audience and asked anyone whose name had been called to stand. Four prisoners, sprinkled throughout the audience, stood. They, too, wore the forest green uniforms. The judges motioned them forward and they took their places next to Damien at the counter for the accused. The table was so tall, the defendants had to reach up to rest their elbows on it.

The judge nodded to Damien to continue his story. "We got into the car to try to find the children. We decided that they could not have taken that many children, more than forty of them, very far and we hoped to catch up to them. But we couldn't find them. They seemed to have disappeared." When he returned to the orphanage, he said, the soldiers had swarmed the grounds. They demanded to know where the Tutsi were hiding. In particular, Damien said, they were searching for a woman named Berta. Damien knew Berta, he explained, because she had come to him earlier in the day asking for some hot water with which to wash her child. "So I found her the water."

One of the officers on the dais broke in. "You are accused of having refused to hide Berta. You are accused of not wanting to risk being killed so you allowed the soldiers to kill her. Is that what happened?"

One of the prosecutors interrupted: "This is outrageous. He is refusing to admit that he took the soldiers to where Berta was hiding. He took them right to her. He may not have killed her himself, but he led the group to her. Did you see Berta in the group of women the soldiers were taking out to be killed? Did you see her?"

Damien shifted from foot to foot. "I can't remember," he said. It was eight years earlier. There was so much he was trying to forget about that time and now he was being forced to recall it in the tiniest detail. He couldn't remember, for certain, whether Berta was in that group.

The crowd giggled nervously when Damien said he couldn't remember. It was clear they were not on his side.

Then one of the military officers on the dais, who had been quiet to that point, cleared his throat and addressed Jacqueline. "There is just one thing I don't understand. If he was in the process of getting buses to take the children to Burundi, if he had risked his life to take them out of Kigali and to drive them to Butare, why, after all that, would he simply kill them?"

Jacqueline shrugged. Damien stopped rocking nervously on his heels. And the courtroom, for the first time, was quiet.

* * *

Sometimes in the night Bonaventure Ubalijoro dreamed of familiar faces or summoned up memories of sitting in the Oval Office with President Ford or hearing the music of grand diplomatic parties in Paris. Other times his thoughts would turn to the faces of half-forgotten friends, people he had met in prison, or he would see himself drifting effortlessly across the landscape, talking about history or politics, his comments flowing easily between French and English and Kinyarwanda. It was this last category, movement and language, that upset him the most when he awoke. Two months after he was released from prison and the government dropped any remaining charges against him, Bonaventure Ubalijoro suffered a massive stroke. His entire right side was paralyzed. His speech was silenced. A man who had been so vigorous now spent his days staring at a television, harboring the uncomfortable feeling that at one time he would have understood what the newscasters were saying, but now comprehension was just out of reach.

"They said he would never walk and never speak again," Ubalijoro's wife, Madeleine, said. "It was the time in prison. It was just so stressful."

Ubalijoro decided his only recourse, as he sat formulating complex thoughts that he couldn't share with anyone else, was to pray. Prayer had been at least partly responsible for his release from prison. Prayer would, in the same way, allow him to escape the malady that trapped him now.

Every morning, an hour or more before dawn, he would stretch his muscles and call his nurse so she could help him to his private chapel downstairs. The process was a painful one. One of his arms was curled against his chest like a broken wing. He had to drag a lifeless leg along behind him. The nurse would pick up the limb and move it for him as if he were taking a step on his own. It took half an hour to go the necessary distance. It was just a hundred feet. Still, six months after his stroke he considered this progress. He had been wheelchair bound, which made chapel visits impossible unless someone came to physically carry him to the room he had set up for prayer. He spent three hours praying in the morning, and three hours praying at night.

One April night in 2003, Ubalijoro couldn't sleep. A flickering presence had awakened him and he was unsure of where he was. He made his way to the window to get his bearings. He looked out into the misty distance and breathed in the smell of wisteria and jasmine from the garden. An unspeakable calm descended on him. He was enjoying that moment when the sky lit up above him. Sparks and stars began pouring over the side of the house; thousands of them fell like a waterfall of light in the darkness. Ubalijoro was not alarmed. This wasn't danger, he thought to himself, this was a sign. Neighbors told Madeleine the next day that they had seen the lights pouring off the roof. Ubalijoro knew he hadn't been dreaming. God, or perhaps the Virgin Mary, was trying to send him a message.

* * *

Back in Arusha, Barayagwiza, Nahimana, and Ngeze had been looking for a hopeful sign of their own. By late 2002, two years into the trial, they needed some indication that the proceedings were turning in their favor. Yet even the most optimistic among them was hard-pressed to see anything playing to their advantage. Judges had already broadened the legal definition of incitement. The precedent set by Taba mayor Akayesu meant incitement could be as simple as encouraging or persuading others to commit offenses. RTLM might have done that by creating fear. Again and again, the radio station told listeners that they would be in great danger if they didn't act against those wanting to do them harm.

While at first the prospect that the minority Tutsi could kill all the Hutu in Rwanda seemed unthinkable, RTLM and *Kangura* worked to turn that on its head. They made it thinkable. Fear can be an effective motivator. It can suspend one's personal sense of right and wrong. It can even make citizens lean on their government, trust officials more. It makes politics more volatile and dangerous. The checks and balances disappear, as authorities don a cloak of paternalism. It isn't just a Rwandan phenomenon. It had happened in America after the September 11 attacks. What was different in Rwanda was the degree of trust. Rwandans believed utterly what their political leaders told them. Americans, when told Al Qaeda was on the ramparts, eventually demanded proof.

Certainly, outside Rwanda, there was a widespread sense of disbelief that so many men, women, and children could have been killed by their neighbors. It was inconceivable that ordinary Rwandans would join in the killing. Rwandans were less surprised. This kind of massacre was, after all, part of a Rwandan pattern. Hutu and Tutsi had been at each other's throats since colonial times, and nothing had happened, not even the murder of eight hundred thousand Rwandans, to fundamentally change the nation's historical curse.

Jean-Paul Chrétien, Nahimana's former professor and mentor who had once lauded Nahimana's "new history" of Rwanda, changed his mind about Nahimana's research after the genocide. He had written a book on the media of the genocide and had, quite literally, become the arbiter of whether words could kill at the Arusha tribunal.

"While everyone was trying to make Hutus and Tutsis understand they were brothers and they would have to live together in brotherhood, RTLM was bent on telling them that they had no relations with each other," he testified. "They were told they were enemies and that their hatred for each other had to grow each day, eternally. RTLM wielded a weapon of lies."

Kangura, he said, employed the same strategy. There was not just a handful of RPF soldiers in Rwanda as part of the Arusha Accords agreement, *Kangura* wrote in January 1994. There were thousands. As usual one couldn't trust the Tutsi to keep their word. "The *Inkotanyi* attack and massacre innocent people and then retreat to the base provided for them under the Arusha 'peace' agreements."

RTLM and *Kangura* created the impression that the entire world was hostile to Rwanda, Chrétien added. "They created a siege mentality. The method used in the extremist press is to remind people that the opposition between Hutu and Tutsi, which manifested itself in the most spectacular fashion in 1959, is the key to everything."

That had been Nahimana's hypothesis in Paris, years before. But Nahimana hadn't produced an important academic work, his former mentor said contemptuously from the stand, he created hate propaganda disguised with faux-scientific objectivity. Nahimana was nothing more than a mean political ideologue. And while he may not have given the orders in the genocide, he did something nearly as bad, he provided the fuel.

In a country like Rwanda it was a very effective strategy, Chrétien told the court.

* * *

The day Nahimana was scheduled to take the stand the seats in the glassed-in spectator booth were filled. For the first time the area was too small to accommodate more than a modest percentage of those who lined up at the door. Workers from the tribunal—clerks and secretaries and aspiring attorneys—filled the best seats across from the witness stand. Nahimana's wife came in from Belgium. A small thick woman with a broad, warm smile, she sat in one of the straight-backed chairs at the far end of the visitor's gallery not speaking to anyone.

The court's television monitors showed a tight shot of her husband, the former professor, as he walked across the courtroom toward the witness stand. He looked uncommonly relaxed. He sat ramrod straight. He looked respectable and trustworthy as any professor would.

Nahimana's goal on the stand was to shy away from the venomous vicinity of RTLM. He could admit to starting the radio station: he could allow that he had helped hire its journalists; but he needed to distance himself from the broadcasts themselves.

The intent of the prosecution's questions was to introduce the very subject that Nahimana was studiously avoiding: the question of his role at the radio station and, more pointedly, his own moral liability in what occurred there. To convict Nahimana of incitement to genocide, they needed to show that he was the man who orchestrated, or at least helped orchestrate, the broadcasts on Radio Hate.

Nahimana's nervousness showed in his tendency to answer the questions prosecutors put to him too fully. He provided too much background, too much unhelpful detail. When asked about his Ph.D. thesis his narrative would begin with his elementary school education. Asked about RTLM, his answer began with 1959. Lawyers tell witnesses to just answer the questions asked. Defendants are supposed to walk an even more careful line, so their words don't come back to haunt them. Judges would say later that Nahimana's testimony, his verbal feints and weaves, ended up sinking him.

For Steve Rapp, Simone Monasebian, and the rest of the prosecution team, it was not just the conceptual leaps of faith that had them concerned about their case against Nahimana, it was the man himself. Who could possibly believe this soft-spoken academic, a man who continually referred to himself as a gentleman, and acted like one, could have set the stage for one of the worst massacres of our lifetime? After watching him month after month in the courtroom, it was clear that there would be no outbursts, no riling of this man on the stand. There would be no big dramatic monument in which Nahimana would be revealed as a deeply prejudiced Hutu who plotted the death of Tutsi. Instead, they had to make their point another way.

"Mr. Nahimana could you tell the chamber why you dealt with the Hutu kingdom of the north as a central point of your historical research," Steve Rapp began when Nahimana took the stand.

It wasn't about prejudice, Nahimana said, anticipating Rapp's line of questioning. It was about proximity. "In my country it is said that a domestic animal which is going to look for grazing starts with grass which is right by the homestead or by the windowsill," he told the chamber. "I'm from the north; I'm from Ruhengeri and it is a region which had Hutu kings, and the last of them died, I think, in 1960. I realized that there are many unclear points in Rwandan historical studies. What is taught is the history of the Tutsi dynasty. So I thought I would begin with my native area." He didn't mention that his native area was the birthplace of the Hutu Power movement. He didn't need to. The audience in the chamber already knew that much.

Nahimana sat impassively, cocking his head slightly as Simone Monasebian rose from her seat to play an excerpt from a February 1994 RTLM broadcast. The transmission crackled through the overhead courtroom speakers. A French translation of the Kinyarwanda transcript rolled across the chamber's computer screens and television monitors so judges, lawyers, defendants, and the audience could follow along. The Tutsi-led army, the RPF, and the Tutsi population were one and the same, the journalist said over the speakers. The Tutsi all needed to be eliminated. The screen continued for a minute or so longer before the prosecution interrupted the broadcast.

Nahimana shrugged, as if the recording was not really something that was his concern.

"Journalists did make mistakes," he said carefully. "But let's be clear, such language is unacceptable to me. It is revolting."

Journalists who made those kinds of mistakes were cautioned and sanctioned, Nahimana told the court. RTLM had announced that a particular Tutsi businessman was driving to Cyangugu with an Inkotanyi in his car, for example. "We were mistaken," Nahimana freely admitted. "We said as much. The journalist involved was told to be more careful, and the Tutsi businessman who was mistakenly identified, he was given airtime to explain himself." These were mistakes, and RTLM tried to correct them.

"Why didn't you resign when these mistakes were made?" Monasebian asked, getting to the heart of the matter. "Why did you stay on as part of the station's managing committee?"

The committee was doing its best to correct the errors RTLM was making, he said, adding that it needed to be stressed that he wasn't the president of the station. He wasn't in charge. "I was just a committee member," he said.

Monasebian pursed her lips and began tapping on the keys of her laptop. A videotape flickered to life on the computer screens perched on every desk in the chamber. It was fuzzy footage from the 1994 meeting Nahimana had had with the former minister of information. This was the meeting in which RTLM was first warned that it was stepping over the line of propriety with its broadcasts.

The 1994 video panned the meeting room. It paused on Ferdinand Nahimana. Jean-Bosco Barayagwiza came into the frame. And finally, it recorded the words of Faustin Rucogoza, the minister of information who had been an early casualty in the 1994 genocide. He had come back from the grave. Nahimana looked a little surprised.

"RTLM has turned into a political party and a mouthpiece of the CDR," Rucogoza told the radio station's leaders. The camera pulled back. Nahimana was shown listening to the minister respectfully. He appeared to be the leader of the RTLM, representing the radio station. He wasn't just an administrator.

"At this meeting you acted as the director of RTLM or a least held yourself out as such," Monasebian said.

Nahimana plucked at his tie. He had never been the director of RTLM, he said. Phocas Habimana held that post.

That had been his story all along. Because no one had ever seen a Radio Mille Collines organizational chart, he could make the case that where he fit in was unclear. Defense attorney Biju-Duval was building his defense on the basic tenet that RTLM had spun out of control soon after Nahimana started the station. There was little Nahimana could have done to stop RTLM's broadcasts once its momentum started building. It was a Frankenstein defense: RTLM was a monster its creator could not harness. The question was no longer whether the radio station had crossed the line. The question was whether Nahimana was partly responsible when it happened.

Nahimana had left Kigali on April 12, just a week after the genocide began, he continued, physically distancing himself from the radio station. He had heard through the grapevine that journalists at the radio station would use drugs and drink before going on the air, he said softly. "I am not saying these journalists were bad before April 6," he said, suggesting there was some unexplained transformation that took place when the presidential plane crashed. "They were the crème de la crème of journalists in Kigali. But using drugs and alcohol before going on the air, that is unacceptable."

Monasebian toyed with asking him whether Georges Ruggiu, a man with no journalism experience whose only claim to fame had been to be invited into the presidential motorcade, was crème de la crème. She decided against it and let Nahimana continue.

The judges needed to understand, Nahimana said, as if explaining the weather to a small child, the journalists drugged themselves after the events of April 6. The journalists were no longer speaking their minds over the air, the drugs had taken over, dulled their senses. There is no question that the authorities at the station, the editor and the director, should have put a stop to it, he said. But the judges needed to remember the context in which all of this took place. The RPF had bombed RTLM's headquarters in mid-April. The attack had seriously wounded a number of journalists. One journalist, Noël Hitimana, was left without limbs. Another employee, Kantano Habimana, lost his entire family to RPF forces.

"On the basis of that you could understand Kantano's hatred of the RPF," he said. "When he says to kill someone with a narrow nose, that is anger speaking." That said, he continued, Kantano should have been removed from his post.

The genocide was "bestial, inhuman, and indescribable behavior," Nahimana insisted. "I went to the French embassy in Kigali out of fear that war or bandits would take advantage of the situation. When the plane went down, I considered that RTLM was no longer ours. It had been appropriated by radicals, extremists, whose way of seeing things and doing things I don't share."

After the assassination of President Habyarimana, RTLM's management committee stopped holding their once a week meetings, Nahimana said. When those meetings ended, Nahimana said he lost touch with the radio station. There were no payments issued to RTLM workers from the radio's bank account. He was no longer passing out paychecks. Instead, he said, the journalists were paid by the army or by Phocas Habimana out of a personal account. "The military took RTLM hostage," he said.

* * *

The case against Barayagwiza was more procedurally complicated. Since he refused to attend the trial and refused to help his lawyer defend him, the court was riding blind. There were few objections, few disputes of fact, because the accused, the man who knew what had happened, declined to participate.

Barayagwiza's defense counsel tried to get around the issue by introducing his book *Le Sang Hutu est-il rouge?* ("Is Hutu Blood Red?"). Barayagwiza's 1995 book provided, just as Nahimana's work had done, an alternate view of Rwandan history, which Hutu said needed to be told and Tutsi saw as patently racist.

Barayagwiza maintained that the RPF was responsible for the downing of Habyarimana's plane and that RPF's main objective was to take power by force. The Tutsi invaders killed thousands of Hutu civilians, Barayagwiza wrote, and they were eager to reduce the number of Hutu so that the Hutu would become the minority in Rwanda. Barayagwiza accused the RPF of violating the U.N. Charter and said it was the Tutsi, not the Hutu, who had committed genocide. Even Amnesty International, he said, had criticized the RPF for their wanton killing. There was no intention to kill the Tutsi generally, he said. The target was the RPF. This was a civil war, not a genocide.

Barayagwiza said he decided to create the CDR out of a desire to serve his country and people. The CDR was misunderstood, he added. It was a pacifist party that espoused the principles of a liberal, open society. It wasn't against ethnic minorities, he said, it was against ethnic minorities trying to install a dictatorship. The distinction, he said, was an important one.

The United Nations, he wrote, had been manipulated by the RPF, and its allegiances were with the Tutsi. Hutu blood could be spilled, he said, without raising any concern among members of the United Nations. "Next to Tutsi blood," he wrote, "Hutu blood is not red. It is black. Therefore it can be spilt without serious consequences."

Knowing that the world would turn a blind eye to the woes of the Hutu majority, Rwanda required men of action, like Barayagwiza, to take matters into their own hands. Starting political parties, cells of self-defense, was a natural part of that process and required no apology.

"I would not blush to be the ideologist of the CDR, no more than I feel in any way guilty about being called such," he wrote.

Barayagwiza's leading role in the CDR party allowed the prosecution, which had little else to go on, to damn him by association. Where it could be proven the CDR's evil hand had been, so too, by extension, was its creator Jean-Bosco Barayagwiza. What the court knew was that Barayagwiza had convened CDR meetings and spoken at them. He was present and participated in demonstrations where CDR demonstrators, armed with cudgels, began to chant "*Tubatsembatsembe,*" or "Let's exterminate them." Barayagwiza himself was said to lead the call for extermination at CDR meetings.

As for RTLM, Barayagwiza wrote, freedom of the press is an essential means of fulfilling democracy. RTLM was the result of an ingenious idea for bringing together a host of political sympathies and ensuring that a Rwandan audience was fully informed on what was at stake as the RPF readied itself for war. RTLM was not created, he said, to prepare massacres.

* * *

Barayagwiza's written defense might have held more sway had it not been for the testimony of a Hutu farmer the court dubbed Witness AHB. He had seen Barayagwiza in Gisenyi, Ngeze's hometown, in southern Rwanda, just days after the plane crash, and he provided such detail and so many names it was difficult to discount his version of events.

Barayagwiza had arrived around lunchtime in a red pickup truck filled with weapons around April 12. We had been expecting him, the witness said, because one of the party leaders in his commune had said that Barayagwiza would be arriving that morning with tools to kill the Tutsi. Those who wanted weapons were told to go fetch them. When they arrived they were told to regroup the next morning. The CDR and MRNDD were starting to collaborate at that time, he said, and they banded together in this instance to kill Tutsi.

Witness AHB, a Hutu who was in Gisenyi at the time, remembered the bloodshed that followed the plane crash and remembered, too, that many of the Tutsi who had survived the first wave of violence were attacked again a week later with the very weapons Barayagwiza had brought to Gisenyi.

Members of the CDR went door to door, AHB said, telling Hutu to come and collect the arms and kill Tutsi. The recruitment campaign, neighborhood by neighborhood, provided details on where Hutu were supposed to go and where they could pick up machetes, guns, and grenades. "The new arms shipment sparked the second killings," AHB told the court. "The second massacre wouldn't have happened if they hadn't had the new weapons and gone door to door."

How this related to charges that Barayagwiza incited genocide by starting RTLM was unclear. So far prosecutors had shown only that he started the radio station, attended CDR meetings with Ngeze, and brought weapons to Gisenyi.

* * *

While Barayagwiza was clearly a man driven by ideology, Hassan Ngeze was more craven. He wanted money and fame and had the Tutsi been working to overthrow Hutu with a newspaper and a radio station, he probably would still have been a participant, even though he was Hutu. Ngeze lived in the moment, for the thrill of the ride, not for politics.

The case against Ngeze included articles in *Kangura*, interviews on RTLM, and witness testimony from citizens in Gisenyi who saw him in trucks with Interahamwe shouting slogans into bullhorns. Yet Hassan Ngeze remained confident that he could convince anyone, including three international judges at a tribunal, that he was vastly misunderstood and should be set free.

"People keep stressing how Ngeze was illiterate and couldn't have possibly done the things he was accused of," Judge Møse said after the trial. "But I found him to be highly intelligent. Of course he could be difficult in court. But think, at the beginning of the trial he hardly spoke a word of English and by the end of the trial he had delivered a closing statement completely in English. He is an easy man to underestimate."

Ngeze made the prosecution's job easier by proudly taking credit for *Kangura*. The law required that every newspaper include a box that said both the author and the publisher of any article was bound by its content. Any newspaper printed without that proviso would be confiscated, he said, so every issue of *Kangura* from 1991 until a month before the genocide, when its publication ceased, had the binding statement on the front page. That statement made Ngeze responsible for what appeared on the newspaper's pages.

That said, Ngeze blithely ignored what it really meant. Ngeze didn't let the facts get in the way of a good story. "Information itself did not interest him," one witness said. "The truth and the quest for truth were not his concern. His concern was this struggle, and that struggle had to be conducted by all means."

Witness after witness produced evidence that Hassan Ngeze used his journal to spark racism and structured anti-Tutsi hatred in the months and weeks leading up to the genocide. It was "us" or "them," *Kangura* said. This was a question of self-defense; otherwise the Hutu would return to the days of Tutsi supremacy.

"The majority people has only one very wicked enemy, who is the RPF," a *Kangura* editorial in July 1991 read. "This enemy is projecting to exterminate the majority people. . . . The Inkotanyi and their accomplices have no place in Rwanda. . . . These murderous enemies have killed our soldiers, our parents, our children, and our friends. Today, they are projecting to exterminate all of us. Who can accept to live with them?"

Six months later, *Kangura* warned its readers that the Tutsi were stockpiling arms for mass destruction. They had more than a hundred fighter planes, the articles said, a great number of armored tanks, missiles, and imported guns. Witnesses said later that Ngeze wanted to warn the Hutu masses so they would take appropriate measures against the Tutsi.

Ngeze saw it differently. He said that he had the duty to report honestly and fairly what was going on in Rwanda. "An independent journalist is also an agent of intelligence gathering," Ngeze told the court. "I investigate so as to inform the masses on what is being hidden from them."

Shouldn't a journalist with such a noble cause, a man merely trying to expose the truth, be protected by the tenets of press freedom? Ngeze asked.

The other question was whether a newspaper that wasn't even being published during the genocide could be blamed for inciting it.

t Rwan-

ay 1923,
e Jewish
egan tak-
nti-Nazi
n against
ier wasn't
ing a war

hat, even
uded the
da media
the Nazi
had writ-
ublishing
ld not be
cient sway
l believed
rney John
ed articles
when the

t to notice
d its Nazi
screaming
. They fol-
ze realized
papers con-
e mayor of
berg Jewry
g to unem-
Nuremberg
s or waged
ned was its

11

Cow Is Gored
e Herd

iis journalism work was part of a
us Streicher saw the creation of
oble endeavor. *Der Stürmer*, or
s anti-Semitism.

!3 to 1945, Streicher used every
iol that bordered on the insane.
e staff helping him produce the
nan in charge. "Streicher and
ie," he would say proudly from
Ngeze, when he took the stand
er, sounded a similar refrain. I
as mine.

hose the name *Stürmer* while
have it," he said later. "Since
, it shall be call the *Stürmer*."
as probably apocryphal. The
ired by the Nazi tendency to
tions. Other arms of the party
ck") and *Die Flamme* ("the
ier would have fit right in.

Ngeze's *Kangura* ("Wake It Up") struck a similar, albe dan, note.

The first issue of *Der Stürmer* rolled off the presses in M and from the start it took direct aim at the Jews. "We will slaves. Therefore he must go." In no time at all, Streicher b ing shots at the Jewish mayor of Nuremberg, a fervent named Hermann Luppe. Streicher used his campaig Luppe to launch more general attacks on Jews. *Der Stürm* just a storm, it was a weapon. Streicher's words were wag against the Jews.

Der Stürmer had other eerie parallels with *Kangura* t if the similarities were coincidence, could not have el three judges weighing incitement charges in the Rwan trial. There had been, for example, attempts to muzzle paper. The director of the German press, Max Amann, ten to Streicher in August 1923 and asked him to stop p the newspaper. He was concerned that Streicher cou controlled and that the Nazi party would not hold suffi over what he published. Prosecutors in the media tria that was why Ngeze was jailed so often. Defense atto Floyd said Ngeze was thrown in jail because he publish the Hutu Power movement didn't like. "He was in jai genocide began," Floyd maintained.

Leafing through the pages of *Kangura* it was hard no the similarities between the Rwandan broadsheet ar predecessor. The layout was remarkably similar—all headlines, venomous cartoons, and vindictive caption lowed a typical tabloid formula. Streicher and Nge early on that scandal kept readers buying. At first the centrated on political rumors. Streicher accused th Nuremberg of abuse of power. He blamed the Nurem for any and all problems facing the city, from housin ployment. As his readership began to grow outside of he turned to sex and crime, either committed by Jev against Jews. By 1926, what made *Der Stürmer* renov pornographic content. Young boys picked up the newspaper and hungrily read it for the salacious details.

Ngeze, for his part, blamed all that plagued the Hutu—from poverty to disease—on the Tutsi minority. It was the Tutsi lust for power that time and again sent Rwanda to the precipice of war, he wrote. One of Rwanda's other newspapers ran a cartoon making fun of Ngeze's preoccupation. The drawing showed Ngeze on a psychiatrist's couch and the doctor asking what ailed him. "Tutsi, Tutsi, Tutsi," Ngeze responded. Ngeze reran the cartoon in his own newspaper in 1992.

Most of Streicher's material came from readers. They sent letters complaining about neighbors or politicians or family members, and Streicher or his staff followed them up and printed the results. The readership for this kind of gossip and rumormongering was made up of precisely the people that the Nazi party was trying to target with its propaganda: the lowest common denominator, the masses who, already aggrieved, were searching for a scapegoat to whom they could affix their problem. The style of the newspaper's editorial content was tailored to fit the Nazi fashion of the time. The sentences were simple, vocabulary limited. The newspaper was conversational and funny and easy to read. Unlike most newspapers of the time geared toward German intellectuals, *Der Stürmer* was clearly written for the common man, complete with rough language and repetitive themes. In this way, too, it provided a template for *Kangura* and Radio Mille Collines.

In December 1925, Streicher hired a cartoonist named Philipp Rupprecht to put pictures to his anti-Jewish message. Drawing under the pen name Fips, Rupprecht provided crude anti-Jewish drawings for the newspaper for more than two decades. The Jews he drew were all the same: short, fat, unshaven, hook-nosed, sexually perverted, and beady-eyed. Each drawing was meant to rob the Jewish people of their humanity. Similarly, unseemly drawings of Tutsi and moderate Hutu found their way into the pages of Ngeze's *Kangura*. In one, moderate Hutu politician Faustin

Twagiramungu was in bed with Agathe Uwilingiyimana, the prime minister. In another, General Roméo Dallaire, the head of UNAMIR, the U.N. contingent in Rwanda, was shown sucking the breast of a Tutsi woman. Ngeze, like Streicher before him, was sending a political message under a cloak of titillation.

The question before the tribunal was whether racist talk, hate speech in some of its worst form, rose to the level of genocide. For the first time since World War II, an international court asked judges to decide and draw a line to mark where press freedom ended and incitement began.

"Press freedom comes with responsibility," Judge Pillay said later. Ngeze, Barayagwiza, and Nahimana were on trial for flouting all the recognized norms of the liberal press. "The press is supposed to hold a position of public trust. It is supposed to maintain a critical distance. They did not."

* * *

Proving the media trio had shirked their journalistic responsibilities was a complicated task. There were ten thousand stages in the cause. Lawyers looked for precedents and technicalities. They waded knee-deep in arguments. They apportioned blame. Prosecutors were chastised for springing last-minute witnesses. There were postponements as defense witnesses failed to materialize. *The Prosecutor vs. Barayagwiza, Nahimana, and Ngeze* dragged on month after month after month. The media case became the most complex and sophisticated of the trials held before the tribunal. It became so complicated it was difficult for anyone not intimately involved to follow it with any precision. There were filing cabinets holding dusty warrants, piles of translation, rulings on evidence. Thousands upon thousands of pages of documentary and tangible evidence in several languages began to eat space in cramped offices. The case came to involve close to one hundred lay and expert witnesses from all over the world. By the time the defense began its arguments, the trial had stretched out for more than two years.

Lawyers had aged. Defendants had grown accustomed to their daily trips to the tribunal. Guards had grown familiar with their charges.

"You have to understand what it was like for those at the Ruhengeri campus of the University of Rwanda in the early nineteen nineties," a former colleague of Nahimana's from the University of Rwanda began for the defense in the fall of 2002. The RPF had been attacking the region since October 1990, and while the initial offenses had been successfully thwarted, with each new push by the Tutsi-led army, the attacks grew in ferocity. "We saw many corpses in Ruhengeri, we learned of the deaths of many civil servants," the witness, known as G99, said of a particularly violent attack in February 1993.

"The RPF wanted to occupy the region," he said. "We actually had to move the Ruhengeri campus of the university to Butare for seven months, the attacks were so frequent."

The RPF was targeting civil authorities, but they also seemed perfectly capable of killing civilians. Naturally those who lived in the area were frightened. And they fled. The university didn't allow its students to return to classes in Ruhengeri until October 1993.

It was in that environment that Ferdinand Nahimana began sending his scholarly papers to friends and colleagues. He was calling on Rwandans to find ways to stop the war, G99 explained. It was a very frightening time.

"In Rwanda, throughout the country's history, cultivated ethnicism has always been at the center of internecine conflicts, culminating in the 1959 revolution," Nahimana wrote in a March 1993 paper that he copied and sent to friends in 1994 because, as he wrote in a cover letter, it was still topical. The first and longest part of the essay was a discussion of the history of Rwanda from 1959. Nahimana described the nation's emerging regionalism, the great divide between people of the south and those from the

trial for the actions of the Rwandan army and the presidential guard, for which he was responsible. Businessman Félicien Kabuga, one of the financiers behind RTLM, was accused of providing cash and weapons to finance the massacres. In that context, prosecutors said the media trial trio provided the final piece: the defendants were in charge of stoking the fires with ideological motivation and justification.

It became increasingly clear that the killing could not have spread so efficiently and so quickly had it not been for RTLM's clarion call. And the people of Rwanda could not have been so quickly organized for action had plotters not found a way to be in every commune, every village, nearly every home. And they did that with the Interahamwe. Here too, prosecutors told the court, the judges would see the hand of Ferdinand Nahimana. In 1993, in his essay laying out the solutions for what ailed Rwanda, Nahimana had provided a blueprint for the organization of the Interahamwe, the killing gangs of the genocide.

Of course, the prosecution began, Nahimana had not overtly called for a Hutu militia. Instead, in his 1993 essay he had focused on the importance of civil defense.

"The will of Rwandans to end the war and their conviction to build a new country will be translated, first, into the acceptance of the existence of this civil defense," Nahimana wrote. "Rwandans have to assist the country to set up a series of measures to make the civil defense effective by giving advice to authorities, particularly on the modalities of the recruitment and organization of the youth who are integrated in the civil defense.

"If the civil defense is rapidly organized," he concluded, "there is no doubt that the enemy of Rwanda will find it difficult to infiltrate the whole country and strike wherever he wants to and when he wishes to do so."

In short, the nation needed to be on alert, Nahimana said. It needed to redouble its efforts against invaders. His message was clear. It was us, the Hutu, against them, the Tutsi, Prosecutor Steve Rapp told the chamber as he introduced Nahimana's writings. Nahimana was laying the groundwork for a genocide more than a year before the first shot was fired.

Nahimana said the prosecution didn't understand. They acted as if a league of Tutsi were not jockeying for power and had not been crossing the border into Rwanda for years. "The Tutsi league had existed. I was suggesting that a civil defense be instituted. The roadblocks existed in 1990, 1991, 1992, up until 1994, in fact. These roadblocks were part of the civil defense I'm talking about. Civil defense is in the public authority's domain, whereas the Interahamwe or militias are in the domain of the political parties." He hadn't supported the Interahamwe. "The Interahamwe was a deviation and I would call it something undesirable. During a war the lawful government has the right to form a civil defense."

No one could argue that the Interahamwe took the idea of a civil defense to a more strident conclusion. It was recruited from the nation's poorest people. There were more than fifty thousand members throughout the country, roughly on par with the number of regular armed forces. The prosecution was arguing that Interahamwe recruiters played upon the Rwandan tendency to embrace authority unquestioningly. They had a herd mentality, a need for group identification. Nahimana had understood that years before; it was the conclusion he drew from his research and a frequent subject in his writings. While Rwandans were judged by their individual characters, the judgment also extended to family, clan, and even the hill on which one lived. Identity had as much to do with the group as with one's own decisions. That was the closest anyone could come to explaining why regular Rwandans complied when authorities gave orders to kill. Individuals were swept along for the ride. Jean-Paul Chrétien called them "innocent murderers," victim-killers who were horrified by what they were doing but killed nevertheless. They were men of the herd. The tribunal was predicated on the fact that in Rwanda the responsibility lay with the educated people in positions of authority, those who knew better—people like Ferdinand Nahimana.

Nahimana knew what he was doing. He knew what his essay

would bring and what a call to arms on RTLM would produce, Rapp said. Nahimana was using the same tools the Nazis had wielded against the Jews. Blaming the Tutsi league for what was wrong in Rwanda resounded like the themes of Nazism. It was reminiscent of *Der Stürmer* screeds that blamed the Jews for the Holocaust.

Nahimana scoffed from the stand.

The difference, among others, he said, was that the Tutsi league and its intention to take the reins of power in Rwanda wasn't the figment of one man's imagination but instead was based in fact. It had been attacking Rwanda for years. "You are talking as if this league did not exist," he told Rapp. "But it did. Historians do not make events, we merely report on them. The league existed, and in the end the RPF brought together these groups."

History proved this. This wasn't a supposition, he said. The prosecution was putting words in his mouth. He had been analyzing and criticizing aspects of the Rwandan regime for years but his solution wasn't genocide, it was peaceful coexistence, he said. "This is the ideology I would want to be accused of, it's the ideology I stood for, not the ideology of genocide which you want to accuse me of."

The essay was written in the context of the resumption of the war by the RPF in February 1993, in violation of the cease-fire agreement, he continued, and had to be viewed that way. "When someone like me dares to talk about ethnicism as a problem, as an issue, you are accused of being an extremist and being involved with ethnicism, as if in Rwanda it is forbidden to be involved in a debate."

Nahimana said that this was a trial looking for a scapegoat, a crime looking for its mastermind. His words were twisted to fit someone else's version of the events. "When we talk about the final solution, I am saying, the prosecutor and some journalists are trying to see in these lines an ideology. They were looking for some fantasy and referring to Hitler's final solution," he said. "This is pure fantasy. They looked for words in my book which could refer to the final word. And when they found 'solution' together with 'final,' they said they had found something. But I'm saying that I'm preaching, rather, for peace and negotiations, so that an end could be put to war."

Radio Mille Collines was not established to incite genocide, Ferdinand Nahimana said from the stand. "At no point whatsoever when we established the RTLM company and set up RTLM radio was that the intention," he said. "There was never any idea of establishing anything that was to be used to kill or to commit other crimes."

So you deny that RTLM was set up as a propaganda tool to mobilize the Hutu against the Tutsi? Steve Rapp asked.

Nahimana shook his head. "I didn't conspire with Félicien Kabuga, Jean-Bosco Barayagwiza, and more than a thousand shareholders of the station to order people killed and call for rapes," he said. "No. We have a saying in our country, we say the fallen cow is always gored by the herd. I am the fallen cow and now I am taking the blame for all that happened in Rwanda."

He found out what RTLM was saying on the radio broadcasts only after the fact, he said. "People came and told me, how could RTLM say such things, and I could not believe it. It was not the RTLM we founded. Yes, we wanted the station to fight the enemy, but what the journalists were calling an enemy was now different. Saying if you see a person with this type of nose, kill him. This was unacceptable."

As to stopping the broadcasts, or voicing his disapproval, Nahimana said he was too frightened. RTLM had targeted him, he said. One broadcast claimed, "Even those like Nahimana whom we expected to be serious have proved not to be so."

"I had a lot of fears. There was a war. I had to think of my fate and that of my family," he said.

* * *

To hear Dr. Helmut Strizek tell it, the Rwandan Patriotic Front was responsible for the genocide. If they had not staged a series of invasions in northern Rwanda in the run-up to the plane crash, there would not have been such antipathy for the Tutsi in Rwanda. The German political scientist had worked in Rwanda and he remembered how the RPF attacks had angered the Hutu. More than a million people fled northern Rwanda and set up squatter camps around Kigali. "One cannot discount this movement of people in lighting the spark," Strizek testified for the defense in May 2003. "This is what I consider the foundation of the genocide. It is this hatred that exploded."

Helmut Strizek was called to the stand to provide evidence about the shooting down of the presidential plane and to discuss evidence on whether there was a clear plan to commit genocide. Defense attorneys said he would provide a historical context to the events in Rwanda in 1994. In the end, however, as defense witnesses go, Strizek was not a good one. In his report provided for the tribunal he focused nearly exclusively on the RPF. One section was entitled "Propaganda and the Choice of Ethnicism." It talked only about the RPF and did not so much as mention RTLM or *Kangura*. Another section on incitement took a similar RPF-centric line.

"Why is there nothing in your report about RTLM or *Kangura?*" Monasebian asked during cross-examination.

Strizek shifted uncomfortably. "I knew this was the very crux of the trial and I didn't want to dwell on it."

"Do you agree or disagree that *Kangura* was the voice of the extremist or radical Hutu?" she continued.

"I heard *Kangura* being criticized," he said. "But I haven't read it." Then, thinking that wasn't enough of an answer, he volunteered that he had read the Hutu Ten Commandments. "They were truly appalling," he said.

Monasebian smiled. She asked if he agreed or disagreed that President Habyarimana's wife, Agathe Habyarimana, and her brother Colonel Sagatwa supported *Kangura*. He shrugged. Some people said so, he said, but he didn't know for sure. "Was Ferdinand Nahimana the chief ideologue at RTLM?" she said at last.

Strizek said he didn't know.

Monasebian opened a binder on the lectern and began to read an excerpt from a 1994 book Strizek had written, in German, about the genocide, entitled *Rwanda und Burundi von der Unabhangigkeit zum Staatszerfall* ("Rwanda and Burundi from Independence to the Collapsing of the State"). He must have assumed no one would bother to read it because what he had written was in direct conflict with his testimony. "*Kangura* is a Rwandan journal founded in 1990, the voice of radical Hutu," Monasebian began reading. "It is said Agathe Habyarimana and her brother Colonel Sagatwa, who died in the presidential plane crash of April 6, 1994, supported it. It synthesized radical positions in the Ten Commandments of the Hutu, that is, not to marry a Tutsi woman." By reading a single paragraph in a book, Monasebian managed to discount most of Strizek's testimony.

She flipped to another section and began reading anew. "The peace agreement had just been signed in the summer of 1993 when the ultra Hutu reinforced their propaganda in the journal *Kangura* and Radio Mille Collines," the book continued. "The genocide was planned and prepared by precise groups, and that radio RTLM called Rwandans to commit genocide after the death of Habyarimana cannot be contested."

Strizek stammered. He had changed his opinion since writing the book, he began. He had only been repeating what he had heard. His views had changed because there was lack of evidence. It didn't matter how many avenues of explanation Strizek pursued; it was clear they all ran into dead ends.

The tribunal would later use his words against the defendants.

* * *

"We're not saying nothing was planned before April 6, 1994," Nahimana's defense attorney Jean-Marie Biju-Duval began in his closing argument in August 2003. "It is obvious to me that in January 1994, following the events in Burundi, on each hill everyone looked at his neighbor differently. Some did organize out of concern that an RPF attack was possible." But to blame Nahimana for that was misguided. To say he had created RTLM to incite genocide was just wrong. It was perfectly within Nahimana's rights to be against the Arusha Accords, he continued. Freedom of expression allows him to have an opinion and voice it. It was also within his right to broadcast that opinion over the airwaves and to encourage debate over whether the peace agreement would be fair to both Hutu and Tutsi. One did not need to be an ideologue to be concerned about a possible Tutsi coup d'état. The RPF had been attacking pockets of Rwanda for years and it would not be a leap to suggest that other, bigger attacks were being planned.

But it would be wrong to say that adds up to a conspiracy, or to some great meeting of the ideological minds. Had Nahimana and Ngeze plotted something sinister? The evidence doesn't support that, Biju-Duval said. Ngeze appeared on RTLM three times, once before April 6 and twice afterward. This is the basis of a conspiracy? The radio station and the newspaper cosponsored a contest. Was this the basis of a conspiracy?

"What is significant here is the absence of collaboration," Biju-Duval said, reading from a notebook lying before him. "There was a split between two ideologues. Nahimana doesn't belong in this extremist labyrinth. His ideology was defending unity and calling for peace." Nahimana's words were twisted by the prosecution to fit a narrative of their own invention, he said. Founding RTLM wasn't enough to convict Nahimana of incitement to genocide or crimes against humanity. "At Nuremberg this kind of thesis was excluded. Belonging to the Nazi party didn't mean you were part of the conspiracy," he said, evoking the international court that loomed large in the minds of all the judges at the tribunal. "Belonging to RTLM didn't mean you were planning a genocide either."

The essay Nahimana sent to his friends was similarly misunderstood. Nahimana wasn't calling for the creation of the Interahamwe. He was calling for a civil defense, Biju-Duval insisted. "Would such an act be criminal if you were worried about an invasion? RTLM was established before the assassination and before Arusha was signed, during a time punctuated by RPF invasions," he said. "Nahimana was trying to establish a way to get information out at a time when government media was eclipsed by Radio Muhabura." RTLM was his answer.

"What is fundamental here is the intention to commit genocide, and Nahimana didn't intend to do that," he continued. "Nahimana is a victim of a political exploitation of events. Right up to 1995, you don't find one word from Nahimana sowing seeds of division between the Hutu and the Tutsi. Nahimana was against the RPF, and that is not the same thing."

As far as leading RTLM, Biju-Duval said, the prosecution is based on the premise that Nahimana remained the director of RTLM thoughout the genocide. There was no undisputed evidence that proved that he was in charge after April 6. Other people claimed he was, but that was hearsay. "We're not saying he didn't hold a position at RTLM," Biju-Duval said. "He was one of three people who could sign checks. That was why he regularly went to RTLM. But he was part of the radio station because of who he was. He was needed because of his reputation. Nahimana didn't have power over journalists. On the morning of April 7, Nahimana hurried to the French embassy. Is that the conduct of a leader?"

The lawyer then went through a short chronology to buttress his thesis. On the eighth of April, Nahimana went to RTLM after getting food at the market. Four days later, the civilian government of Rwanda escaped to Gitarama, just outside of Kigali. Nahimana was evacuated to Burundi with the French embassy staff. The army, at that point, was in charge of RTLM, and it was the army, not Nahimana, that commanded its broadcasts.

"Even in times of peace, a radio station can't be remote-controlled," Biju-Duval said. "Who was in charge? Phocas slept at RTLM. Gahigi got a house close by. These were the only two people to which RTLM was responsible. It is clear that those who had influence before the sixth of April had no power after that." Because they had died in the genocide, Nahimana became a convenient target.

Finally, Biju-Duval turned to Nahimana's interview on Radio Rwanda, his opportunity to distance himself from RTLM. The record, the defense attorney said, was incomplete. The Kigali government, which had provided the tape to the prosecution team, had provided only a snippet of the interview. As the judges weighed the guilt or innocence of the three men, they should remember that they were doing so based on just ninety excerpts from RTLM, excerpts provided by the Kagame government in Kigali, which had a stake in the trial's outcome. Out of all the recordings from RTLM, only nine admitted into evidence were from April, when the genocide began. Two were from April 13 and April 15, and one was from April 25. Nahimana's radio interview at the end of April on Radio Rwanda didn't include a condemnation of the genocide for a very simple reason, the attorney said. Nahimana, who had been evacuated and taken out of the country and had only just returned, didn't have enough information to condemn the killings because he didn't know about them.

Because so many people had taken part in the genocide, the tribunal's job was not just to try the masterminds of the killings. The tribunal's mission was something more: it was holding the people who came to personify what went wrong in Rwanda accountable. When people around the world thought of RTLM they thought of the media gone crazy. Broadcasting license plate numbers and compiling Tutsi death lists were not protected speech by any stretch of the imagination. Even in the United States, which had the most liberal speech protection laws, a court would have found that RTLM went over the line, he said. But the prosecution had failed to prove that Nahimana had ordered journalists to say those things.

It was natural to believe that there must have been an organization, a grand plan, that had envisioned RTLM as an integral cog in the machine of genocide. And every organization, every plan, needed a leader. Nahimana was the ideal candidate. He was one of the founders of the radio station. Certainly he must have built it with the intention of using it as a tool of genocide, Biju-Duval said. But a trial can't be built on ambiguity. Can Nahimana be convicted of incitement to genocide without having said anything? Will he be found guilty of crimes against humanity for what others said when he was being evacuated out of the country?

"We must try to rule on certainties," Biju-Duval concluded. "That's the honor of Nuremberg. It handed down judgments that stand up to the test of time. No innocent person was convicted at Nuremberg. Will we be able to say the same thing here?"

* * *

John Floyd nodded to Biju-Duval and stood up to begin his closing remarks. It was August 2003, nearly three years since the trial had opened and the three defendants had pleaded not guilty.

"We've been talking for three years as if doubt never existed," Floyd said with a cadence reminiscent of his old fraternity brother, one of O.J. Simpson lawyers, Johnny Cochran. "If there are two, three, four, or five explanations for something that took place, and if the prosecutor hasn't provided beyond a shadow of a doubt one particular option, then my client, Hassan Ngeze, has to be acquitted."

Floyd's lament was similar to that of the Nahimana defense team: there had been only a small sample of material from *Kangura* that had been translated from Kinyarwanda or available to the lawyers with which to build a defense. Floyd had asked for translations of all the *Kangura* issues so he could put the articles in a larger context, but only the most offensive tracts were made available, he said. The judges ruled that translating so many issues of *Kangura* would strain the tribunal's resources, and as a result the defense of Ngeze was prejudiced; the tribunal saw only snippets of the newspaper. Those excerpts, Floyd said, were not representative of Ngeze's publication.

Ngeze never directly advocated that Hutu kill Tutsi. Was his talk racist? Floyd asked. Of course it was. But did that mean it was genocidal? Absolutely not, he said. What was even more fundamental, he continued, was that *Kangura* was never published during the genocide. The tribunal was able to admit the back issues only because of the March 1994 radio contest with RTLM—otherwise all the evidence stacked up against Ngeze would have been inadmissible since the court had jurisdiction only from January 1, 1994, to December 31, 1994. Hassan Ngeze published only six issues in 1994, the last of which predicted (correctly) that Habyarimana would be assassinated. Ngeze was on trial for telling the truth, Floyd said. The events he predicted in his newspaper came to pass. To send him to jail for that would be an outrage, he said. It would muzzle the press. It would cast a pall over intellectual freedom. It would be a mistake.

Then Floyd went one step farther. He gave the floor, reluctantly, to Hassan Ngeze.

"Is providing information a crime?" Ngeze asked, reading from a handwritten statement on loose-leaf paper. "Journalists the world over want to know, if a journalist is given information that can save humanity, do they have to keep it to themselves? By publishing articles in *Kangura* that provided the people with the information that was going on behind the scenes inside the Habyarimana government, am I guilty?"

Ngeze paused for effect, before continuing in a different vein. "My role as a journalist in the Great Lakes region prevented me from getting married, it made it difficult for me to feed my family. It is not because I am not handsome that I don't have the love of a woman."

Smiles pulled at the corners of the judges' mouths.

"They have told me that I am a handsome man," he continued. "They haven't married me because I was always in prison in

Rwanda, my life was always in danger. That's why I am not married."

Judge Pillay cleared her throat and tried to keep her composure.

"You are not on trial for being not married," she said.

The courtroom erupted in laughter.

Ngeze didn't miss a beat. "I have been in prison for seven years. There is but one Hassan Ngeze who saved the lives of thousands of Tutsi."

For Ngeze, an issue that was entirely beside the point for the tribunal was key. "Shouldn't Hassan Ngeze be given some mercy for having saved so many innocent lives during the tragic events between April and July 1994?" he continued. "Shouldn't he be accorded some mercy for having defied the orders of the Interahamwe and continuing to aid others during this difficult time? Shouldn't it be noted that he went to prison on numerous occasions for trying to help others during this period?"

Hassan Ngeze, he continued, tried to warn the world what was going to happen in Rwanda. If only the United Nations had listened, Ngeze continued, there would have been no genocide and no need for the tribunal.

"I declare in front of this chamber that I, Hassan Ngeze, from the bottom of my heart, I forgive those who killed my family, all the people who testified against me. The time has come to reconstruct our country and to reconcile. I am waiting for the day of my acquittal, the acquittal which is well in my rights, and the day I will be set free, and the day I will be married. . . . Madame President, honorable judges, we Rwandans are what you want us to be."

He sat down and tidied his papers.

12

All Thumbs

There was no fanfare when the authorities told Damien Nzabakira that he could go home. Judges in the military tribunal had cleared him of all charges, a guard told him. In the end they did not believe that a man would risk his life to drive forty children from Kigali to Butare only to murder them in cold blood. So while his accuser and her family appealed the verdict, Damien was free to return to his family.

There was no apology. No reparation. No return to his old job. No offers of employment. Instead, he emerged from the gates of the prison in the summer of 2003 with nothing more than a letter from the military court that said he was innocent. At first Damien didn't know what to do with himself. He had been in jail for nearly eight years and now, suddenly, he was free. In the beginning he spent long minutes in the morning trying to decide what to wear. One shirt would seem just right, only to have him change his mind and slip on a different one. Making the choice, and then changing his mind, pleased him.

His daughter, closing in on nine years old, was more of a problem. She hardly knew Damien. She demanded to know what this stranger was doing in their home. She had visited her father occasionally in prison, but that was there, and he was more remote. Now she saw him every day. The situation might have been frustrating, even tense, if Damien had not been practiced in the art of winning over reticent children. The Red Cross training he had received in the orphanage, the instructions to hold back and let the child come to you, helped him reconnect with his daughter. It took her months to accept that her father, a man she barely knew, had returned. It took just days for the child to decide on the merits that whoever this man was, she liked him. For the time being, that was enough.

The summer Damien returned from prison, more than nine years after the genocide, a new threat was surfacing. While the details were murky and the view slightly distorted, it was clear Rwanda faced a new enemy. The new menace was not the tall, thin, elegant Tutsi that had been scurrying into Rwanda under cover of darkness. Instead the new threats were smaller and stouter. They were the surviving members of the Hutu Power movement, the band of *génocidaires* who had slipped across the border into the Congo and who were lying in wait, intent on overthrowing the Tutsi government. These were the men who wanted to return Rwanda to the days before the genocide, to a time when the Hutu were in charge of the nation, the officials in Kigali warned. The nation needed to be vigilant. Rwandans had to view their neighbors through narrowed lids. They had to watch for signs of divisionism. The threat to the nation hadn't disappeared, it had merely found a new disguise. This evil force, the government hinted, looked remarkably like the Hutu.

It was to guard against this threat, to make sure that genocidal violence could never again erupt in Rwanda, that President Kagame said he sent Rwandan troops into the Congo. The nation was too fragile. The end of the genocide was too hard won to allow a small group of Hutu radicals to put Rwanda's future in peril. Laws needed to be passed, safeguards placed. Kagame felt it was his duty to ensure that genocide would never again return to Rwanda. His country's cycle of violence needed to end with him.

The discussion of a constitution, a document that unequivocally protected Rwandans from the shadowy divisionists in their midst, began in 2000. There was to-ing and fro-ing as a special committee cobbled together a series of bylaws, some would say commandments even, that would prevent ethnic violence from gaining a toehold in Rwanda. By the summer of 2003 they had forged the nation's first homegrown constitution and had put it to a referendum. For the first time since independence, Rwandans were given the opportunity to decide their own fates peacefully. All that was required was a thumbprint. With so much illiteracy in Rwanda the system had to be simple. Citizens needed only to press their inky thumbs in a box printed on a piece of paper as thin and translucent as a moth wing. There was only one question asked and its simplicity belied its importance: "Do you agree with the new constitution?" Below the question were two empty squares: one marked YES and the other labeled NO. Voters were to put their print inside the appropriate box.

Less than a decade after the genocide, Rwanda was still cautious by nature. The voting process had to be closely monitored. To ensure that every voice was heard, citizens were given time off work to register to vote. More than 4 million did. The government ordered shops shuttered on referendum day—May 26, 2003—to boost turnout.

While the American constitution is about what its citizens have every right to do (bear arms, freely assemble, speak their minds), the Rwandan version is more focused on what is not permitted. A twelve-member commission handpicked by President Kagame had come to the conclusion that while pluralism was a fine idea, Rwandans weren't ready for full democracy. As a result, the constitution was premised on a lack of trust—on the fundamental belief that Hutu-Tutsi relations left unchecked would only lead to more bloodshed. To ensure that genocide could never revisit the people of Rwanda, the founders of the constitution decided to bar any one ethnic group from gaining the upper hand. The constitution declared that no one party could hold more than half the seats in the cabinet. The president and the prime minister could not be from the same party. The word "party" was code, of course. It was a euphemism for ethnicity.

The constitution also laid the foundation for Rwanda's first ever multiparty elections. While it was unclear when elections would be called, the constitution did say that the winner would be permitted a seven-year term renewable only once. What the constitution didn't say, however, was whether that meant that if President Kagame were to emerge victorious in a presidential contest, the former Tutsi general could end up serving as head of state for seventeen years. Kagame said he had asked the committee to limit the presidential term to five years, but the parliament thought seven years was a better alternative, and who was the president to argue?

Outside Rwanda, human rights groups from the International Crisis Group to Human Rights Watch cried foul. The constitution was not laying out the tenets of a free society, they complained; instead it was entrenching the status quo. It was a blatant attempt to keep the minority Tutsi in power. Their protests fell on deaf ears. Rwandans demonstrated an obedience for which by now they were renowned. Eighty-seven percent of those registered showed up to cast a ballot. The referendum won by a landslide: 93 percent of those who inked their digits pressed the meat of their thumbs in support of the constitution.

* * *

From his self-imposed exile in Belgium, Faustin Twagiramungu was waiting for his moment. The former prime minister had been in Brussels since 1995, awaiting a time when he felt Rwanda was ready for real democracy and real reconciliation.

That time arrived, Twagiramungu decided, in the spring of 2003 when the Rwandan parliament announced that the nation would hold its first ever multiparty elections. The elections would be called in August, the parliament announced in May 2003. Twagiramungu had three months to mount a campaign.

If Twagiramungu had been an unknown, a man without a constituency in Rwanda, the mere idea of contesting Kagame in the election would have been folly. But in gross political terms Twagiramungu had nearly the same name recognition as the former general. Rwandans knew him as a moderate who had led the kinder, gentler wing of the Democratic Republican Movement, or MDR. Twagiramungu had been on the early Hutu Power hit lists precisely because he advocated sharing power with the Tutsi minority. But it wasn't Twagiramungu's political past that worried members of the current administration. What concerned them was the one thing that no one dared utter aloud: a Kagame-Twagiramungu contest for the presidency pitted a Tutsi candidate against a Hutu one. If Rwandans were to go to the polls and vote even marginally along ethnic lines, Twagiramungu would emerge as the next president of Rwanda.

The freshly minted constitution authorized a body called the Forum of Political Parties to serve as watchdog over the nation's political activities, and under the new laws of the land the group was able to take disciplinary measures against any politician or political party that "displays obsequiousness, plots against others, betrays one's country, or works in secret." Rights groups like Human Rights Watch worried aloud that the law as it was written could be used to justify all kinds of authoritarian acts.

It was out of concern that Twagiramungu's MDR party might stir up old resentments that parliament decided to act preemptively. The party was showing a tendency toward "divisionism," authorities warned. The MDR talked about Rwandans in terms of Hutu and Tutsi. The mere use of such ethnic distinctions was seen as potentially inflammatory. There was only one thing to do: protect the nation against such a scourge. The parliament decided to dissolve the MDR. An arm of the MDR, called MDR-Power, they helpfully reminded Rwandans, had supported the genocide. The fact that Twagiramungu led a moderate faction of the party and had been in the transitional government after the RPF took power in Kigali and restored peace was beside the point. Rwanda needed protecting. The battered nation was still fragile. The government could not countenance a return to such volatile language. Certainly no one wanted to risk reopening old wounds and resurrecting divisions between Hutu and Tutsi. The MDR, by a unanimous vote in parliament, was abolished in a matter of days. Human Rights Watch protested, saying that "by banning the MDR, which is the most credible contender against the RPF during the forthcoming presidential elections, the RPF is paving the way to ensure itself an easy victory." The RPF began referring to Human Rights Watch by a new name: Hutu Rights Watch.

Rwandans following the events on the radio secretly suspected the problem was not the MDR at all. The problem, more likely, could be laid at the feet of Twagiramungu. The mere suggestion that he would challenge Kagame in elections had precipitated the dissolution of the MDR. Kagame, Rwandans knew, had no intention of handing over the reins of power. The president would do whatever was necessary to win. Anyone who thought otherwise was naive. To oppose Kagame was to take on a powerful force. Those who dared defy him took their lives in their own hands.

Even months before the race began, there were rumors of mysterious disappearances. A short time after Twagiramungu announced his decision to challenge Kagame in the election, a key MDR deputy, Léonard Hitima, vanished. His car turned up near the Ugandan border. The Rwandan government suggested that he had defected to Uganda. Twagiramungu suspected foul play. Kagame drew a bead on Twagiramungu as well. "There are some people who are saying good things during the day and preaching divisive ideology during the night," Kagame warned, without naming names. "Soon we shall relieve them of their duties so that they can go away also."

In June, Kagame spoke before parliament about the upcoming presidential race. He vowed to "wound" all those who opposed him. Human Rights Watch, which had been monitoring the speech, sounded the alarm. Kagame's aides said that "wound" was just a turn of phrase. The president meant nothing sinister. Human Right Watch, it said, was overreacting.

* * *

Kagame's threat was not lost on Faustin Twagiramungu, the man who had to escape from the genocide under the cover of darkness. The problem with Rwanda, as he saw it, was no longer just the frisson the genocide sent through the hearts and minds of ordinary Rwandans, it was the heavy-handed rule of Kagame. "There is no peaceful climate in my country and I think I can do better," he said in early 2003. "What Kagame wants is a typical one-party system and he wants a kind of military dictatorship. There is a tendency to say in Africa people aren't ready for democracy, but that is a lie. I think people who say that are the so-called intellectuals who simply want to keep the population in a kind of political slavery."

Kagame's political forces responded by accusing Twagiramungu of seeking to return Rwanda to the dark days before the genocide. Twagiramungu was a divisionist, Kagame declared, and would not stop until the Hutu had returned to majority rule. The charges sounded familiar to anyone who followed Rwandan history. It was the mirror image of what Habyarimana had claimed were the Tutsi's intentions in the months before the 1994 genocide.

Some objected to Kagame's proclamations, but there was a curiously widespread and enduring fear caused by the genocide that tended to override common sense. In the end, no one was quite sure of the point at which a national preoccupation with domestic security crossed the invisible line dividing prudence and paranoia.

* * *

For Bonaventure Ubalijoro the coming election was just another in a string of unexpected and happy events. In particular, God had decided to show himself again to the aging diplomat. Ubalijoro had descended the stairs to the chapel one morning, as was his habit, and had sat on his favorite bench to begin his prayers when something caught his eye. The white curtains and cloth on the altar looked different. Spotted, or stained. He called his nurse and she helped him get up to take a look. In fact, the curtains and the cloth in the chapel were not stained at all. Instead the linens were festooned with hundreds of small crosses: light and gently imprinted, but there nonetheless. Everywhere he looked another peeked out to surprise him. He held his breath with delight, smiling with the discovery of each little mark. He began to lose count. Just how many there were hardly mattered. What was clear was that God had sent him another sign. Another miracle had taken place. It made Ubalijoro pray even harder.

* * *

The Rwandan government spokesman, Joseph Bideri, sat back in an oversized leather chair in his office in the Bureau of Information (ORINFOR) and began to discuss with a guest the rules of journalistic engagement ahead of the Rwandan elections. Bideri was sitting in the very same office where Ferdinand Nahimana had sat, as head of ORINFOR, ten years before. Bideri, a soft-spoken former wire service journalist who had worked in Europe and Canada, was in charge of ensuring that the press in Rwanda acted responsibly during this pivotal time. It was late summer 2003. Bideri had held journalism seminars in the run-up to the balloting in a bid to turn Rwanda's ragtag team of reporters into a professional force that faithfully reported the news. "We have only public broadcasting in this country," he began, "so we have to have rules and we have to follow them."

Those rules, in 2003, had not changed much from the regulations that RTLM was supposed to follow nearly a decade before. The Ministry of Information had established elaborate guidelines to ensure that all the presidential candidates got equal time. By law, each candidate was to get thirty minutes of prime time television coverage every week, he explained. Radio, still the information medium of the nation, would also be strictly apportioned. Each contender would get two hours a week of coverage on the airwaves. Newspapers, he continued, would be required to provide equal coverage on each of the candidates. "The idea," he said, "is to guard against the kind of biased coverage that we had in 1994. We can't let that sort of thing reemerge."

That evening Rwandan television provided some early election coverage. It was a seven-minute piece on a Kagame rally in Cyangugu, in the southern part of the country. The newscast ended before there was a chance to feature any of the other candidates.

* * *

Twagiramungu had expected a huge crowd to meet him at the airport when he touched down at Kigali International Airport in June 2003. Instead, he stepped off the plane to see a small knot of people, all of whom, he learned later, had heard about his arrival by word of mouth. The state-controlled media neglected to mention, much less cover, his return.

"It didn't even occur to me that the Rwandan media would ignore it," he said. "Imagine, a former PM, known as a moderate, a candidate for the office of the president, coming back after eight years—and nothing. I'm not a journalist, but that sure sounds like a story to me."

It took three more days, in fact, before Twagiramungu got any airtime at all. Rwandan television ran a two-minute humorous interview with the former prime minister. Observers could be forgiven if they neglected to notice that Twagiramungu was running at all. There were no "Twagiramungu for President" posters anywhere. Twagiramungu's campaign staff had put them up all over town, but the posters seemed to disappear almost as soon as they were posted. Rwanda was running, it became clear, a stripped-down, starter election. This was just a tentative attempt at a presidential campaign with an even more cautious contingent of journalists paddling in its wake.

Two months before the August 2003 elections, the U.S. State Department issued a warning. The Rwandan government's human rights record remained poor in part because of evidence that it was trying to intimidate voters and limit political opposition. The missive from America didn't affect Kagame's political game plan. Twagiramungu rallies were broken up. Attendance was discouraged by local leaders. Newspaper articles warned of Twagiramungu's sinister intentions. He would return Rwanda to a time of violence and strife, they said. Rwanda couldn't afford to fall back into its old patterns.

NOW TWAGIRAMUNGU CALLS FOR ETHNIC LOYALTY read the twenty-four-point front-page headline of the *New Times*, Rwanda's leading newspaper. "Presidential aspirant Faustin Twagiramungu launched his campaign at the weekend with a call for ethnic loyalty," the article began. "Twagiramungu told his supporters in Kigali to stick to their history. 'The history of Rwanda does not start with the RPF's ascent to power. National unity shouldn't rob you of what you are. Stick to your history.'"

The front page featured a photograph of Twagiramungu, Kagame, and two minor candidates who had also decided to join the race. Beneath the article about Twagiramungu's "call for ethnic loyalty" was another unsigned piece, with the headline TWAG'S TOP CAMPAIGN MANAGER DEFECTS TO RPF. A key aide to Twagiramungu, the article said, joined President Kagame's RPF party. "Damascène Ngirinshuti also rubbished Twagiramungu's campaign policies, adding that the former premier had nothing but ethnicity to offer Rwanda."

Twagiramungu thought he could offer reconciliation, but he never really got the chance.

* * *

In 2003 in Ruhango township, an hour outside of Kigali, the people began arriving in the early morning: a colorful late-summer procession made its way to the football field on the outskirts of town and gathered in the blazing sun on the dusty hillside to hear the first presidential stump speech of their lifetime. Those who arrived early were given Kagame presidential rally favors for their trouble: there were tricolored scarves, plastic RPF flags, and T-shirts with Kagame's likeness on the front. When the Kagame staffers had finished passing out the RPF paraphernalia, the landscape was dotted with the red-white-and-blue hues of Kagame's ruling party. Organizers had obviously spared no expense.

While assuredly this was a joyous event for Rwandans—the first democratic multiparty elections in forty-one years of independence—there was an uneasiness in the crowd as well. It could have been the armed soldiers who stood with their guns at the ready along the perimeter of the field. It could have been the RPF plainclothes police officials stationed in the crowd taking the temperature of the audience to ensure President Kagame would witness nothing less than unmitigated adulation when his campaign convoy arrived. Or more likely it was the feeling among those who had come that Kagame wasn't coming here to win them over so much as to ensure that they knew their responsibility was to give him the mandate he was seeking if they wanted Rwanda to avoid violence. This T-shirt-donning, flag-waving, air-punching event was, for the most part, just for show. There was no doubt about the outcome of the election. Though Twagiramungu and two other candidates were running, it was clear that Kagame would prevail. The only suspense was in finding out by how much.

Half an hour before the president's arrival, rally practice began. Kagame's campaign theme song, a Congolese tune entitled "We Shall Vote for Kagame," blasted from speakers set up around the pitch. The crowd exploded into the campaign's battle cry: "*Kagame! Oee! Oee! Oee!*" ("Kagame! Hurray! Hurray! Hurray!"). Each *oee* should be punctuated by punching the air, Kagame campaign workers told the crowd. They did several practice *oee*s until the crowd got the idea. Like a game show audience, they were cajoled into shouting louder, clapping more enthusiastically, dancing with abandon to the Kagame song.

"I am going to vote for Kagame because he has, most of all, brought us peace," said Mayunranda Iram, a farmer from Ruhango, with rote earnestness. "There is no other candidate for me." Others around him nodded in agreement.

Take some of these people aside, though, and they spoke out of the corners of their mouths and with furtive glances. There was widespread voter intimidation going on, they said. They didn't feel they had a choice but to vote for the president. One woman said her mother attended one of Kagame's earlier rallies and was reported to security when she failed to punch the air during the Kagame cheer. She was forced to explain that she wasn't subversive, she was just arthritic. That kind of harassment was commonplace, some in the crowd said.

When Kagame arrived before the carefully prepared crowd in Ruhango, he was riding in something that looked like the popemobile—an open-air car fitted with a guardrail he could use to keep his balance as the vehicle bounced along the field. He waved to the crowd, focusing on something in the middle distance. A woman pulled up the front of her "Vote Kagame" T-shirt and doubled it back so she could kiss the lips of the president's printed face on the front. The president gave her a benevolent wave. Kagame staffers jogged alongside the car, wearing identical black tennis shirts with the president's name stitched on the front. They wore matching black baseball caps. For a moment, the scene looked more like a campaign stop in rural America than a rally in East Africa.

Several campaign journalists from the state-run Radio Rwanda and Television Rwanda were also wearing the Kagame campaign uniform. The novelty of covering a presidential campaign had temporary trumped even the appearance of objectivity.

For presidential hopeful Twagiramungu, setting up for a rally just a town away, there was no bus, no popemobile, not even a van. With few campaign resources, he had taken to asking those who had cars to give him a ride to campaign venues. His first public rally attracted about a thousand people. He was surprised by the turnout.

In the end, this was a campaign about campaigning, not about political platforms. There were issues, but no one bothered to discuss them. There was no rallying cry to bring Rwanda up from its ranking of having the lowest per capita income in the world. No one mentioned taming rampant inflation. And when the revelers left, no one seemed to notice the thin, ribby, curly-tailed dogs digging in heaps of garbage outside the stadium. Twagiramungu's rally rated a quick mention on Radio Rwanda. Rwandan Television buried the story deep in the lineup of its evening newscast. A day later, a similar Kagame event in the northern city of Gisenyi led all the major newscasts on radio and television. State television ran a seven-minute-ten-second piece that provided little beyond the descriptions of ebullient crowds. When the station went to commercial, it happened to be a Kagame campaign piece. There was a montage of film clips of dancing crowds in "Vote Kagame" T-shirts. The music swelled and a chorus of African singers started chanting: "*Kagame Paul Tuzamutora*" ("Paul Kagame, we shall vote for him").

Given the track record of Rwanda's media and the ongoing proceedings in the media trial, the uncritical coverage of Kagame could not have surprised anyone. It wasn't hard to understand why free and unfettered access to candidates and aggressive campaign-style reporting were nonstarters. There was still a sullen, raw, postgenocide mood in Rwanda. Simmering below the surface was the fear that these elections could reopen the wounds of 1994. That concern went a long way toward encouraging self-censorship. The Rwandan press failed to mention, for example, that top opposition candidate Twagiramungu was a Hutu and Kagame was a Tutsi. "The election is an experiment," said a Kagame staffer. "This is supposed to help us build confidence that we can live together. So we have put in place a measured democracy."

And measured media coverage to go with it. Kagame won 98 percent of the vote. Twagiramungu returned to Belgium.

13

Tribunal in Chains

December 3, 2003

Rumors about the verdict in the media trial began to circulate early in the morning. Steve Rapp and Simone Monasebian were on the eighth floor of the conference center, in their offices, when the first whispers of a prosecution victory drifted down the corridor. The leaks always originated in the language section. Charged with translating the verdicts from English to French to Kinyarwanda, they were the first people, after the judges themselves, to learn how justice would be served. The media trial, by virtue of its duration and complexity, inspired more speculation than any other case at the tribunal. Everyone knew that it could set some sort of standard for freedom of the press, and they were curious to know how far-reaching it might be.

By the end of 2003 the case had garnered so much attention, the judges had purposely held the pages with the verdicts spelled out until the last minute, out of concern announcements would be made before the judges were ready. The translators in the language section were given the three-hundred-page judgment in such small bites they were forced, when the day's work was done, to pull together in their own minds a piecemeal impression of where Judge Pillay and her team were heading.

Steve Rapp had spent the previous evening pretending he wasn't preoccupied with the verdict. He was performing in a French play in two days' time and he had lines to learn. He tried to focus on that. Simone Monasebian had flown in from New York only the night before. Between jet lag and anticipation there was no hope of sleep. So she baked: eight chocolate cakes that would be served, win or lose, in the Prosecutor's Office after the judges revealed their ruling. The after-verdict party was an ICTR tradition, a way to cap a difficult task and to show, after the case was finished, there were no hard feelings between the defense and prosecuting attorneys.

The former head of prosecution at the ICTR, Carla Del Ponte, also appeared in Arusha in the days before the verdict. One official smiled at her in the elevator and remarked how fortunate it was that Del Ponte's trip coincided with the media trial conclusion. The prosecutor smiled. "I came for the media judgment."

Half an hour before the court was to convene, the public gallery was already full. The overflow crowd was sent to a conference room in another wing where the ruling would be simultaneously broadcast. When the media trial judges finally filed into the courtroom, two of the defendants—Nahimana and Ngeze—were already seated. Barayagwiza, after three years of boycotting his own trial, had refused to show up. Nahimana sat quietly. Hassan Ngeze, full of nervous energy, had brought along a small hand mirror, which he set up on his table. He had told the guards the mirror was necessary so that he could control his reaction to the verdict. He would not be looking at the judges, he told them; instead he would staring at his own face. He put the mirror so close, his breath fogged it.

By the time the media trial drew to a close, the International Criminal Tribunal for Rwanda had made considerable progress. It had taken fifty-three Rwandan *génocidaires* into custody and indicted twenty more. The genesis of the genocide was now understood. The former Rwandan prime minister Jean Kambanda admitted that the genocide had been planned in advance. He had been in charge of the administration of the genocide. He was responsible for doing away with those who didn't want to take part. He helped local officials organize citizens so the massacres would be more efficient. It was all planned years before the plane crash, he said. And, as expected, there had been a single goal: the extermination of the Tutsi.

Other precedents had been set. The mayor of Taba, Jean-Paul Akayesu, had become the first man ever charged with rape as a crime against humanity. For standing watch and encouraging Interahamwe to ravage Tutsi women, he was sentenced to three life sentences plus eighty years' imprisonment. He was transferred to a U.N.-sponsored prison in West Africa. Rwanda's minister for family and women's affairs, Pauline Nyiramasuhuko, incited Hutu to rape thousands of female Tutsi. She became the first woman ever to be put on trial for genocide. And now three media executives, Barayagwiza, Nahimana, and Ngeze, would hear whether they would be held responsible for abusing their power as journalists.

"It seems to us most probable that the idea of genocide emerged only gradually, possibly in late 1993, and accelerated in determination and urgency into 1994," Judge Pillay began, reading from the media trial summary judgment. After almost three years of testimony, the big dispute was not about the facts in the case, but rather over the analysis of what had been presented.

The tribunal had found that the Tutsi-led RPF invasions into Rwanda from Uganda were indeed a factor in precipitating the genocide. It was clear that the Habyarimana government immediately saw that the invasions would give them a rallying point, an opportunity to consolidate their power, which had been eroding in Rwanda for some time. By focusing on the RPF attacks, Habyarimana provided Rwandans with a distraction—and an excuse—for all that was not working in Rwanda in the early 1990s.

Up to this point, the Tutsi had not been singled out for abuse by the government in some seventeen years, Judge Pillay said. Now, as news of the invasion broke, it appeared that even many Tutsi were initially unsympathetic to the invaders. The government had a perfect opportunity to unite the country against the alien raiders, Pillay said. But the Habyarimana administration took a different route. They decided to vilify all Tutsi in a bid to get Hutu to rally behind the president. There was no single meeting, no dusty document discovered in a vault, that could be traced as the definitive first step in the genocide's master plan, she said. But the tribunal found that in looking back as the story unfolded through 1991 and 1992, there was a pattern the world community had missed. Radicals and military officials in Rwanda were working together, testing various killing techniques. Their experiments taught them two things: they could massacre large numbers of people quickly and efficiently and, based on early reactions both in Rwanda and abroad, they could get away with it. When there were massacres in Bugesera in 1992, the world community turned a blind eye.

All this was happening as a backdrop to the Habyarimana government's first faltering steps toward democracy she said, continuing to put the massacre in context. Political parties were flourishing and the state had relaxed its controls on the media. Habyarimana critics began to express themselves publicly. But liberty soon took a backseat to license when extremists began to take advantage, she said. Those who could read got a dose of anti-Tutsi rhetoric from *Kangura.* Those who could not had the hip radio station Radio Mille Collines. After three years of testimony, Pillay said, the tribunal had concluded that the station was a business proposition between like-minded friends. Instead it involved close relatives of the president, two cabinet ministers, and top militia leaders. And Ferdinand Nahimana, one of a new generation of Rwandan historians to emerge in the postcolonial period, was the driving force behind it. He had become a Hutu intellectual who used his skills for the cause of ethnic hatred, the court found. He used RTLM to promote the idea that there were accomplices everywhere. He made every Tutsi a suspect, the judges said, citing a May 1994 broadcast as an example.

"Let me congratulate thousands and thousands of young men I have seen this morning on the road in Kigali doing their military training to fight the Inkotanyi," that broadcast said. "At all costs, all Inkotanyi have to be exterminated, in all areas of our country. Some may say they are refugees, others act like patients, and others like sick-nurses. Watch them closely, because Inkotanyi tricks are so many."

If the Tutsi had been saying the same about the Hutu, the judges indicated, they might have rendered a different verdict. But speech that was "align[ed] with state power rather than in opposition to it" deserved less protection and warranted more restriction and scrutiny than press that questioned the government, they decided technically that meant journalists who opposed the government would be given more latitude, more freedom of expression, than those who didn't. The judges decided that in some cases press freedom could be relative. The judges also linked liability with the intent of the author. (It was just the kind of precedent American freedom-of-expression advocates were worried they would use.) They cited a 1996 decision, where the European court found an editor guilty of incitement for publishing an anti-semitic article cloaked as academic research. Nahimana's new history of the Hutu fell under similar restrictions, they said. The ICTR endorsed the state's right to restrict freedom of expression if it was necessary to respect the rights of others. The U.N. judges went further. They agreed that it was enough in some situations to decide that statements that do not meet the strict legal criteria of incitement but are part of some sort of pattern could be as "pernicious as explicit incitement, if not more so."

Article 19, a British organization that promotes free expression, had studied RTLM and decided that the genocide would probably have occurred with or without the station, Pillay continued. Article 19 had concluded that banning it would have had little impact on the way the events unfolded in Rwanda. "RTLM was an instrument, not the cause, of genocide," they concluded. "[It] did not provoke the genocide, but rather was one element in a premeditated plan for mass slaughter. . . . [It] played the specific role of conveying orders to militias and other groups already involved in the slaughter."

The court, Judge Pillay said, agreed. The genocide would have occurred whether or not RTLM had existed. At the same time, she said, speaking for the panel of three judges, the station's significance could not be minimized. "Without a doubt, it played a prominent role in keeping passions at a fever pitch during the final months before the genocide. It significantly raised the bar of permissible hatemongering. Under any sensible criminal code, RTLM would have been silenced soon after it went on the air." Similarly, the judges found, the *Kangura* offices should have been shuttered as soon as Ngeze decided to publish the Ten Commandments of the Hutu, years before the genocide even began.

The commandments had one purpose: they were meant to incite divisiveness and resentment. They specified that any Hutu who married or was involved with Tutsi women or who did business with any Tutsi at all was a traitor. They insisted on the need to maintain Hutu purity and to avoid contamination from the Tutsi. It was the kind of propaganda that white racists had commonly and effectively used in the American South and in South Africa.

It was established without a doubt that a systematic attack against the Tutsi population started soon after President Habyarimana's plane was shot down on April 6, 1994, Pillay continued. It was also accepted that the attack had taken place in the context of a war between the RPF and the Rwandan government that began when the RPF attacked Rwanda from Uganda in 1990. What was in question was how much of a role Barayagwiza, Nahimana, and Ngeze played in the events that followed.

RTLM started endearing itself to the people of Rwanda by

about the content in *Kangura*, about articles that said Tutsi never liked sharing power with the Hutu in peace because of their boasting nature and there determination to reestablish their monarchy, he said it wasn't incitement, it was reality. In Rwanda, he had said, a Tutsi was often described as a snake because he was malicious. The Hutu were referred to as gorillas, and the Hutu were said to be dirty. Ngeze had said that that was the reality of Rwandan society. It may have been unseemly, but that was the way it was. The lists of Tutsi collaborators that he published, he said, were the normal course of business when a country was at war. The RPF was recruiting people inside Rwanda, and Ngeze said he was merely uncovering that. Ngeze claimed that he was doing what he could to stop the war, the judges said.

He was trying to put information out so the public could lecide whether to go to war or stop the violence in its tracks. Ngeze said the articles he published, including the one that prelicted Habyarimana's assassination before it occurred, were varnings, Judge Pillay said. The court thought they were a threat. Ngeze equated the RPF with the Tutsi population, and that ıelped lead to the death of countless innocent civilians, she said.

Though *Kangura* did not publish during the genocide, the nessage it sent during the first three months of 1994 was tantanount to incitement. The witness code-named AHA had said ıat the truth or a quest for truth was not of concern to Ngeze. 'he judges agreed, Pillay said. The ethnic hatred that permeated *Kangura* had the effect of poison. At times *Kangura* called xplicitly on its readers to take action. More generally, its message f prejudice and fear paved the way for massacres of the Tutsi opulation, the court ruled.

If someone had been looking over Hassan Ngeze's shoulder at ıat moment, they would have seen that he took a deep, frighted breath, and then, when he exhaled, the mirror before him ıddenly fogged.

Jean-Bosco Barayagwiza, once a prominent lawyer in Rwanda,

playing music, three weeks of nonstop Congolese tu teners were wooed, RTLM began presenting oth cluding the idea that the Tutsi constituted dange majority. And according to one witness, the peopl message like dogs.

Many of the individuals specifically named in casts were subsequently killed, the court said. A extent of causation by RTLM broadcasts in thes have varied somewhat, depending on the circun killings, the judges ruled that there was a caus "The chamber finds that RTLM broadcasts eng stereotyping in a manner that promoted contemp the Tutsi population," the judges said.

RTLM broadcasts called on listeners to seek c arms against the enemy. The enemy was identi and their accomplices, all of whom were effectiv the Tutsi ethnic group by the broadcasts. RT exploited the history of Tutsi privilege and Hu and the fear of war, to whip Rwandans into a fren violence. The Interahamwe and other militias li and acted on the information that was broadcast encouraged them to kill, relentlessly sending the Tutsi were the enemy and had to be eliminated Judge Pillay concluded. That was tantamount t

It was clear that the radio station, had it bee would have been found guilty.

Nahimana looked stricken. The question no would be found guilty of having been respon outbursts. Judge Pillay, by this time, had been r of the judgment for fifteen minutes. The de defendants already knew, was not tending in th

* * *

Pillay's voice became even more somber as actions of the defendants themselves. When had never denied that he was one of the founders of RTLM or a ranking member of the extremist CDR party. Instead, Barayagwiza had opted for defiance. He spent three years in jail refusing to participate in what he saw as a kangaroo court doing the bidding of the Tutsi-led Kagame government. He had already convinced himself that he would be found guilty. He saw, therefore, little reason to attend the proceedings. Judge Pillay was forced to address an empty chair.

The chamber found that Jean-Bosco Barayagwiza was one of the principal founders of the CDR and made decisions in the party, she said. As to his involvement with RTLM, the judges said he was equally pivotal. Nahimana had been referred to as RTLM's top man and Barayagwiza was number two, the judgment continued. The duo were the real ideologists of RTLM, and, they concluded, Nahimana was the "brain behind the operation."

When called into the Ministry of Information to explain RTLM's incendiary broadcasts, Nahimana and Barayagwiza defended RTLM's programming. The two men had the ultimate responsibility for RTLM, the judges said. When the French government complained to Nahimana about broadcasts blasting the commander in Rwanda, General Roméo Dallaire, that had an effect; a short time later, the targeting of Dallaire over the airwaves stopped. It was a telling example of how much control over RTLM Nahimana actually possessed after the genocide began, Judge Pillay said.

Nahimana claimed RTLM was hijacked and that he did not have de facto authority to stop the broadcasts after the genocide began. The Dallaire incident suggested otherwise. "This evidence suggests that Nahimana had de facto authority to stop transmission but he did not exercise it other than once. Barayagwiza was in a similar position, but there is no evidence that he ever intervened in an effort to stop RTLM."

The chamber agreed with the defense that the downing of Habyarimana's plane was the trigger for the genocide. But if the plane crash was the trigger, Pillay said slowly, then RTLM, *Kan-*

gura, and the CDR were the bullets in the gun. "The trigger had such a deadly impact because the gun was loaded," she said.

The tribunal had weighed the evidence and believed beyond a shadow of doubt that Ferdinand Nahimana, Jean-Bosco Barayagwiza, and Hassan Ngeze loaded that gun. "They acted with intent to destroy, in whole or in part, the Tutsi ethnic group," Judge Pillay said, summing up the conclusions of the three-judge panel. Barayagwiza and Nahimana represented the radio at the highest level during meetings with the Ministry of Information; they controlled the finances of the company; and they were both members of the steering committee that functioned as the station's board of directors. While the two men didn't necessarily make decisions about each particular broadcast of RTLM, they were responsible for Radio Mille Collines's message, and by extension, the two men were guilty of genocide, incitement, and crimes against humanity.

Similarly, she concluded, the chamber also found Hassan Ngeze—as founder, owner, and editor of *Kangura*, a publication that advocated the killing of Tutsi civilians, guilty of genocide, incitement, and crimes against humanity.

The judges had revisited the Nuremberg trial of Julius Streicher when they assessed the criminal accountability for direct and public incitement. The Nuremberg judgment didn't find any direct causal link between Streicher's publication and specific murders. Rather, the military judges decided that Streicher's views in *Der Stürmer* worked like a poison injected into the minds of thousands of Germans, which caused them to follow the policy of Jewish persecution and extermination.

The Nuremberg judges did not think that Streicher was in Hitler's inner circle, or even fundamental to the formulation of his anti-Semitic policies, but he was convicted nevertheless of crimes against humanity. Forty-five years later, Barayagwiza, Nahimana, and Ngeze were found guilty of incitement to genocide and crimes against humanity by application of the same standard.

"This case raises important principles concerning the role of the media, which have not been addressed at the level of international criminal justice since Nuremberg," Judge Pillay continued. "The power of the media to create and destroy fundamental human values comes with great responsibility. Those who control such media are accountable for its consequences." Nahimana slumped in his chair. Pillay asked him to stand up.

"You were fully aware of the power of words," Judge Pillay said. "You used the radio—the medium of communication with the widest public reach—to disseminate hatred and violence. You may have been motivated by your sense of patriotism and the need you perceived for equality for the Hutu population in Rwanda. But instead of following legitimate avenues of recourse, you chose a path of genocide. Without a firearm, machete, or any physical weapon, you caused the deaths of thousands of innocent civilians." Though witnesses had attested to Nahimana's good character, she continued, the court didn't find that testimony to be mitigating. Instead they showed how much of the public trust Nahimana had betrayed. "The chamber sentences you in respect of all the counts on which you have been convicted to imprisonment for the remainder of your life."

Hassan Ngeze's gaze had hardly wavered from the small mirror in front of him. Judge Pillay asked him to rise. "Hassan Ngeze, as the owner and editor of a well-known newspaper in Rwanda, you were in a position to inform the public and shape public opinion toward achieving democracy and peace for all Rwandans," Judge Pillay said. "You have significant media networking skills and attracted support earlier in your career from international human rights organizations who perceived your commitment to freedom of expression. You did not respect the responsibility that comes with freedom. You abused the trust of the public by using your newspaper to instigate genocide. The chamber notes that you saved Tutsi civilians from death by transporting them across the border out of Rwanda. Your power to save was more than matched by your power to kill. You poisoned the minds of your readers, and by words and deeds caused the death of thousands of innocent civilians." He, too, was sentenced to life imprisonment.

Barayagwiza was not there to stand before the three judges for sentencing, but Judge Pillay read a statement about him for the record. "Jean-Bosco Barayagwiza is a lawyer by training and his book, *Hutu Blood, Is It Red?* processes a commitment to international human rights standards. Yet he deviated from these standards and violated the most fundamental human right, the right to life. He was the lynchpin of the conspiracy, collaborating closely with both Nahimana and Ngeze." For his role in the events, the judge said, the chamber had wanted to sentence him to life in prison. But because his rights had been violated early in the trial with a slow indictment, his sentence would be reduced. With credit for time served, Barayagwiza's sentence was reduced to twenty-seven years. For a man nearing sixty years of age, it was, essentially, a life sentence.

* * *

Defense attorneys Jean-Marie Biju-Duval and John Floyd issued a press release after sentencing. The judges, in order to establish the facts, "began by rejecting the testimonies of direct witnesses," Biju-Duval said. The tribunal did not find the Belgian Georges Ruggiu's testimony to be credible, even though he was one of the few people who testified who had actually seen events unfold at the radio station. Judges simply rejected Nahimana's version of events. They ruled that Nahimana was "responsible for the RTLM's editorial line" when there was no proof. They said he "did nothing to stop the radio from becoming a machine for war and genocide" but he wasn't even in the country when that happened. Ferdinand Nahimana never exercised any management responsibilities, never expressed any opinion in 1994, and cut all ties with the station at the very beginning of the massacres, before its broadcasts became criminal, Biju-Duval declared.

No act, no word, no speech linked Ferdinand Nahimana directly and personally to the genocide and crimes against humanity committed in Rwanda during the months of April through July 1994, and yet he was convicted of conspiracy to genocide. Nahimana was convicted "so that 'radio genocide' ends up with a criminal made to measure," Diju-Buval said.

John Floyd was no less hyperbolic. He said the judgment was "the worst decision ever in terms of international justice. I have never seen any thing like this in my thirty years of practice," he said. Both he and Biju-Duval intended to appeal.

Barayagwiza declared in a press statement that he had been "judged and condemned by a tribunal in chains." He continued that "it has become evident that its objective is not to judge those responsible for crimes, regardless of their ethnic group, but to hunt Hutu leaders, pretend to judge them, and condemn them to such heavy sentences that they would forever be excluded from power."

Hassan Ngeze sent a note to his friends and copied Simone Monasebian. With this verdict, he said, he no longer believed in God.

* * *

Initially, the international community applauded the verdict. Some groups, like the Committee to Protect Journalists, immediately distanced the media trio from real working journalists. The legal precedent set, the group said, applied to a radio station that had essentially become a form of military communication. This wasn't about freedom of the press. Others chimed in. University of Michigan law professor Catharine MacKinnon said the conceptual breakthrough in the media case was "its understanding that the media itself committed genocide through instigating it, holding media leaders accountable accordingly."

The verdict represented a clear warning to journalists and broadcasters that they risk prosecution. It would provide a starting point for modern international law, analysts said, because the International Criminal Court would take its cues from the Rwanda tribunal's work. The ICC would build on this verdict and use the criteria the three judges laid out to create a uniform legal definition of incitement to genocide, and set a standard for press freedom.

It took months before the pundits realized what the media trial verdict had wrought. As they read through the more-than-350-page judgment it became clear to them that the judges at the ICTR had massaged and stretched the definition of incitement. The highlights from the RTLM broadcasts that had been sent around the world were so extreme they clearly would not have been protected speech. They would have been considered beyond the pale even in America, with its broad First Amendment protections. What the analysts failed to see initially was how a set of bad facts on the ground in Rwanda had made for bad law. The tribunal had put limits on the press that had the potential to send a frisson through freedom of expression the world over.

The judges had cited precedents from European law in which journalists were prosecuted for hate speech and incitement. The ICTR judges said that countries had the right to limit expression if they were protecting national security and public order. That was a broad definition. Legal scholars worried that it would open the door to criminalizing the telling of the truth if it had the potential to incite. The Pentagon had asked CBS News not to air the photographs of abused prisoners in Baghdad's Abu Ghraib prison out of concern that they would create a violent backlash against American soldiers stationed in Iraq. The CBS newsmagazine *60 Minutes* did anyway. Could producer Don Hewitt have been prosecuted for incitement after mobs gathered in Iraq when the pictures were broadcast?

The way the judgment had been written, the news reports about Abu Ghraib didn't even need to be directly linked to the violence in Iraq. The very thing that had worried American advocates of freedom of expression had come to pass: the media trial verdict had set a very broad standard for what could be considered incitement.

The judges relied on cases from Canada and Europe, where hate speech and incitement to discrimination were against the law. And they went further. They cited a Chinese law that prohibited broadcasts that "incite hatred on account of color, race, sex, religion, nationality, or ethnic or national origin." They pointed to Vietnamese law; it prohibited the "sowing of enmity."

The judges cited the German Gunther Deckert case, in which a defendant was convicted of incitement for hosting a speech by a man who denied the gas chambers of Auschwitz had ever existed. John Floyd warned, when he took Ngeze's case nearly three years earlier, that the tribunal was playing with fire. An overly broad interpretation of the facts would allow repressive countries to use hate speech laws to suppress legitimate dissent. The way the judgment was written, Floyd said, American rap artists could be guilty of using "insulting material likely to stir up hatred" and could be tried for incitement in an international court. First Amendment legal scholars, once they understood what had happened, offered to write amicus briefs for the appeal.

14

The Aftermath

April 2004

On a hillside overlooking downtown Kigali a swarm of Rwandans worked feverishly to finish the Kigali Memorial Center before April 7, 2004, when foreign dignitaries of every stripe and variety would arrive in Rwanda to mark the tenth anniversary of the 1994 genocide. Workers were hurriedly planting grass, setting brick, and shoveling gravel onto the long drive that led to the memorial complex.

It was a massive project and had been rushed to completion because the $1.5 million needed to build the memorial had been slow in coming. In 2002, former President Clinton had returned to Rwanda. This time he traveled beyond the airport and was greeted by cheering crowds. Rwandans lined the roadways twenty-deep just to catch a glimpse of the forty-second American president. Clinton went to lay a wreath at the half-completed Kigali Memorial Center, and when he found out that the government didn't have money to finish the building, he wrote a personal check. Eventually the William J. Clinton Foundation and the Swedish and Belgian governments provided the funding for the building. The checks arrived in late December 2003. That gave the British charity Aegis Trust precious little time to build mass grave sites and gardens and to design an exhibit that would be a testament to the tragedy that had rocked Rwanda.

The Kigali Memorial Center is housed in an enormous pale yellow stucco building that looks more like a southern California mansion than a genocide memorial in the heart of Africa. And just as the center does not look the least bit African, neither does the exhibit that it houses. That is not so surprising given that the Rwandans had farmed out the project. While the exhibit's displays read as if a Rwandan wrote them, in fact the entire enterprise was imported. The words, the displays, the pictures were all produced in Britain. There was something faintly unsettling about watching Rwandan workers unpack a genocide memorial conceived by people who weren't even in Africa when the killing happened.

The retelling of the genocide, to anyone who had studied the issue, was decidedly a Tutsi version of the events (Kagame's figures for the death toll were always over a million killed; most international aid groups and the U.N. put the figure at closer to eight hundred thousand) and a little hyperbolic.

"Every minute of the day, someone, somewhere was being murdered, screaming for mercy," one exhibit panel read, "receiving none. And the killing went on and on and on . . . 10,000 each day; 400 each hour, 7 each minute. The genocide resulted in the deaths of over a million people. But death was not its only outcome. . . . The *génocidaires* had been more successful in their evil aims than anyone would have dared believe. Rwanda was dead."

There was only one small room in the entire exhibit that focused on the Hutu. The builders of the memorial had singled out five Hutu who risked their lives to save the Tutsi among them. One of the Hutu featured was a Gitarama woman named Sula who protected seventeen Tutsi during the genocide. She was a traditional healer, some said a witch, and she used her reputation to her advantage, the exhibit said. She threatened to put a curse on any Interahamwe who dared harm those she was sheltering. Frightened, the Interahamwe retreated, machetes at their sides. Another man dug a trench in his yard in anticipation of having to hide from the RPF. Instead he used the gully to hide Tutsi. He put planks on top, then green banana leaves, and then piled earth on top of that. He even planted sweet potatoes on top. The Tutsi he had secreted beneath were never discovered. As good as these stories were, though, one could understand why the Hutu majority had bristled at the exhibit. The entirety of their positive contribution during the genocide was summed up in stories that could be counted on one hand.

The short shrift in the exhibit was a telling example of a larger problem in postgenocide Rwanda. The Hutu majority felt systematically disenfranchised. By 2004, most of those who held the key positions in the government were Tutsi. The good jobs, Hutu muttered, were all held by the Tutsi as well. Walk into any tourism office or air-conditioned bureau and the odds were high that the people behind the desks would be Tutsi. Never mind that they were less than 15 percent of the population. Somehow they had managed to secure the most favored positions in both the public and the private sectors. It was, in many ways, exactly as the Hutu Power leaders had predicted. If the Tutsi were given an opportunity to rule, the Hutu would be relegated to a second-class citizenship. While there was little question that RTLM and *Kangura* had crossed the line with their fiery rhetoric in the months leading up to the genocide, their predictions about Tutsi domination over the Hutu had been realized. Bubbling beneath the surface was a deep Hutu resentment for the Tutsi's heavy-handed favoritism for their own. "This isn't over," one Hutu university student said, summing up the feelings of countless others. "There will be another genocide. Maybe not as bad as the killing in 1994, but there will be another. The majority people won't let this stand."

For the creators of the Kigali memorial, this resentment didn't come as a surprise. "None of this is easy," said one of the founders of Aegis Trust, James Smith. "Imagine telling people in New York who lost loved ones in 9/11 that they would have to be living next to the people who caused that tragedy and would just have to find a way to get along."

In one room there was a series of shelves where family members could put portraits of victims for all to see. "It is not going to be complete," said Mr. Smith. "We're going to leave a space blank so people can leave their photographs after the tenth anniversary. You can pick them up, feel them, and it is going to make it very intimate."

Mr. Smith likened the room to the impromptu 9/11 memorials that went up all over New York as people searched for loved ones they hoped would still be alive. "It is their way of participating. It is their own memorial," Mr. Smith said. "And for the international visitors who come here it will help to change the perception of this being a tribal war, a tribal conflict somewhere in the middle of Africa. Here are people who are no different to anybody else."

Outside the exhibit, the sidewalk opened out onto the hillside and eight mass grave sites. They were not the tangle of bodies one usually associated with mass graves. Instead, these were neat, sanitized concrete crypts—eight feet deep, each filled floor to ceiling with coffins that held the unidentified remains of fifty Rwandans found in shallow makeshift graves throughout the capital city after the genocide.

Only six of the crypts were full and sealed. The two others were awaiting the arrival of more remains. One worker named Paul helpfully suggested that they would find enough bodies around Kigali to fill all the empty spaces. When asked if he thought this memorial would help Rwandans put the genocide behind them, he shook his head. "This isn't for us," he said. "This is for the foreigners."

The memorial for Rwandans is half a country away, in northwestern Rwanda, in Nyamyumba commune. It was there, in what was once a hotbed of Hutu rebel activity, that the Kagame government decided to erect a memorial in 1998. Kagame had sent his minister of internal affairs to unveil the monument—a great eruption of concrete block with a hand holding a machete aloft seemingly glued on top. It was meant to signify Rwanda's impending reconciliation.

The minister was one of a handful of Hutu members of the Kagame government and he told an assembled audience of villagers that the memorial showed how much Hutu and Tutsi had in common. "Do Hutu speak a different language?" he asked. "Do they worship a different God? Do Tutsi and Hutu marry and live side by side?" The crowd had heard all this before. Years later they still see the memorial, the arm with the machete at the top of the hill, as an affront, not a symbol of reconciliation.

A day after the minister departed, the memorial was defaced. The concrete machete blade had been knocked out of the sculpture, leaving just a raised fist. By 2002, the government had replaced the blade on the sculpture four times. "As soon as they repair the monument someone knocks out the machete blade again," a villager said. "It is still too sensitive."

* * *

While projects like the memorial and institutions like the International Criminal Tribunal for Rwanda were meant to help the Rwandan people compose a single narrative, a true accounting of what took place in 1994, there were still disagreements over the details.

There was no argument that the event that launched the killing was the downing of President Juvénal Habyarimana's plane, but who was actually responsible was still in dispute. The Kagame government said Hutu extremists had taken out one of their own as part of a political coup. Weeks before the tenth anniversary of the genocide, the French government revealed that it had evidence that laid the assassination at the feet of Paul Kagame.

In March 2004, the French newspaper *Le Monde* reported that a French magistrate investigating the death of Habyarimana had concluded that Kagame, as one of the leaders of the RPF, had given the direct order to fire two rockets at the plane in April 1994. Kagame denied the allegations, saying that the "RPF and myself have nothing to do with this. That information has no credibility."

Placing blame for the assassination that sparked the genocide had become a perennial event. But this time, the accusations came from a stronger source. Jean-Louis Bruguière, a judge in the National Anti-terrorism Division in Paris, had been investigating the plane crash since 1998. He said it was in his jurisdiction because the pilot of the plane had been a Frenchman.

For some time it had been rumored that the United Nations had a document proving the RPF was behind the attack. The ICTR tried to have the information released publicly in June 2000, to no avail. Bruguière's report was said to have come through interviews with several former members of the RPF whom he now described as "dissidents." The judge also claimed to have deposed a member of the commando unit sent to carry out the attack. Bruguière's informants said that Kagame was aware the assassination could spark a genocide but he was willing to "sacrifice" the Tutsi population in some areas to take power in Kigali.

Kagame administration officials ridiculed the French investigation. Bruguière had not even set foot in Rwanda, and his report, a government spokesman said, was just rehashing old information. "It brings no new element, no new proof to back up the allegations," the spokesman said.

Even to those who disliked Kagame, the thought that he would knowingly spark a genocide seemed a little far-fetched. The problem was that a convincing argument could be made for either a Kagame-inspired assassination attempt or a Hutu Power movement offensive. The RPF had been looking for an occasion to take the reins in Kigali, and the assassination of the president would have provided just such an opportunity. The Hutu Power movement was aggrieved because Habyarimana had signed the Arusha Accords. Too many people had a good reason to want to see President Habyarimana's plane go down.

In April 1994, just as the French were making their allegations, the Canadian former leader of the U.N. peacekeeping forces in Rwanda in April 1994, General Roméo Dallaire, released his own analysis. He said the evidence seemed to support the case that Hutu extremists downed the plane. He said that the junta ordered the presidential guard to seal off the crash site. They wouldn't permit an independent inspection of the wreckage. Dallaire said that several senior members of the junta smirked when they were told that some of debris from the plane had landed in Habyarimana's own garden.

* * *

Months after he was released from prison, Damien Nzabakira got an unusual phone call. A lawyer from the International Criminal Tribunal for Rwanda wanted him to testify. A military trial was getting under way that sought to hold the soldiers behind the Butare massacre accountable for the killing. Damien, they had heard, had been a witness to the events. Would he be willing to talk to investigators about what he had seen? They knew he had been on trial for participating in the episode, the lawyer continued. But they knew, too, that he had been completely exonerated. Damien couldn't help but laugh at the irony. Of course he'd be happy to testify, he said.

* * *

On February 29, 2004, just weeks shy of the tenth anniversary of the genocide, President Kagame announced a limited amnesty for the nation's prisoners. Some forty thousand Hutu awaiting trial behind bars—the old and the sick, those accused of lesser crimes—were released. They were sent to reeducation camps and then back to their villages to try to assimilate. *Gacaca*'s traditional justice, after several years of experimentation, still had procedural shortcomings. The accused did not have lawyers. Some witnesses seemed, ten years after the genocide, more intent on settling long-held grudges than in finding the truth. There were rumors of murders, people who disappeared before they had a chance to testify. Many of the judges were illiterate. And President Kagame's political control was still ever-present: *gacaca* courts were still not allowed to discuss crimes Tutsi might have committed during the genocide. Hutu citizens saw this as patently unfair.

While the *gacaca* were not perfect, they did clear out some of the backlog of prisoners in the system. There were still sixty thousand Rwandans behind bars in 2004, but the Kigali government had managed to cut the inmate population in half. The government had installed a counseling system for women rearing children of the genocide, *enfants de mauvais souvenirs*. Programs began to help them cope not only with the trauma of rape but with the daily reminder, in the form of a child, that the sexual violence had taken place. AIDS was still a problem, but the government had installed a system to distribute antiviral drugs. While there were complaints aplenty about who got which drugs, organizations were at least seeking to address the problem and to help the mothers still struggling with the aftermath of genocide.

The national assembly had written a constitution and the people of Rwanda had ratified it. And while it seemed as much a document to keep the Tutsi in power as it was a safeguard for individual Rwandans, it was a start. Similarly, the government had passed a media law. It looked strikingly similar to the regulations that had allowed RTLM and *Kangura* to incite Rwandans to kill, but officials in the Ministry of Information said they were more alert now. They were better prepared in 2004, they said, to leap on any outlet that might wield the media as a weapon of war. The government had the power to effectively bar any discussion of ethnicity. Just as Twagiramungu had been labeled a divisionist during the elections, branded with what had become Rwanda's scarlet letter, journalists too had to dodge that epithet. Those who wrote or spoke about divisions between Hutu and Tutsi could go to jail, or worse. Rwanda's police were the arbiters of good and bad journalism. If they felt some articles could harm the country, they were permitted to act. It was an issue, they said, of internal security.

One couldn't help wondering how long it would take before fear would once again be officially authorized. One could almost hear the Kagame government warning of Hutu Power members amassing at the border, raising anxiety among an audience of radio listeners. They would hint of possible catastrophe. Certainly all this concern about internal security meant that they thought that death and devastation could happen again.

Robert Subufirira, managing editor of *Umuseso*, Rwanda's largest weekly newspaper, learned that firsthand. He went into exile in Tanzania in March 2004 after tangling on various occasions with Rwanda's media police. He had, the authorities said, crossed the line when his newspaper began investigating corruption in the Kagame government. He was jailed twice for criticizing the government and for publishing a political cartoon that showed President Kagame proclaiming that only he, as a Tutsi, was fit to lead the government. The cartoon, the government said, was divisionist. After two years of enduring government pressure, Subufirira left Rwanda and sought asylum in Tanzania. There could be newspapers in Rwanda apparently, but the Kagame government didn't want them to talk about the nation's most pressing issues. The Kagame administration seemed to have decided that ethnicity in Rwanda would go away if people would just stop talking about it.

For some, the introduction in February 2004 of a new radio station, Radio 10, was an indication of the nation's progress. Eugène Nyagahene, a Tutsi, was the man behind Radio 10. A successful businessman from Burundi, he had managed to become a media mogul of sorts in the neighboring nation, beaming radio broadcasts and television channels to a population of East Africans hungry for information. Nyagahene had known key members of the Kagame government when they were struggling against the Habyarimana government in the 1980s, Kagame officials said, and he understood that launching Radio 10 in Rwanda had to be a carefully managed enterprise. The media had such a checkered past in Rwanda that anything that came over the airwaves or was printed in the papers was immediately suspect. That's why Nyagahene went on the air with a promise that Radio 10 would not repeat the mistakes of RTLM.

Radio 10's business plan, to begin, was modest. It would broadcast in French, English, and Kinyarwanda, and initially it would broadcast only to Kigali and some other major towns, just as RTLM had done. The plan was to gradually expand Radio 10's reach to the rest of Rwanda. The Kagame government was quick to add that the new radio station would be monitored to prevent any incitement of ethnic hatred.

"We're here to inform, entertain, and educate the people of Rwanda," the station's communications director, Chantal Zingiro, said in early 2004. This was Zingiro's first foray into Rwanda. A Tutsi reared in Paris, she spoke beautiful French and no Kinyarwanda. As she walked through the broadcast booths of Radio 10 she said she knew little about the details that surrounded RTLM. "I've bought some books about RTLM and I certainly know what it did in 1994. But I haven't read all about it yet."

Zingiro said Radio 10 was eager to offer Rwandans something beyond the fare provided on the government's Radio Rwanda. Instead of replays of long-winded speeches by government officials, Radio 10 listeners would be treated to Congolese music and call-in shows. The station had four staff journalists, and the rest of the contributors were freelancers. They didn't need to be journalists necessarily, she said, just willing to learn. Radio 10 would train them. "We want to bring new voices to the radio," she said. "Voices that smile."

That was only the beginning. Radio 10 wanted to give Rwandans a chance to express themselves. Unhappy about petrol prices? Call it in to Radio 10. Questions about AIDS? A phone call to the radio station would clarify. Zingiro predicted that Rwandans would relish this kind of interaction. Rwandan radio would finally come of age. For the first three weeks it was on the air, the station played nothing but music twenty-four hours a day. The ploy worked. Droves of Rwandans tuned in.

"Someone told me that RTLM started the same way," she said.

Epilogue

On June 30, 2004, the Rwandan parliament took a more tangible step against those enemies lurking in the shadows. It embraced the findings of a special commission charged with rooting out those who were spreading a "genocide ideology" in Rwanda. No one, it appeared, was above suspicion. The Catholic Church, schools, national and international nongovernmental organizations were all named as part of a vast conspiracy secretly supporting genocide or disseminating its principle tenets. Amnesty International said the vote was reminiscent of the attacks against Twagiramungu and the MDR during the national elections. It appeared that the Kagame government was wielding the concept of genocide as a weapon to silence its critics. Those found guilty of harboring a "genocide ideology" could, among other things, be sentenced to death.

"If these measures are enforced by the government, the loss to civil society, already under sustained attack from the Rwandese authorities, cannot be underestimated," Amnesty International said at the time.

Bonaventure Ubalijoro's name appeared on a new government list in the summer of 2004. "During the presidential elections campaign Major [Félicien] Ngirabatware and Mr. Ubalijoro went around the area of Bugesera preaching divisionism," the short sentence about the former diplomat read. Parliament leveled the accusations, failing to mention that Major Ngirabatware, Ubalijoro's coconspirator, was in jail. Ubalijoro, in August 2003, could not walk without a nurse's help and could barely speak. Ever the optimist, Ubalijoro said he wasn't worried by the latest salvo. The Lord would see him through, he said, and those who lie will face the wrath of God.

At the ICTR, by June 2004, twenty-one *génocidaires* had been tried—eighteen convicted and three acquitted—and another forty-three Rwandans were either on trial or in detention and a handful were indicted but still at large. The media trio had appealed their sentences, though the law of averages was working against them. While particular counts and charges had been reversed on appeal, nobody had ever been released or fully acquitted. By July 2004, the ICTR was still working to translate the judgment into French before it could be sent to the appeals chamber in The Hague.

* * *

JEAN-BOSCO BARAYAGWIZA couldn't have held out much hope for a victory in the appeals process, even though some legal analysts said there were grounds for overturning the verdict. Though he was one of the three stars in the media trial, the prosecution proved only that he was the leader of the extremist CDR party and that he helped found RTLM. He was found guilty of crimes against humanity and, among other things, incitement to genocide in connection with the radio station, but there was never any conclusive proof that he was running Radio Mille Collines when its broadcasts turned violent. The prosecution had an eyewitness that placed him in Gisenyi distributing weapons to the Interahamwe. He is unlikely to beat those charges.

FERDINAND NAHIMANA was dubbed chief ideologue of RTLM by various prosecution witnesses. His former neighbors in the hills of northern Rwanda, however, said his guilty verdict wasn't about the radio station, it was about politics. Several of Nahimana's childhood friends said they had followed the twists and turns of the trial on the radio. They said the government was scared of Nahimana because he was an intellectual and showed the Hutu had as good a history as the Tutsi. Nahimana remained in the U.N. Detention Facility in Arusha awaiting a decision from the Appeals Court in The Hague. His appeal, filed by Jean-Marie Biju-Duval, focused on the fact that the prosecution never proved conclusively that he had control over the radio station after the April 6 plane crash. While what the radio had broadcast before April 6 was certainly racist, it was unclear whether there were grounds for the incitement-to-genocide charges.

HASSAN NGEZE's appeal brief was filed with the court on June 19, 2004. Ngeze asked the chamber to remove Floyd from the case two days later. Ngeze objected to Floyd's decision to include questions about his mental health in the appeal. While a court may have found Ngeze guilty of incitement to genocide and crimes against humanity, his neighbors in Gisenyi still thought of him as a hero. "He had hired guards to protect the street," Afsa Nyinawingi, a neighbor on Nyakabunu Street, said when asked about Ngeze. He didn't charge the neighbors for protection, as many people who had Interahamwe friends did. He saved her family, she said. "He should be found innocent just because of the people he managed to save," she said. "He was publishing *Kangura* before the genocide happened and he never killed anyone, but he was found guilty. I knew him. I don't understand."

SIMONE MONASEBIAN emerged from the case as the prosecutor most responsible for the landmark convictions of the media trio. She left the ICTR soon after the media trial ended and took up a post as the principal defender of the Special Court for Sierra Leone, where she oversees thirty-six defense attorneys, as well as investigators and administrative staff. Though the media trial was a big win internationally, she said that "when it comes to America, I want the truth in all its dangerous versions to come out. The remedy to false and evil speech is more speech, not enforced silence." When she is not defending alleged war criminals in Sierra Leone, you can find her teaching the media case to law students in her international criminal law class at the American University in Cairo.

STEPHEN RAPP, still at the ICTR, had turned to two other high-profile cases. The first zeroed in on President Habyarimana's oldest brother-in-law, the head of the Akazu, Protais Zigiranyirazo. The case was particularly challenging because his position was entirely unofficial. Rapp also began building a case against Simon Bikindi, the so-called rock star of the genocide, who sang ironic Congolese tunes like "I Hate These Hutu," a staple on RTLM. "I Hate These Hutu" was an anthem meant to warn moderate Hutu about the dangers of aligning themselves with the Tutsi.

DAMIEN NZABAKIRA was flown to Arusha, Tanzania, to testify against the very men he had been accused of helping during the Butare massacres. The ICTR had checked and rechecked his version of events in Butare and were convinced in their own minds that he was innocent. Nevertheless, by July 2004, the harassment of people in Rwanda who had been acquitted of genocide charges began anew. While no one had pointed the finger at Damien by the summer of 2004, he had his documents—including the letter that authorized his release from prison—at the ready. Damien got a job teaching at an elementary school in Rwanda, and on July 8, 2004, his first son, Bernard Estival, was born.

BONAVENTURE UBALIJORO seemed to take the prospect of once again being on the wrong end of a politically motivated smear campaign in stride. Friends said Ubalijoro was under fire because he regularly took food to friends who were still in prison. He told his family that he was carrying out the will of the Lord and he was not afraid of returning to prison on the basis of lies. A third miracle had occurred in the summer of 2004. A local prophet had laid her hands on Ubalijoro during a church service and called upon him to walk. He struggled to his feet and shuffled down the length of the church. It was the first time he had walked without help in years. He was smiling broadly when he returned to his pew. He had always expected, he said, the miracles would happen in threes.

GEORGES RUGGIU was found guilty of direct and public incitement and crimes against humanity. He was sentenced to twelve years for each crime but judges said he could serve the two sentences concurrently. In July 2004, he was still in the U.N. Detention Facility in Arusha, Tanzania. He is supposed to serve out the rest of his sentence overseas.

JOHN FLOYD filed Ngeze's appeal and washed his hands of the International Criminal Tribunal for Rwanda. Floyd said in good conscience he couldn't continue to minimize Ngeze's irrational behavior. The chamber allowed Ngeze to testify, even encouraged it, when the judges were well aware that Ngeze was mentally ill, he said; they eventually crucified Ngeze for his inconsistencies. The appeal challenged the fairness of the trial, the chamber's refusal to translate all the *Kangura* issues, and the pressure President Kagame had brought to bear on the tribunal for a guilty verdict. Floyd said he raised more than seventy points of legal and factual error in the trial. He had not been paid by the tribunal for nearly six months, he said. After the court digests his brief, he added, he might never be paid.

JEAN-MARIE BIJU-DUVAL was working on Nahimana's appeal by July 2004. He returned to Paris, where he was an *avocat à la cour,* determined not to do any more work for the ICTR.

MONIQUE MUJAWAMARIYA had tried to work in Rwanda after the genocide but ran into conflict with President Kagame over investigations of Tutsi reprisal crimes. She thought it would be safer to move to Canada. She testified in numerous trials in the ICTR in her capacity as Rwanda's most famous human rights activist. Now a resident of Quebec, in 1998, she established Mobilisation Enfants du Monde, an organization dedicated to teaching nonviolence to African youth.

NAVANETHEM PILLAY was elected one of eighteen judges at the International Criminal Court in The Hague in 2003. The media judgment was grounded on hard evidence, both eyewitness accounts and documentary record, she said after the verdict attracted criticism. After eight years of listening to the testimony of survivors, she said, she left the ICTR convinced that the rule of law had triumphed over the rule of force.

RADIO MILLE COLLINES went off the air on July 14, 1994.

Notes on Sources

I arrived in Africa eight years after the genocide, wondering if prejudice in Rwanda—Hutu versus Tutsi—would be any different from the prejudice I had studied in deep East Texas after the racially motivated murder of James Byrd Jr. in 1998.

My first book, *A Death in Texas*, focused on how the small town of Jasper, Texas, struggled to make amends after three white men chained James Byrd to the bumper of a pickup truck and dragged him three miles down a country road to his death. At the time, everyone was wondering if there was something about Jasper that made three men think they could commit the worst racially motivated crime in America since Emmett Till's murder and get away with it. Many of the same questions swirled around the 1994 genocide in Rwanda. There had been tremendous complicity, tens of thousands of murderers who killed eight hundred thousand people in the space of a hundred days. The investigations had only just begun when it became clear that those who killed or ordered the killing were certain they would get away with it.

"We always got along all right," one black resident in Jasper told me in 2000. "But we always knew the whites were prejudiced."

Claver T. said precisely the same thing, word for word, in a banana grove in a small Rwandan village called Mbilisi in 2002. I was there with a documentary film crew from Internews, and Claver, one of a handful of Tutsi in the village who had survived the genocide, was to be interviewed about the killings. Where there had once been hundreds of Tutsi, now there were less than a dozen left in the village. "How did Hutu and Tutsi get along in the village before the genocide?" we asked him.

Claver tightened his mouth. "I guess we got along all right, but we always knew the Hutu were prejudiced."

The themes I had focused on in Jasper seemed to apply in this African context as well. This time, however, I decided to broaden the story. It would focus on an entire country instead of just a single town; I would map Rwanda's struggle for redemption by looking at its entire court system instead of just a single case.

RTLM had the dubious distinction of being renowned all over the world—from the smallest hamlets of Rwanda to big cities in the west—so it provided the perfect vehicle to look at how Rwanda was faring ten years after the genocide. Most everyone has a general sense of what happened in April 1994, though most can't keep straight whether Hutu killed Tutsi or it was the other way around. People outside of Africa also seem generally aware that a radio station used fiery broadcasts during the genocide to encourage killers to do their work. What I found interesting was that few people realized the men behind Radio Mille Collines were on trial in an international court—or that their case could end up setting a crucial precedent regarding freedom of expression for the rest of the planet.

I did not find Rwandans particularly secretive or unfriendly. Quite the opposite. I traveled to Rwanda six times between March 2002 and April 2004 and spent close to a hundred days there and in Arusha. I was never denied a single interview, including a two-hour session with President Kagame a week before the elections, and never had a question left unanswered. I had been told that women wouldn't talk about the gang rapes they experienced or discuss the children who were born of such violence. Nothing could be further from the truth. I spoke with nearly a dozen women who were incredibly open about what had happened to them and how it made them feel, even ten years later.

I remember one meeting in particular in which I was interviewing a woman who was rearing one of the *enfants de mauvais souvenirs*. She was having a particularly hard time coping after the genocide and had sent her child off to live with her father, hoping that if the child was out of sight, the rape would be out of mind. After an emotional discussion, I asked the woman if she had any questions for me. I was a foreigner. I thought, perhaps, there was something she had always wanted to ask a stranger but had been afraid to until now. It seemed only fair, given that she had just opened herself up to me.

She looked up and said, "Yes, can you tell me how I learn to love my child?"

This is a work of nonfiction; all the characters are real, as are their names and the details of their lives. Interviews were conducted directly with me either in French, in English, or in Kinyarwanda with a Rwandan or Ugandan interpreter translating into French. I used a single initial for a last name when I thought the publication of unedited answers might cause trouble for Rwandans who had to remain in the country after this reporter left. Similarly, it was the practice of the ICTR to assign witnesses initialed pseudonyms so that those who testified in the tribunals would not be open to reprisals when they returned home, either from the families of those they testified against or from the government in Kigali.

Rwanda also has a convention of putting last names first, such as Ubalijoro Bonaventure instead of Bonaventure Ubalijoro. I decided not to use this system, for the sake of clarity. Where I used dialogue, it was based on the recollection of at least one participant or was spoken in my presence. In some cases, opinions that were expressed in e-mails were paraphrased.

I attended part of Damien's military trial and visited him in prison as a "relative" several times (the fact that I was white didn't seem to matter to prison guards, who dutifully wrote down my passport number and waved me through the gates). Portions of Damien's trial that I did not attend were pieced together through accounts by Damien and members of his family. Because Damien subsequently testified at the ICTR I was able to corroborate his story with records kept in Arusha.

The details of Bonaventure Ubalijoro's incarceration and the miracles he experienced were recounted to me directly over a great many dinners at his house in Kigali. I saw the miraculous crosses in his chapel with my own eyes. I also was in Rwanda during the presidential campaign and elections and know (contrary to the latest charges leveled by the Rwandan parliament) that Mr. Ubalijoro was at home during this time. He would have had trouble getting to Butare given that he was barely walking and speaking because of the effects of a stroke. I visited him in August before the elections on two separate occasions.

The media trial was the *Jarndyce v. Jarndyce* of the tribunal—the most complex and sophisticated of the ICTR trials. It involved close to one hundred lay and expert witnesses from all over the world, and thousands upon thousands of pages of documentary and tangible evidence in French, German, English, and Kinyarwanda. For the sake of the narrative I was forced to make difficult choices to simplify a three-year trial. Lawyers came and went from the case with regularity. While Simone Monasebian and Steve Rapp take center stage in the book, they were only half of the final prosecution team. Charity Kagwi-Ndungu and William Egbe made up the other half. The decision to minimize their roles in the book is in no way meant to be a reflection on the work they did. Nor does it suggest that their contributions were not vital to the prosecution of the media trio. Monasebian and Rapp were, I decided, more accessible to a reading audience because touchstone events in their lives were easily anchored in the minds of readers. Kagwi-Ndungu and Egebe's contributions, when they appear in the book, are usually referred to with the shorthand "the prosecution."

The choice to focus on two lawyers from each side—prosecution and defense—was mine and, again, was motivated by a drive toward clarity. On the other side of the aisle, Mr. Giacomo

Barletta-Caldarera admirably represented Jean-Bosco Barayagwiza. The fact that Mr. Barayagwiza never attended the proceedings made it difficult to provide Mr. Caldarera a larger role in the book. For the reasons laid out above, I chose to focus on John Floyd and Jean-Marie Biju-Duval, the defense attorneys for Hassan Ngeze and Ferdinand Nahimana, respectively. This also should not be seen as a reflection on the work of Canadian René Martel or Queen's Counsel Diana Ellis, who defended Ngeze and Nahimana with great vigor over 241 days in chamber. There were also dozens of witnesses who, in a longer book, might have deserved mention, but for the purposes of this narrative were left out so I could focus on those who had the most bearing on the judgment.

The conclusions I have drawn in the book are my own, and the people who counseled and educated me over the past two and a half years (including Simone Monasebian, Stephen Rapp, John Floyd, René Martel, Jean-Marie Biju-Duval, Erik Møse, Alison Des Forges, Mary Kimani, Wanda Hall, Pierre Ubalijoro, and Bonaventure Ubalijoro, just to name a few) bear no responsibility for my errors of commission and omission. I hope I was a good student.

Because I arrived in Rwanda years after the genocide, details of what occurred during the massacres had to be gleaned from survivor interviews, news reports, and those who went before me. I was the White House correspondent for *Bloomberg Business News* in 1994 and knew many of the people who were making the Clinton administration decisions while the genocide was raging. They were helpful in piecing together the events in the run-up to the genocide. I still remember the back-and-forth with the White House press secretary, Dee Dee Myers, over whether the killing in Rwanda was an example of tribal warfare or deserved the sinister moniker "genocide."

For background on those hundred days, Philip Gourevitch's award-winning book on Rwanda, *We Wish to Inform You That Tomorrow We Will Be Killed with Our Families,* was invaluable. I hope this book successfully picks up where he left off. General Roméo Dallaire's recently published *Shake Hands with the Devil* was worth the ten-year wait. It pulls back the curtain on the day-to-day tragedies unfolding in Rwanda during the genocide and provides a window on a man who wanted to do the right thing but was foiled by a bureaucracy at every turn. *Leave None to Tell the Story*, Alison Des Forges's comprehensive study for Human Rights Watch about the planning, organization, and execution of the genocide, is the gold standard of Rwanda research. I have tried to cite each of these three works in the following chapter breakdown on sources every time I used them, but should say all three books influenced me so much it would be impossible to give them their full due.

Similarly, reports from Internews, Diplomatie Judiciaire, and Hirondelle News Agency provided daily coverage of the ICTR trials. The reporters there filled vital holes and were critical to my fact-checking process. I still check their Web sites to see how the ICTR is faring.

I attended large portions of the media trial and tried to be in Arusha during key junctures—including the closing arguments—so that I could observe the courtroom firsthand. I also watched a roster of videotapes of various witnesses and key moments in the trial so that I could accurately depict them in the book. RTLM excerpts and *Kangura* translations were taken from the official translations approved by the ICTR. I had numerous interviews with the main players over the course of two years. Because of the vast distances involved, I would conduct interviews in person while I was in Africa and then would follow up with phone calls and e-mails for clarification when I had returned to New York. There were literally thousands of e-mails exchanged and I can't thank everyone enough for their patience and their time. Simone Monasebian, in particular, saved me from embarrassing mistakes, and for this I will always be grateful.

Prologue

Details about the evening of the plane crash were drawn from more than twenty interviews with Kigali survivors over the course of two years. Interviews with Monique Mujawamariya and Alison Des Forges and transcripts from the ICTR were also helpful. I relied as well on newspaper articles written at the time, including the *Washington Post*'s superior coverage in the summer of 1994, which tracked Paul Kagame's march toward Kigali with great detail and precision. Paul Taylor and Keith B. Richburg's coverage was first-class and helped me re-create the early days of the killing, the glacial pace with which the world responded, and how that indifference embittered survivors. There was a roster of editorials and news articles that provided an understanding of the careful line the new, Tutsi government had to walk after the genocide so it could prosecute the Hutu extremists who slaughtered hundreds of thousands while reaching out to the Hutu masses who made up 85 percent of the population. (Some people would say that in the end, this was not done very successfully.) Thomas W. Lippman's editorials were also helpful in jogging my memory as to what was being said and done in the White House in the spring of 1994. Lynne Duke's *Mandela, Mobutu, and Me: A Newswoman's African Journey* put this into context. She lambastes the Clinton administration for the myth that Kagame, Uganda's Yoweri Museveni, Ethiopia's Meles Zenawi, and the Congo's Laurent Kabila were a "new generation of African leader" committed to democracy and free markets. Samantha Power's "Bystanders to Genocide," in the September 2001 *Atlantic*, was also helpful in reconstructing the details of the early hours of the genocide.

The National Security Archive provided copies of actual memos circulating in the White House and the State Department in the run-up to the massacres and after they began. Faxes from Roméo Dallaire, force commander for UNAMIR in Kigali; memorandums from Ambassador Prudence Bushnell, principal deputy assistant secretary, including a memorandum entitled "Rwanda: Jamming Civilian Radio Broadcasts," from May 1994; Alison Des Forges's, *Leave None to Tell the Story: Genocide in Rwanda;* Philip Gourevitch's *We Wish to Inform You . . . ;* Dallaire's *Shake Hands with the Devil;* and Samantha Power's award-winning *A Problem from Hell* were also critical research aids. Similarly, reports from Hirondelle News Agency, Diplomatie Judiciaire, and Internews informed this section of the book. *Frontline*'s "The Triumph of Evil: 100 Days of Slaughter" also provided context.

Chapter 1: Beginnings

Interviews with Damien Nzabakira, his family, and friends over the course of two years were the basis for the story of his life and his whereabouts in the hours and days after the plane crash. Details were also gleaned from his case file after he was acquitted of all the charges in a Rwandan military court.

Mahmood Mamdani's *When Victims Become Killers* is one of the best books I have read on how and why a genocide was able to gather momentum in Rwanda. Mr. Mamdani strings history and current events together in an easily accessible way, and when one finishes his book, one comes away with a real sense of life in Rwanda. He is the one who introduced me to the concept of Tutsi not begging for their lives, and subsequent interviews confirmed this. The media trial transcripts were also helpful in this regard.

The sections on John Hanning Speke were researched with primary materials at the Royal Geographical Society in London, England. I was given four boxes of his letters and notebooks, white gloves to wear, and an entire day to leaf through the actual pages he wrote in the nineteenth century. I remember the librarian said I had five hours and I wondered how I would fill that time, given that I had absolutely no idea what I was looking for. I went through letters with handwriting that was almost undecipherable. I paged through hundreds of watercolors. And then on the last page of the last notebook was a drawing of a Hutu and a Tutsi. I think I shrieked. I got sour looks from the real scholars around me. Speke's *Journal of the Discovery of the Source of the Nile* helped in researching his Hamitic theory. Philip Gourevitch introduced this idea in his *We Wish to Inform You . . .*, and I pursued it at the Royal Geographical Society. Details on East African history came from Adam Hochschild's *King Leopold's Ghost*, an immensely readable book about Belgium's colonization of the Congo. Dallaire's book was helpful on Rwandan military history, as was Des Forges's tome. Ferdinand Nahimana's new history came from trial transcripts of his direct testimony and from translations of the work. The analysis of his research came from testimony by Alison Des Forges and Jean-Paul Chrétien at the ICTR. Interviews with Des Forges and Monique provided details on the massacres at Bugesera. Investigations by the ICTR also helped me in writing this section. Details about the negotiations for the Arusha Accords were gleaned from interviews with John Shattuck, Alison Des Forges, and Nahimana testimony. Roméo Dallaire's book and the coverage in the *Washington Post* and from the Hirondelle News Agency were also used as resource material.

Chapter 2: Murderers or Patriots

The RTLM-and-*Kangura* contest was a key piece of evidence in the trial. It allowed the prosecution to admit many more issues of *Kangura* than it might have otherwise because the mandate of the court allowed it to focus only on crimes committed during 1994. Most of the *Kanguras* used in the incitement charge were from 1990 and 1992. Because the contest involved back issues, attorneys were able to skirt that provision. I interviewed John Floyd, Hassan Ngeze, Simone Monasebian, René Martel, Steve Rapp, and numerous others about the contest and the early days of RTLM. *Leave None to Tell the Story* was also helpful in putting together this section.

The mood in Kigali in the run-up to the genocide was gleaned from interviews with survivors and with Monique. Her testimony at the ICTR reinforced what she had told me privately. Hirondelle News Agency, Diplomatie Judiciaire, and Internews also provided detail. Monique's visit to the White House was reconstructed by me from Monique, Alison Des Forges, and a friend who worked at the National Security Council at the time who declined to be further identified. There was also a *New Yorker* article on Monique in 1994 that was helpful in putting together notes for her interview.

Paul Kagame's biography came from an August 2003 interview in Kigali, Dallaire's book, Steven Vogel's reporting for the *Washington Post* in August 1994, and *The Secrets of the Rwandan Genocide: Investigations of the Mysteries of a President*, by Charles Onana and Deo Mushayidi, a Tutsi who worked for the secretariat of the Rwandan Patriotic Front. *The Kangura* translations came from the ICTR, and their interpretation owes much to Alison Des Forges and Jean-Paul Chrétien and their testimony at the trial. Ngeze's reputation in Gisenyi was gleaned from interviews with his neighbors in November 2003 and again in March 2004.

Details on the RPF troop movements came from Dallaire and State Department briefs on the events on the ground in Rwanda in the spring of 1994. Monasebian and Rapp were both interviewed extensively for details on their legal careers before the media trial.

Chapter 3: "Contours of the Monster"

Georges Ruggiu's testimony and deposition provided a wealth of detail on how he came to be a cub reporter at RTLM. The shareholder documents, first outlined in Des Forges's book, were admitted into evidence in the trial. Particularly instructive was a small book called *Broadcasting Genocide: Censorship Propaganda & State Sponsored Violence in Rwanda 1990–1994.* (article 19, International Centre Against Censorship, October 1996). I also did preliminary research on RTLM and the tribunal that appeared in Yale Law School's *Legal Affairs* magazine. The resulting article, "Radio Hate" (September-October 2002), helped clarify my thinking on how the verdict might end up muzzling the press. Emily Bazelon, my editor there, was particularly helpful.

Details about Bonaventure Ubalijoro came from one-on-one interviews conducted from 2003 through and 2004 and numerous conversations with his son, Pierre Emmanuel Ubalijoro, over the same period. The discussion of political parties in Rwanda came from *Leave None to Tell the Story*, news reports, and help from Mary Kimani, a brilliant reporter at Internews. Ubalijoro's early political woes and discussion of what was going on behind closed doors came from a report from the Office of the President of Rwanda entitled *Rwanda Presidential Report on Rwandan Political Parties* (Kigali, August 1999).

Damien's harrowing bus ride to Butare came from his case file and numerous interviews with Damien, his friends, and family over the course of two years. Faustin Twagiramungu's escape details were provided in interviews with the former prime minister from February 2003 through August 2003 and Dallaire's *Shake Hands with the Devil*.

Stories about Monique's escape were legion and were published in many news outlets soon after she appeared in the United States in mid-April 1994. In addition to interviews with Monique and Des Forges, sources included the *Washington Post*, the *New Yorker*, and the *New York Times*.

Additional information on Rwandan history and its emphasis on 1959 came from Philip Gourevitch's *We Wish to Inform You . . .* and Mahmood Mamdani's *When Victims Become Killers*. John Shattuck's attempts to silence RTLM were corroborated with internal memos and interviews with the main players. The National Security Archives provided some of this primary source material.

Nahimana's meeting at the Ministry of Information was caught on videotape, which I have watched in its entirety. There was also a written transcript of the meeting admitted into evidence at the media trial.

Details on Rafael Lemkin came from Samantha Power's Pulitzer Prize–winning book, *A Problem from Hell,* and from his autobiography and private papers housed in the New York Public Library. I would never have known about him were it not for his main role in Power's book. Details from *Axis Rule in Occupied Europe* came from a draft of his book available at the New York Public Library and from Power's reporting.

There are a variety of rich sources for those interested in the details of the Nuremberg trials. Court TV has *A Look Back at Nuremberg,* which provides a great primer. Randall Bytwerk's *Julius Streicher: The Man Who Persuaded a Nation to Hate Jews* (New York: Stein & Day, 1993) was very helpful, as was Telford Taylor's *The Anatomy of the Nuremberg Trials* (New York: Knopf, 1992). Rebecca West's reporting for the *New Yorker* from Nuremberg is collected in one volume called *A Train of Powder.* Joseph E. Persico's *Nuremberg: Infamy on Trial* and Whitney Harris's *Tyranny on Trial: The Evidence at Nuremberg* also informed my reporting.

Chapter 4: "I Want a Big, American Lawyer"

Nahimana's whereabouts in the early days of the genocide are part of the court record, as are his comments to Radio Rwanda in which he described meeting the former Burundian ambassador to Kigali on the tarmac. Military advancement and details on Kagame came from Dallaire's book and other media reports from 1994, including in particular, stories from the *Washington Post.* Details from John Shattuck's meeting with Kagame came from interviews conducted by me with both men in late 2003.

The mechanics of setting up the tribunal came from John Shattuck interviews, news accounts, and interviews with Faustin Twagiramungu and the press secretary for the ICTR at the time, Tom Kennedy. Details on what the Clinton administration provided to set up the court came from a State Department press release at the time and an interview with Shattuck. Two other articles—one in the *New Yorker,* called "An African Nuremberg," by John Ryle (October 2, 1995), and another from The Atlantic Online, entitled "A New Kind of Justice," by Charles Trueheart (April 2000)—also informed this section of the book.

The *Washington Post* provided stellar coverage of the U.N. vote to establish the tribunal. Interviews with Alison Des Forges about attitudes in Rwanda regarding the tribunal were also very helpful. This was a perennial question I asked any Rwandan I interviewed, so I feel I had a good representation of how ordinary Rwandans view the ICTR. An interview with ICTR judge Erik Møse in 2002 and again in 2003 helped flesh out details on what was at stake in the media trial as it proceeded. The details of Nuremberg in this chapter were drawn from Rebecca West's *A Train of Powder*, Joseph E. Persico's *Nuremberg: Infamy on Trial*, and Whitney Harris's *Tyranny on Trial: The Evidence at Nuremberg.*

News reports, my own reporting as White House correspondent for *Bloomberg Business News* during the crisis in Yugoslavia, Rebecca West's *Black Lamb and Grey Falcon*, and Richard Holbrooke's *To End a War* were all used as resources in pulling together the section on the former Yugoslavia and the tribunal set up in The Hague to try the war crimes committed there.

The ICTR indictment is on the court's Web site (www.ictr.org). Steve Rapp, Simone Monasebian, and Tom Kennedy interviews helped to put the indictment into context. Reports from the ICTR, Diplomatic Judiciaire, and Internews were also used as resources.

John Floyd's arrival at the tribunal and the story of his background came from numerous interviews with him in Washington and in Arusha over the course of two years. Phone interviews with Ngeze from the UNDF confirmed Floyd's version of events as he came to represent the Rwandan newspaperman.

Chapter 5: When Two Elephants Fight, It Is the Grass That Suffers

Analysis as to what was at stake in the media trial came from dozens of interviews with people involved on both sides of the case and outside legal analysts who could better explain how the precedents set in the media trial could cast a pall over freedom of expression more generally. Steve Rapp, Simone Monasebian, First Amendment attorney Floyd Abrams, and Joel Simon of the Committee to Protect Journalists all provided analysis. Details of press-freedom precedent in America were originally published in an article I wrote for *Legal Affairs* magazine ("Radio Hate," September-October 2002).

The Akayesu trial was part of the ICTR record: *The Prosecutor v. Jean-Paul Akayesu.* Rapp first alerted me to the importance of Akayesu in the media decision. Philip Gourevitch also covers some of the Akayesu story in his *We Wish to Inform You.*

Judge Pillay's background was gleaned from interviews with her associates and with the judge herself in New York.

I saw the conditions at the UNDF firsthand and also relied on a special report by Mary Kimani from Internews. Tom Kennedy from the ICTR was also helpful in this regard, as were articles from Diplomatie Judiciaire. Del Ponte's concern about Barayagwiza's release came from interviews with those directly involved in the arguments and discussion. The original indictment, all eighty pages; and news reports from Internews, Hirondelle, and Diplomatie Judiciaire; and interviews with the principal players were the basis for the reporting on the opening moments of the trial. Transcripts were also used.

Chapter 6: "We Had No Control"

Damien provided details about his time in prison and I made numerous prison visits to see both Damien and other prisoners over the two years I spent writing and researching the book. Damien's case file provides a list of the charges leveled against him. Internews allowed me to tag along with their documentary film team during one of their shoots in late 2002 and permitted me to accompany them into several prisons, including Cyangugu Central Prison, described in the chapter. I learned a great deal about transitional justice from a seminar on Rwanda justice held by the New York Bar Association in 2003 and from another briefing, at the Ninety-second Street Y, in New York City, in 2004. Also helpful were detailed conversations with Karen Murphy, a director of Facing History and Ourselves, which works, among other things, to build transitional justice. Details on Pasteur Bizimungu's government were gleaned from *Washington Post* coverage and interviews with Twagiramungu and Ubalijoro. I also obtained a Rwandan presidential report called *The Reflection Meetings,* which contains minutes of the discussions held in the president's office after the genocide.

Nahimana's view of history and his defense came, in part, from his own direct testimony. Ngeze's early newspaper days came from interviews with him from the UNDF, interviews with John Floyd, and *Leave None to Tell the Story.* Witness AHA's testimony came from the ICTR transcripts, as did the official translation of *Kangura* number 6 and the Hutu Ten Commandments.

Nahimana's work at ORINFOR was detailed in *Leave None to Tell the Story,* his own direct testimony, and reports from Diplomatie Judiciaire and Internews.

Chapter 7: Merci, Génocide

The story of Sammy Weza first came to my attention in September 2002, when Victor Peskin wrote an article entitled "Rwandan Ghosts" in *Legal Affairs* magazine. I did additional reporting on the case and interviewed the ICTR's Tom Kennedy, Simone Monasebian, and Stephen Rapp on the troubles behind the scenes at the tribunal. Samantha Power's article "Never Again: The World's Most Unfulfilled Promise," in the *Atlantic,* also helped me write this section. Interviews with officials from Ibuka also informed my reporting, as did conversations with Mary Kimani of Internews.

Bonaventure Ubalijoro's case was closely followed by Amnesty International. Their briefs and interviews with Ubalijoro's family and friends aided in pulling the section on his trials together.

Monasebian, Rapp, Ngeze, and Floyd provided information

on the notes and gifts Ngeze began circulating and sending to Monasebian. The *gacaca* reporting was done firsthand: I attended several *gacaca* in 2003 and 2004. The television show and billboards were ubiquitous in Rwanda at that time. A Facing History and Ourselves seminar in New York, conversations with Karen Murphy, one of its directors, and research by Michelle Wagner at the University of Minnesota all helped me access *gacaca*'s successes and shortcomings. Amnesty International's April 2003 report *The Troubled Course of Justice* helped illuminate the problems with justice in Rwanda, including arbitrary arrests and detention. Mary Kimani of Internews also had a very interesting series, "Victims Meeting Their Killers," which helped inform this chapter.

Chapter 8: The Rape Babies Arrived in the Spring

Witness FW details came from speaking with the attorneys, trial transcripts, and interviews with Monasebian, who questioned and prepared him. Ruggiu's book *In the Rwandan Torment*, was excerpted as one of the exhibits in the trial and it provided more detail on Ruggiu's whereabouts and defense of RTLM during the genocide. The Phil Donahue–like moderator was part of the Internews team, and that particular session occurred in 2003. In 2004, AVEGA, a group helping women who were victims of rape during the genocide, put me in touch with nearly a dozen women rearing children of the genocide. Large portions of this chapter are gleaned from those interviews. Two reports were also invaluable: *Shattered Lives: Sexual Violence During the Rwandan Genocide and Its Aftermath* (Human Rights Watch, September 1996) and Peter Landesman's article "A Woman's Work," *New York Times Magazine*, September 15, 2002.

Chapter 9: Words Can Kill

Transcripts of Monique's testimony and subsequent interviews with her were vital to the understanding of RTLM and its role in the genocide. The media trial prosecution strategy was gleaned from numerous interviews with Simone Monasebian, Charity Kagwi, and Steve Rapp. Alison Des Forges's testimony was part of the record, as were the Omar Serushago details. Interviews with John Floyd helped me divine the defense strategy, as did reports from Hirondelle, Internews, and Diplomatie Judiciaire. Chrétien's testimony was part of the court record.

Chapter 10: Hutu Blood, Is It Red?

I attended Damien's trial and received e-mails from his family when he was released. A mutual friend of ours taught him how to get online and send e-mails himself (the e-mail revolution had occurred while he was behind bars). The Nahimana testimony, that of prosecution witness AHB, and the translations of *Kangura* were all part of the court transcripts. I interviewed Ngeze's neighbors in Gisenyi for their reaction to the guilty verdict for Ngeze at the tribunal.

Chapter 11: The Fallen Cow Is Gored by the Herd

Randall Bytwerk's *Julius Streicher: The Man Who Persuaded a Nation to Hate Jews* was particularly helpful in explaining the Streicher verdict and its implications, as was Rebecca West's *A Train of Powder* and Joseph E. Persico's *Nuremberg: Infamy on Trial.* The essays attributed to Nahimana were taken from excerpts by ICTR translations and they were part of the trial record. I interviewed attorneys on both sides of the aisle in the closing days of the trial. For details on other ICTR cases, the ICTR Web site provides updates and summations. Diplomatie Judiciaire is also very helpful in this regard. The detail of the Strizek verdict came from Hirondelle News Agency and an interview with Simone Monasebian. I was at the ICTR for the closing arguments.

Chapter 12: All Thumbs

I was with the candidates during the campaigning in Rwanda and attended several of their rallies. Trouble was afoot, however, before I arrived. Human Rights Watch produced a comprehensive paper by Alison Des Forges in May 2003 entitled *Preparing for Elections: Tightening Control in the Name of Unity*. Amnesty International also produced a report in April 2003 called *Rwanda: Escalating Repression Against Political Opposition*. Both reports were helpful in preparing me before my trip and helped form the analysis in this chapter. Also helpful was more general reporting from Hirondelle News Agency, the *Washington Post*, BBC News, *New Vision* newspaper (Kampala; Internet version), and the *East African* (Nairobi; Internet version). A report by the International Crisis Group in 2003 entitled *Compte rendu de la réunion discussion sur le problème du parti MDR*, informed this chapter as well. *Rwanda and Genocide in the Twentieth Century*, by Alain Destexhe, was also used as source material.

I had an exclusive interview with President Kagame in August 2003, just before the election.

News of strong-arming ahead of the balloting was rife. Some of the proof appeared in the Kigali newspaper *New Times* as quoted in the chapter. I also interviewed Bonaventure Ubalijoro and Joseph Bideri before of the elections. For details on the results I turned to the Panafrican News Agency, BBC Worldwide Monitoring, and interviews with Twagiramungu while he was in Rwanda and in Belgium.

Chapter 13: Tribunal in Chains

Details about the trouble at the tribunal were gleaned from interviews with a variety of players at the court, from judges to attorneys to others who worked there. The legal analysis in this chapter is not just my own, but rather my reading of the combined conclusions of many, including Floyd Abrams, Aryeh Neier, and Joel Simon at the Committee to Protect Journalists. While they informed me, the flaws in legal logic are all my own.

Chapter 14: The Aftermath

I was in Rwanda for the tenth anniversary of the genocide so that the book would encompass ten years: from the moment the genocide began to exactly ten years later. The book is also meant to follow the lives of its main characters over that span of time. I interviewed members of Aegis Trust and toured the memorial the day before it opened. Details about President Clinton's donation appeared in his 2004 autobiography, *My Life*. I also used reports from Hirondelle, the BBC, *Le Monde*, Human Rights Watch, and Amnesty International in pulling together the concluding chapter. Helpful as well were Mary Kimani's "A Case Study—Rwanda: Media in Conflict" (Internews) and an article in the *Wall Street Journal*, "Horror Recedes in Time, Rwanda Still Restrains the Press," April 30, 2004. Ubalijoro was put on the government list of "genocide ideologues" just as this book was going to the publisher.

Acknowledgments

My heartfelt thanks go out to all those who helped me put together a complicated book. Some provided vital information, others provided insight and advice, many were patient enough to listen to yet another story about my latest trip to Rwanda or Tanzania without knowing I was testing out material before it made it onto the page. I started this project in January 2002 and finished it in August of 2004.

I learned from my first book that narrative nonfiction depends on the kindness of strangers. The Rwandans who told me their stories, who were so open about their harrowing days during the genocide and their lives after, made this book possible. They shared their feelings about Hutu and Tutsi, prejudice and the future, with grace. They allowed me to ask the most basic questions about being Rwandan while enlightening me about their culture and their beliefs. Without them this book would never have happened.

In particular, I would like to thank Flora and Obed. I use only their first names so they can maintain some semblance of anonymity. Flora helped me set up a team in Rwanda that permitted me to travel and report in Africa with great efficiency. Obed, my driver, translator, fixer, and eyes and ears on the ground, may have studied politics at university but he should have been a journalist. Even without my suggestion, he would sit in the car and prod local Rwandans with the very questions that needed asking. My prompting became unnecessary as he got into the spirit of the project and tried to help me understand, and appreciate, his country. We could go for hours on end without talking, but the silence was the comfortable variety that develops between friends. I depended on him to make things happen in Rwanda and in two years he didn't disappoint.

Similarly, Damien, even from prison, managed to be helpful as I set out to write this story. He is one of the kindest, most thoughtful men I have ever met. He harbors no resentment toward the Tutsi, or against the government that was partly responsible for his wrongful incarceration. The Hutu had their chance to rule and we didn't do it well, he told me, now it is the Tutsi's turn to try to govern us. He voted in the nation's first contested elections in 2003 just months after he got out of prison. He cast his ballot for Paul Kagame.

My agent, John Thornton, has a calm way about him that soothes the jangled nerves of a newish writer. He read the entire manuscript, twice, and provided invaluable suggestions to improve the book's clarity and narrative thread. He had a way of appearing just when I needed him and fading into the background when I didn't. I appreciate all his help and hope to work with him for years to come.

My editor at Free Press, Elizabeth Stein, is everything I think an editor is supposed to be: a cheerleader, a dispenser of tough love, an endless supplier of razor-sharp wit and sarcastic humor, and, most of all, a guide for the occasionally overwhelmed. I have worked with her on two books and hope we will work together on twenty more. She makes me laugh, keeps me writing, and holds me to a high standard. For all those reasons, she remains one of my favorite people in the world.

My copy editor, Chuck Antony, saved me from myself. He found flaws in logic, repetitions, and asked smart questions that helped me dramatically improve the book. Every author should be as fortunate as I was to have a copy editor of such quality looking over his or her shoulder. Thank you, Chuck.

George Hager, a veteran editor at *USA Today*, took weekends and evenings out of an already packed schedule to edit the book while it was still taking shape. His suggestions were always right on point and insightful, which made teasing him about the little nits he insisted on pointing out that much more difficult. We used to work together at *USA Today* and I am glad that we have continued our relationship. He is smart, funny, and a great friend.

Special thanks also goes out to Robin Meszoly and Simone Monasebian. Robin was my editor at the White House for nearly eight years and knows my writing (and my tics) better than I do. She managed to read my manuscript at a time when literally a dozen competing things were going on in her life. She has always found a way to clear her schedule for me and for that I can't thank her enough. Similarly, Simone Monasebian graciously went over the trial portions of the book to make sure they were accurate. The lengthy memo she wrote suggesting improvements and changes in the book was a godsend.

Encouragement and support from the editors at the *New York Sun*, particularly Seth Lipsky, Ira Stoll, and Stuart Marques, were also vital to the completion of this project. They permitted me to go to Africa to report for the book at times when it might not always have been in the newspaper's best interest to let their City Hall bureau chief disappear. They never complained. They always encouraged.

For my other friends, those who were always supportive, including Alexandra Iselin, Joanne Murphy, Meg D'Incecco, Peter Bakstansky, Peter Beardsley, Lois Conner, Jenny Rider, Timothy Williams, Jim Bradley, Minky Worden, Sam Jacob, and Pierre Ubalijoro, thank you for your friendship, patience, and for making New York so fun.

Bibliography

Balakian, Peter. *The Burning Tigris: The Armenian Genocide and America's Response.* New York: HarperCollins, 2003.

Barnett, Michael. *Eyewitness to a Genocide: The United Nations and Rwanda.* Ithaca: Cornell University Press, 2002.

Bergner, Daniel. *In the Land of Magic Soldiers: A Story of White and Black in West Africa.* New York: Farrar, Straus, and Giroux, 2003.

Bytwerk, Randall. *Julius Streicher: The Man Who Persuaded a Nation to Hate Jews.* New York: Stein and Day, 1993.

Carr, Rosamond. *Land of a Thousand Hills: My Life in Rwanda.* New York: Penguin Putnam, 1999.

Courtemanche, Gil. *A Sunday at the Pool in Kigali.* New York: Knopf, 2003.

Dallaire, Roméo. *Shake Hands with the Devil: The Failure of Humanity in Rwanda.* Canada: Random House, 2003.

Danticat, Edwidge. *The Farming of Bones.* New York: Penguin Books, 1998.

Des Forges, Alison. *Leave None to Tell the Story: Genocide in Rwanda.* Human Rights Watch, March 1999.

Destexhe, Alain. *Rwanda and Genocide in the Twentieth Century.* New York: New York University Press, 1996.

Dugard, Martin. *Into Africa: The Epic Adventures of Stanley & Livingstone.* New York: Doubleday, 2003.

Duke, Lynne. *Mandela, Mobutu, and Me: A Newswoman's African Journey.* New York: Doubleday, 2003.

Farwell, Byron. *Burton: A Biography of Sir Richard Francis Burton.* New York: Penguin Books, 1963.

Fuller, Alexandra. *Don't Let's Go to the Dogs Tonight: An African Childhood.* New York: Random House, 2001.

Gourevitch, Philip. *We Wish to Inform You That Tomorrow We Will Be Killed with Our Families: Stories from Rwanda*. New York: Picador, 1998.

Gunther, John. *Inside Africa*. New York: Harper & Brothers, 1953.

Harrell, Peter E. *Rwanda's Gamble: Gacaca and a New Model of Transitional Justice*. New York: Writers Club Press, 2003

Harris, Whitney. *Tyranny on Trial: The Evidence at Nuremberg*. Dallas: Southern Methodist University Press, 1954.

Hochschild, Adam. *King Leopold's Ghost: A Story of Greed, Terror and Heroism in Colonial Africa*. New York: First Mariner Books, 1999.

Holbrooke, Richard. *To End a War*. New York: Random House, 1998.

Kapuscinski, Ryszard. *The Shadow of the Sun*. New York: Vintage Books, 2002.

Krog, Antjie. *Country of My Skull: Guilt, Sorrow, and the Limits of Forgiveness in the New South Africa*. New York: Three Rivers Press, 1998.

Lamb, David. *The Africans*. New York: Vintage Books, 1987.

Mamdani, Mahmood. *When Victims Become Killers: Colonialism, Nativism, and the Genocide in Rwanda*. Princeton, N.J.: Princeton University Press, 2001.

Melvern, L. R. *A People Betrayed: The Role of the West in Rwanda's Genocide*. New York: Zed Books, 2000.

Neuffer, Elizabeth. *The Key to My Neighbor's House: Seeking Justice in Bosnia and Rwanda*. New York: Picador USA, 2001.

Pakenham, Thomas. *The Scramble for Africa: White Man's Conquest of the Dark Continent from 1876 to 1912*. New York: Avon Books, 1991.

Persico, Joseph E. *Nuremberg: Infamy on Trial*. New York: Penguin Books, 1995.

Pierce, Julian. *Speak Rwanda*. New York: Picador USA, 1999.

Power, Samantha. *A Problem from Hell: America in the Age of Genocide*. New York: Basic Books, 2002.

Scroggins, Deborah. *Emma's War, An Aid Worker, a Warlord, Radical Islam and the Politics of Oil: A True Story of Love and Death in Sudan*. New York: Pantheon Books, 2002.

Sehene, Benjamin. *Le Piège Ethnique*. Paris: Editions Dagorno, 1999.

Shattuck, John. *Freedom on Fire: Human Rights Wars & America's Response*. Cambridge, Mass.: Harvard University Press, 2003.

Speke, John Hanning. *Journal of the Discovery of the Source of the Nile.* Mineola, N.Y.: Dover Publications, 1996.

Taylor, Telford. *The Anatomy of the Nuremberg Trials.* New York: Knopf, 1992.

West, Rebecca. *Black Lamb and Grey Falcon: A Journey Through Yugoslavia.* Penguin Books, 1940.

———. *A Train of Powder: Six Reports on the Problems of Guilt and Punishment in Our Time*. Chicago: Ivan R. Dee, 1946.

Index

About the Author

Dina Temple-Raston is the author of the Barnes and Noble Discover Award–winning *A Death in Texas*. She has worked as a foreign correspondent in China and Hong Kong and covered the White House for *Bloomberg Business News* for eight years. She is currently the City Hall bureau chief for the *New York Sun*. She lives in New York City.